The World After Alice

Lauren Aliza Green holds an MFA from the Michener Center for Writers and was one of Forbes' '30 under 30' in the 2024 media category. Her work has appeared in *Conjunctions*, *American Short Fiction*, *Glimmer Train* (winner of the New Writers Award) and elsewhere. She is the author of *A Great Dark House*, which won the Poetry Society of America's Chapbook Fellowship, and the inaugural recipient of the Eavan Boland Emerging Poet Award, sponsored by Poetry Ireland and Stanford University. Her writing has received support from the Kenyon Review Workshop, Bread Loaf and the Carson McCullers Center. Lauren lives in New York City.

The World After Alice

LAUREN ALIZA GREEN

MICHAEL JOSEPH

PENGUIN MICHAEL JOSEPH

UK | USA | Canada | Ireland | Australia
India | New Zealand | South Africa

Penguin Michael Joseph is part of the Penguin Random House group of companies
whose addresses can be found at global.penguinrandomhouse.com

First published in the United States of America by Viking,
an imprint of Penguin Random House LLC 2024
First published in Great Britain by Penguin Michael Joseph 2024

001

Typeset by Jouve (UK), Milton Keynes
Printed and bound in Great Britain by Clays Ltd, Elcograf S.p.A.

The authorized representative in the EEA is Penguin Random House Ireland,
Morrison Chambers, 32 Nassau Street, Dublin DO2 YH68

A CIP catalogue record for this book is available from the British Library

HARDBACK ISBN: 978–0–241–68465–8
TRADE PAPERBACK ISBN: 978–0–241–68466–5

www.greenpenguin.co.uk

To my parents, Helen and Rich —
the greatest people I know

We hang like clouds between heaven and earth,
                              between something and nothing,
Sometimes with shadows, sometimes without.

                              Charles Wright, *Negative Blue*

Prologue

She stood coatless on the bridge in the cold. Cars pulsed by her, a ceaseless string of light. She did not see them. All, to her, was dark. Even the glittering city shone black.

There would be reports later – commuters who'd spotted her as they sat in traffic, joggers hoping to cover a few miles before the snowfall. That morning, salt trucks had whirred across the city's grid, dusting the asphalt to keep it from icing over. And there the girl stood in only a skirt and a blue sweater, the raw wind lifting strands of her hair and setting them gruffly back down. The Hudson River lay in wait below, vast and uninviting.

She struck those who noticed her because she'd been carrying something: a violin case (which one passerby mistook for a gun).

For six days, until the surveillance footage emerged, the police considered her missing. Rumors circulated the quiet Upper West Side where her family lived: she'd been kidnapped, had run away, had been lured into prostitution. She was so young, people said, their voices threaded with shock and intrigue. So young, with such potential.

Only one man saw the girl set down the case before she stepped forward, hoisted herself onto the bridge's waist-high guardrail, and jumped.

PART ONE

PART ONE

I

In the midsummer week leading up to the wedding, the bride wondered whether they should get married at all. This predicament beset her as she sat cross-legged on the floor of her and the groom's Brooklyn apartment, the seating chart before her. Where to put his parents, who had been divorced for twelve years, since his sister's death? Where to put her own father, who opposed the marriage on the grounds that it was too hasty? She threw down her pen, the end of which had been chewed to disfigurement. It was hopeless.

The bride's name was Morgan Hensley; the groom's Benji Weil. He had light hair, rosy lips, and dilated pupils, inside of which the world appeared stripped of its perils, like a flame on glass. She opposed him physically in every way, though it was the inward sullenness telegraphed through her eyes that most definitively set them apart. Gently, Benji assured her such anxieties were for naught. Yes, their parents existed in perpetual strife, but a ceasefire could be brokered for one weekend. He was sure of it.

Benjamin Weil, the ultimate optimist. To his core, he did not believe anyone would wish to spoil such a celebratory occasion. Nevertheless, he rang first his mother and then his father on speakerphone. Each parent averred in turn their enthusiasm for the weekend ahead, refusing to admit their dread. And Morgan watched as Benji, who insisted on traveling the circuitous route to convince himself all was well, everyone was happy, deftly overlooked the note of strain in their voices.

'See?' he said, triumphant. 'Told you so.'

Yet in the ensuing days, the darkness tugged at both their confidences with the finesse of a magician whisking a tablecloth out from beneath a dining set. As their union drew nearer, preparations hovered in midair, threatening collapse, and neither party slept.

2

Nicholas Weil awoke in a panic, feeling the bedside table for his phone. He swiped to his savings account. No, one more minute of sleep. He burrowed deeper into the comforter, clinging to the last shreds of oblivion. Fat chance. He threw off the covers. The room swam to him in the morning light. The trophies, the school pennants, the Hardy Boys books stacked upon the writing desk – alienly these objects hovered, until Nick remembered he was in Maine, in his childhood bedroom, and their strange forms resolved. Two days until his son's wedding.

The drive from Westchester to Maine had taken eight hours, with an unexpected detour into New Hampshire when the SUV's gas light blinked yellow. For forty miles Nick had been without cell service, a deprivation that left him nervy, on edge, snapping at Caro when she suggested they play the license plate game. He pulled over as soon as the bars reappeared, saying he had to send an email. In reality, he only wished to monitor the grim performance of his stock portfolio. He begrudged every gas pump, every toll. Shouldn't a man be able to traverse his own goddamn country without the burden of compensating all fifty states? Were not said states *united*, after all?

By the time they arrived at his mother's house, the razor of a migraine had carved a deep incision into his skull. They were greeted at the door by his mother's aide, Raina, a former nurse who'd cared for many elderly patients and so knew the routine well: the flurry of initial visits that gradually tapered off to the occasional holiday appearance as the adult child weaned themself from their parent's love. Eleven guilt-charged months had passed since Nick himself had last ventured here.

Up the three flights Nick ushered his young wife ('*Younger*, not young,' Caro would amend) and their six-year-old daughter, Avery, his eyes crossed with exhaustion. Quads aflame, he collapsed onto the chenille bedspread while Caro tucked Avery away in the guest room. When she returned, she hesitated by the window, moonlight spreading over her like zinc. 'Do you want to . . . maybe,' she said. She slid a hand into his briefs, breathlessly adding: 'We'll make it fast.'

This morning, Nick was relieved to find himself alone, the voices of Caro and Avery drifting up through the ancient floorboards. He performed the usual rituals: checking his trading accounts (abysmal) and crypto wallet (even worse). Next he navigated to the dreaded Citibank app, whose digits laid bare the incontestable horrors of recent months. His phone dinged with a reminder that he'd soon have to retrieve Benji and Morgan from the airport. In not two hours, this weekend would lurch inexorably forward through the dark tunnel that awaited.

He tugged on his jeans. The insects outside the dormer window were already in a tizzy. Sunbeams streamed through the space, illuminating the frayed edges of the wallpaper. The entire room was marooned in a bygone era: Sony stereo system in the corner; flip clock on the bedside table; a TV in whose VCR he'd once, in a pinch, discarded a condom. (Did he dare check . . . ?) The shelves upon which he'd once proudly displayed his trophies now housed an array of peanut butter and tomato sauce jars. Downstairs, the garage held enough water bottles to quench a small village. He resented his mother's scarcity mindset because he knew he possessed it too – a fear that at any moment, the winds would change, whisking everything away.

A metallic clatter alerted him to Matisse, his brindle-coated dog who was much more than a pet. Matisse stood a regal fifty pounds, with ears that perked into tri-angles even when he was exhausted. He had one lazy eye, the other shrewd. Two observers on either side of him might assume rivaling impressions of his intelligence.

'I know, bud,' Nick said. 'But we're only getting started.'

In the kitchen, Avery sat with her legs dangling off a barstool's edge. 'Daddy, Grandma doesn't believe I can spell *school*. If I spell it right, you gotta give me a dollar, okay?'

'Morning, monkey,' he said, spinning the milk carton on the counter until the pasty cow smiled at him. 'Sleep well?'

'S-C-H-O-O-L. Too easy. Do a harder one.'

'Invincible.'

She frowned and reluctantly sounded out the letters. After a moment, she gave up. 'Do one from the *list*, Daddy. How about *wolf*? W-O-L-F, wolf.'

'Any good dreams to share with the class?'

Oh, yes, Avery lied, embellishing her answer with fanciful details (a princess, a UFO, a talking lizard) in an attempt to capture one of her father's smiles. Believing his eyes had drifted away, she stealthily plugged her thumb into her mouth – a habit that grew more concerning with each passing year. Her teacher had gone so far as to devise a system wherein she'd clap each time Avery's fingers lifted, to either startle or embarrass the girl out of the practice. On the contrary, this had only trained her to be more discreet.

'Is that Nick?' Judith asked.

She was lazing in the recliner, a handheld radio pressed to her cheek. Once, she'd been an avid gardener; now she spent entire days listening to the news, rising to outrage at the prescribed moments. Whenever Nick suggested she might find a more pleasant hobby, she said all her friends were dead, and she would soon be dead too, so she could listen to whatever she damn well pleased.

Nick stooped to kiss her cheek. 'Hi, Ma.'

'Nicky! When'd you get here?'

'Last night, late.'

'What a nice surprise.'

'It's not a surprise, Ma. We're here for the wedding.'

Judith's eyes grasped his, holding tightly. Around the locus of her bright lipstick, her face appeared wan. She'd weighed one-sixteen at her last doctor's visit, an alarming decrease for a woman who'd once worn her corpulence with aplomb. The doctor suspected an internal bleed, but there was no use in doing surgery, not now.

'We're here for Benji's wedding,' Caro supplied. 'Your grandson, Benji.'

'How long will you be staying?'

'Just a pit stop,' Nick said. 'We're here to pick you up. The wedding's in Sugar Hill.'

'Sugar Hill?' Judith made a face. 'They didn't give you trouble taking off work, *nu*?'

Nick's cheeks flamed. It was the same question Caro had raised. The Nick of yore would have been loath to take even a single day off. That the firm where he'd squandered three decades of precious time had terminated him six months ago was an unfortunate matter he hadn't yet disclosed to his wife. Only Matisse – the trusty and, chiefly, mute dog – was aware of his troubles.

Nick had planned to tell Caro about the layoff straight-away, but she'd been late from the gallery, and when she came in, she wanted to know if he'd gotten the groceries as she'd asked. He had not. She launched into her one-woman show of browsing the fridge, carping about leftovers. Nick sulked off to the couch. Fine, then she didn't deserve to know.

How could Kerr & Co. fire *him*? After all that work, that energy and devotion. *Corporate restructuring*, Kerr had called it, a fancy term to obfuscate the brutal real-ity. If they'd asked Nick to retire, he would've done so willingly. Great men before him had stepped down from their posts: Bobby Orr, Tom Landry, George

Washington. But no. He had been *involuntarily separated.* He didn't know how to admit this. To admit it, he would've needed to accept it.

He had measured his and Caro's financial runway to the last cent. There were the kids' trusts, though to siphon funds from those would be considered embezzlement. He sold off his season tickets to the Rangers, canceled his memberships to the Whitney and the Met, unsubscribed from *Men's Health* and *The Economist.* It wasn't enough. Once you threw in the private school tuition, the housekeeper, the mortgage on the gallery, the gymnastics lessons, the swimming lessons, the tennis lessons, the Brownie meets, the summer jaunts, and dinners out, there was little left. He researched how to relocate his family to Vermont or Wisconsin, some place cheaper than Westchester. His assets were bleeding out at a catastrophic rate. He'd lost a sixth of his wealth in the past quarter alone, with no salary to reinforce the gap.

To avoid confronting his shame, he invented stories: the young jaspers at the firm were envious; they'd slandered him as part of a witch hunt. Some days, he almost believed these lies. Others, he was swept up by a tornado of irrational urges. When he saw a deliveryman leave his cart of packages unattended, he imagined reaching in to snatch one. When he passed an idling police cruiser, he pictured himself hopping in and speeding away. Reckless – his precarious situation made him reckless; made him tip restaurant servers and baristas extra so that they wouldn't get suspicious. He was spending more now than ever.

'Is Linnie coming to the wedding?' Judith asked.

Nick turned, shirking Caro's gaze. 'I should hope so. It is our son who's getting married, after all.'

'Don't be fresh with me, Nicky. Come, help me with the crossword.'

His mother gestured to the open magazine section on the armrest. Though she didn't do the puzzle anymore, she liked maintaining a perception that she did so that no one would grow wise to the precipitousness of her decline.

'In a minute,' Nick said.

From the vantage of the kitchen island, he appraised the house: the cabinetry faded to beige, the scalloped valance collecting salt in its folds. He could already imagine the day a real estate agent would throw out her arms and say, 'Look at that view. We can work with that. Clawfoot tub, access to a shared dock, east-facing windows, and this – tell me this is the original trim. Old charm is a big selling point up here where everything is new, new, new. Imbues the home with *character.*' He pictured the families parading through with their strollers, skimming their sanitized fingertips over the countertops, inspecting the baseboards for damage.

In the adjoining living room, where the bleu celeste walls once conjured a sense of cloudless skies, bric-a-brac congested every surface. Judaica on the shelves. Plastic bags bulging out the sideboard cabinet. The wooden mallard had lost its bill. Beyond the atrium doors sprawled the backyard, and beyond that, the estuary where he and his friends used to play cops and

13

robbers. The apple trees were in bloom; a pair of cinnamon-colored bunnies schemed among the knobby roots. Six tote bags were by the door, ready to be loaded into the car.

'Think you packed enough?' he asked his mother.

'Always with the tsuris.' She jabbed an attenuated finger in his direction. 'You better watch that beast near my couch. I just got it cleaned.'

'Oh, please. That thing's been collecting dust since Bush Senior. Anyway, Matisse is a good boy. His teacher says he's the star of his training group.'

'If I had a nickel.'

Nick grinned. Over the years, his mother had derived no shortage of satisfaction from depreciating his inborn sense of exceptionalism. He was glad this part of her, at least, remained intact.

'Who's getting married again?' Judith asked. 'Did you say there's a wedding?'

'Benji – your grandson. And yes, there's a wedding, which you'll be attending, so I hope you managed to fit your dancing shoes into one of those bags.'

'I remember my father used to say, "When you're looking for a husband, don't look for looks, the looks can go. Don't look for money, the money can go. Just look for somebody with a fine character."'

'Good one, Ma. I'll write it down.'

'Don't start with me, Nicky. Come, let's do the crossword.'

Nick advanced to the fridge, where magnets in the shapes of various countries pinned up holiday cards and invitations from years past. An Alzheimer's Association binder clip anchored a typewritten living will, vesting him with power of attorney.

The sound of Matisse's nails against the floor gave the dog away before he loped into the kitchen, his nose guiding him to the English muffin in the toaster.

'No begging,' Nick said.

He loved his dog as he loved little else. Much energy went into ensuring Matisse was well trained, gourmet fed, impeccably groomed. A perfect specimen of the canine species. Was it selfish, he wondered, to own a dog? Some in his training group referred to themselves as *pet parents* rather than *owners*, but the former implied that your progeny would one day be freed from beneath your thumb. If all worked as it should, your children would outlive you; your pets would not.

On the kitchen counter, an envelope with familiar handwriting caught Nick's attention. He opened the flap and removed a penguin-themed birthday card from within. 'Happy birthday, Mom. Here's to many happy returns. Hope to see you soon. Love, Linnie.'

'What's that?' Caro asked.

Nick stuffed the card back into the envelope. 'Just a hospital bill I have to take care of.'

He followed his wife's eyes to the framed photographs on the counter: Avery at three on the tire swing, his father in uniform, Benji striding across the stage to receive his diploma. In the center was a picture of him and Linnie on their honeymoon. A turquoise beach, the water translucent enough that he could see their limbs in the shallows. Linnie was laughing, a small gap between her teeth, sun on her neck. He had the strapping body of an athlete. They looked radiant, their dreams as infinite as the waters around them.

How long since they'd last seen each other, last touched? Alice would've been twenty-eight now, an adult. Numbers were reassuringly tangible, an objective way to affirm how much time had elapsed.

Nick reached out and turned the honeymooners facedown.

Caro curled her hand over his. 'Should we—'

'What, now?'

Across the room, Avery was explaining to her Jewish grandmother why she preferred Santa Claus to the Easter Bunny. 'Toys last longer than candy,' she said, with a cognitive prowess that relieved her father. Who cared if she was a thumb-sucker? What other six-year-old could wrap her head around delayed gratification with such assurance?

'Yes, now,' Caro said. 'Don't you have to go to the airport?'

Any coyness surrounding their sex life had been discarded in the doctor's office. There had been no bleeding, just a heartbeat there, gone. Had Caro not scheduled a routine ultrasound, weeks might have passed before she understood the precise cruelty with which her body had betrayed her.

How young and exposed she'd looked lying there as the sonographer glided the probe across her middle, a rover seeking life on a desolate planet. The screen filled with haze. 'Looks about six weeks,' the sonographer said.

Caro's grip on Nick's hand tightened. No, there must be some mistake. She was ten weeks along; she was sure of it. Her voice was distant and echoey, as if the doctor's office had unfurled into a cathedral around them. Nick visualized the calendar on her nightstand where she kept track of such things. Ten weeks: today, your baby is the size of a kumquat.

He couldn't bear it, the thought of losing another child. Really, he couldn't. He'd wanted to walk out of the room right then. Her doctor had warned them that there were risks to having a baby at thirty-eight. Risks, further, to conceiving when Caro had already suffered one pregnancy loss. Now Nick was the one to protest. He'd always favored her propinquity to girlhood. How, in this regard, could she, his young wife, Caroline DeLuca, be considered *geriatric*?

Then the familiar crying, the agony, the questions. Caro was in pain, and he hated it. He couldn't stand seeing her like this, so he avoided her. He felt like a jerk when she called out his defense mechanisms, which she did so kindly and empathetically. She understood. She didn't have to, but she did. She said she was hurting too, so maybe they could hurt side by side. Maybe they could lie together in silence and absorb each other's pain. She could take away his, and he could take away hers – didn't that sound nice? She was showing him the supernatural lengths of her compassion, the underbelly of her resilience. That was Caro.

Yet Nick couldn't mourn with his wife, not really. Emotionally, materially, they couldn't afford another kid.

He was an old father as it was. Other parents at camp pickup mistook him for Avery's grandpa. He'd already had three children – two (Alice, Benji) with Linnie and one (Avery) with Caro. Memories of domestic bliss crowded his mind, and he worried that establishing new ones would require him to record over the old, like a cassette tape with finite capacity. Was it so far-fetched to assume that a man had some quota he couldn't exceed of diapers, first haircuts, and field trips?

No, he couldn't start anew. To articulate this, however, would be akin to taking a hammer to Caro's heart. So he kept his distance, made excuses. On nights she was ovulating, he'd text her from the Starbucks where he now spent the bulk of his days, saying he had to work late, and pray she'd be asleep by the time he tiptoed into the bedroom.

On the final stretch of spiral staircase, he put his hands on her behind and said, 'I don't trust this butt.'

She wiggled into him. 'This butt's capable of all sorts of things.'

'All sorts of evil.'

In the bedroom they drew the organdy curtains closed and undressed in practiced haste, pausing by the mirror to greet their reflections. Nick was, to his pride, a full head taller than she. The hair that blanketed his chest had long ago silvered. Concealed behind two obstinate inches of fat (which he hated but she found endearing) were the remnants of his former body, more compelling for their mystery, like the wreckage of some great ship.

He reclined onto the bed, stacking the pillows behind him to better admire Caro's breasts. He'd developed a newfound fondness for them. That this fondness coincided with the decline of his mother's health was a correlation too Freudian for either to dwell on.

'Get on top?' he suggested, a rusty nail poking through his tone.

Both knew the best position for conceiving was with Caro on her back so that gravity could assist – how many times had they reviewed that? Now she'd have to remind him, and he'd sigh but agree, making it seem like he was doing her a favor by bending to her will. Their eyes met with grim intent. Reluctantly, she rolled off him, the talk of pregnancy a turnoff for them both.

Again, the word *geriatric* flashed across the jumbotron of Nick's mind. Ever since that dispiriting conversation with Caro's doctor, he sensed she'd given up trying to get pregnant in earnest. More often than not, their intimacy would end as it did now, with both unsatisfied. But she'd made such a big deal of wanting a child, importuning him to her side at every possible moment, she couldn't very well say, 'It just occurred to me, sweetums, maybe you're right. Maybe trying for another *is* a terrible idea.'

For her to double back would entail more than simply admitting defeat. In espousing the arguments Nick himself had workshopped on her for months ('It's not the right time'; 'We haven't thought it through'; 'Isn't Avery a handful enough?'), she'd have no choice but to expose herself as a hypocrite – something she'd never do. Her resolve delighted him. Every month, he fought to hide his smile as she performed the charade of emerging from the bathroom saying, 'Call me crazy, but I swear I can feel the egg implanting itself.' Prompted, he'd rise to false excitement, applying a garnish of caution to remind her they shouldn't get their hopes up. Every pimple, mood swing, bout of nausea – it was hard to decipher what was a symptom of pregnancy and what of the stress.

Nick's phone buzzed on the nightstand. 'Shoot, that'll be Benji. They must've landed.'

'All right, then. Go.'

Nick detected, in the rhythmic ticking of Caro's pupils, that she was counting the days until this entire ludicrous affair was over and she could return to an existence in which she didn't question her status as his wife. They had both hoped that their marriage might recast their sins; prove she was not the mistress, as reputation would have it, but the one Nick had been destined to be with all along.

In the dozen years since Alice's death, Linnie and Caro – ex-wife and current – had glimpsed each other only once, at one of Benji's ice hockey games, when the two women avoided linking eyes across the arena. The chance meeting had been an unfortunate scheduling error. To maintain the balance between them, Nick and Linnie had agreed to divide their attendance at Benji's events. Nick took his college graduation, while Linnie attended his induction ceremony into some obscure leadership society Nick had never heard of. They each laid claim to but half of their son's life. Nick liked to think that he had secured the more desirable portion, but it was still only half.

'You think Benji considered telling us sooner?' Caro asked. She lifted her sunglasses from the nightstand and opened and closed the arms, feigning fascination with the hinges. 'Remember that time at Yankee Stadium, when he said he had to talk to us?'

'That was about his taxes,' Nick answered curtly. He didn't like Caro rubbing in his son's silence. 'Frankly, it's presumptuous of him to think we'd be so thrown by the relationship that he'd need to hide it. To each his own, I guess.'

'How long do you think Peter's known?'

'Beats me, Car. I'm just as in the dark as you. To tell the truth, part of me wonders whether this isn't all some cockamamie ploy for attention.'

'Benji's not like that.'

'See, a few months ago, I'd have agreed. But to date on the sly like this? Who knows.'

Nick didn't want to be cynical; he wasn't a cynic at heart. Lately, though, he'd begun to bewail the state of his home life, his marriage, the nation at large.

'I still owe Peter for the band,' he said. 'Need to get that wired.'

'And what do you owe me?' Caro asked thickly.

'Oh, plenty. Add it to my tab.'

'You're a goof.' She spun the sunglasses and set them on the bridge of his nose. The room turned agreeably dark, a shadow of itself.

'Honestly,' Nick said, one last maneuver to initiate the

conversation he'd been putting off for months, 'I must be in the hole to Peter a few grand by now.'

She yawned. 'God, this air's killing me. We should get your mom one of those heavy-duty air filter things.'

His snare had been too subtle. What choice had he now but to pray that by some stroke of providence, Morgan and Benji would cancel their nuptials, relieving him of the obligation to pay? When the bills arrived in the mail, he set them aside, telling himself they'd get taken care of somehow. He flirted with refusing to cover his portion altogether, but how would he justify it when Peter and Linnie had already fulfilled their shares? The rope between him and his son was worn down to its last thread already. A single twist, and snap.

He climbed into the SUV and set off. Sunlight, pure and yellow, buttered the sleepy, looping roads – a light wholly of this place, deep and penetrating. He felt he was less moving through the light than into it, descending toward some white-hot nucleus. The sea hovered so close he could taste it. The air, the smell, the swirling quiet . . .

The beauty persisted only so long before thoughts of work intruded. Nick had seen the warning signs, his encroaching redundancy. When he sat down at his desk, the numbers on the screen jumbled. Around him hovered the faces of men who'd been hired long after him, men still determined to prove themselves. His world had changed, leaving him and those like him behind.

The money game had two kinds of players: passive investors and active ones. The passives shot their wads into an index fund and waited for the market to rise.

The actives were the big shots. They researched and chose individual stocks to outperform the S&P 500. Nick belonged to this kind. Once, men of his ilk had thrived, overseeing accounts worth hundreds of millions of dollars. But over the past decade, the paradigm had shifted. Perhaps spooked by the market's volatility or the high expense of portfolio managers, the large-scale endowments had gone soft. This state of affairs was more dismal than the average hobby investor might realize. If those controlling the nation's capital suddenly decided to sit on their hands and leave their fates up to the market – if they decided *not* to play – then nobody was directing those resources to their most fruitful end. Small companies with promise were left in the lurch, while big companies continued to grow irreflective of their performance. Entire faculties were deprived of the financial nourishment they required. If this kept up, the whole market would enter gastrointestinal stasis – the end of capitalism; bye-bye, big, beautiful American dream.

The young men around Nick didn't grasp this. They'd come up in a different era – the post-9/11 era, the era of the participation trophy, the ubiquitous gold star. They were rah-rah Big Tech; let's wave our crypto-revolution flags and squeeze the Big Man. They didn't want to be the best at the game; they wanted to dismantle the rules entirely. They were the ADHD generation, antsy if any one stock sat in their portfolio too long. Their favorite phrase was *big moves*. 'Making big moves,' they'd say.

How absurd, the way these men arrived with their

Banana Republic chinos and leather briefcases, as if playing the part of a Wall Street broker in some Enron parody. Absurd, how they kept their pomaded heads down like some cabal of conspiracy theorists decoding the Dead Sea Scrolls. Whenever Nick suggested they ought to research this stock or that, one of these spirited bucks would boast about how he'd already done it and posted the results on the office's Slack channel – did Nick need a refresher on how to access it? Between their cubicles, these men ricocheted ticker symbols at such a lightning pace, he feared he'd get caught in the cross fire.

For some in his cadre, job loss would scarcely qualify as cause for concern. For those, there were options: assets to be liquefied, second and third homes to sell off. And though Nick, a skilled interloper, had metabolized enough rules to play in the sandbox of the Old Money crowd, he again perceived the canyon that roared between himself and his peers.

Overhead, signs for the airport appeared. Nick followed a line of cars onto a ramp. Arrivals. Departures. Short-term parking. The thought of the wedding weekend – of Benji and Linnie – surfaced in his consciousness only briefly. He had bigger matters at hand.

3

The seventy-seat regional jet touched down in Bangor ten minutes ahead of schedule. At the chime of the seat belt sign, the passengers stood to retrieve their belongings, sloughing off the morning's lethargy. Some hauled hiking packs with CamelBaks affixed to the side, while others wore woven sun hats and airy caftans, a Birkin bag dangling from the crook of a bangle-laden arm. Morgan and Benji waited until the others had deplaned before rising themselves. The slower they moved, Morgan reasoned, the more they might postpone the imminent reunion, prolonging for a few minutes the peace she sensed was on the verge of rupture.

At baggage claim, her eyes lingered upon two boys attempting to hoist each other onto the carousel. A symphony of hellos and goodbyes filled the hall, lovers parting and greeting. A tribute wall advertised the airport's former life as a military base.

'Thataway,' Benji said, pointing.

Outside, the sun blazed down with force. Spots of color bloomed on Morgan's vision. She held a palm to her forehead.

'You okay?' Benji asked.

A forced smile. 'Great.'

Why she'd ever dared hope this weekend might be

easy, even pleasant, Morgan could not say. When it came to their families, little was. Her mother, Sequoia, had recently boarded herself up in an ashram in Goa and refused to fly home for the wedding, which she rebuked for its contribution to the *marital industrial complex*. Her father, Peter, though ordinarily not one for vehemence, proved no better. This whole shindig was shortsighted, he'd argued, slicing his hands ardently through the air. Morgan had shrugged off his warnings. Now, though, with a hiss, the nozzle of panic came loose, and his words billowed inside her.

'There he is,' Benji said. 'Brace yourself.'

He waved at Nick, who swerved between angrily bleating vehicles to reach the curb. Nick popped the trunk, and Morgan carefully laid the garment bag containing her wedding dress inside.

Up front, father and son awkwardly embraced. 'And so the prodigal son returns,' Nick said.

How many times had they seen each other since the Syracuse commencement ceremony two years before, when Benji could barely muster a hello? A handful at most.

'Thanks for picking us up,' Benji said.

'You got it, champ.'

Morgan winced at Nick's affectation. He had a habit of falling back on terms of endearment when uncomfortable. He used to do it with Alice – *pickle, alley cat, sweet pea*. In his mouth the nicknames sounded clunky, an attempt to compress his children into people they were not.

'How was the trip?' Nick asked.

The two men talked, as people do when burdened with too much to say, of nothing at all: Benji detailing the travails of the toddler-strewn family seated behind them, Nick asking after Morgan's job as an assistant conductor for a Brooklyn youth chorus. It was going well, she said; the choir had just performed at the Macy's Fourth of July Spectacular.

'We'll have to watch that. Grandma would love it. And you, Benj – am I allowed to ask how work is going? You still thinking of pursuing that PhD? Might be worth the salary boost.'

'I'm not in it for the money.'

'No, of course not.'

Morgan narrowed her eyes, the palaver washing over her. It was obvious Nick had little capacity to appreciate Benji's career as a school social worker – a job for which the New York City Department of Education paid him $69,000 a year.

Nick flicked on the radio to hear the traffic. Out the speaker crackled an advertisement for the sailing competition that took place every August on the peninsula. 'Already ten,' he said. 'The trading floor's been open thirty minutes by now.'

'You're working today?' Morgan asked.

'When am I not?'

'You and my father both.'

'How *is* Peter? I was hoping to talk to him about the hospital. Maybe flex my expertise into the healthcare sector.'

27

'Why?' Benji asked, with a touch of suspicion.

'Can never be too curious. How's Mom?'

'Fine.'

But Nick must have sensed this would be his only opportunity to prod his son for information, because he said, 'Is she bringing a plus-one?'

'Yeah. Some new guy she's dating.'

'You haven't met him?'

The radio program changed. 'Coming up,' the host said, 'we have a professor from Johns Hopkins University, here to discuss his new book: *Artificial Intelligence and the Forgetful Mind*. Stay tuned.'

Morgan rested her head against the windowpane. Aspens lined the highway, their branches like flagstaffs upholding the sky. Pastures, ponds, an overturned canoe. The brush turned to a smudge, a fissured line of green. Clapboard houses blended into the fringes – human life, an afterthought.

Maine had been Benji's decision. It was neutral ground, he said. Far enough away that only the essential people would make the trek, close enough that anyone who wished could be there. Morgan, however, sensed the real reason: their lives in New York were a musical rondo, the refrain of what *was* continually disrupting the hope of what *could be*. Until she reached college, she had believed this force field of the past was inescapable. Only once she'd arrived at Vassar did she discover she could amble for hours without thought.

College had trained Morgan to differentiate between the high and the low, to distinguish art from noise. Her friend group, a salmagundi of pseudo-intellectuals, decidedly praised the former and derided the latter. Morgan liked these peers but did not trust them. They were too quick to reach for irony when expressing weakness or doubt, too quick to couch their vulnerabilities in self-effacement. Her chorus colleagues were the opposite. They were do-gooders, passionate about arts education and community engagement. Morgan fell somewhere in between these contingents – neither as acerbic as her college friends nor as altruistic as her colleagues. No one understood her, not fully. She ached for the bond she'd had with Alice, a claustrophobic vortex of obsession and possession. Would she ever know such unbridled closeness again, or had it been one of those fleeting wonders of youth one doesn't think to treasure until it's too late?

The Hopkins professor launched into a spiel on neural networks. Nick turned up the volume. As if the car were moving through time rather than space, Morgan envisioned the years paring away until she was back in high school, with Alice beside her and Nick at the wheel. They had planned a tour of several Northeast colleges, ending with Bowdoin and Colby. Through each information session, Nick dutifully jotted down notes about the student-faculty ratio, number of applicants, and extracurriculars, while Alice sat with her chin in her hand, looking bored. This was before her self-imposed hunger; before she and Morgan were swept apart on the rapids of adolescence; before her fixation on Mr Newman, her philosophy teacher, burned her up . . .

'So, lovebirds,' Nick said, 'what's in store for this weekend?'

Benji twisted in his seat. Morgan gestured for him to go ahead; he knew the itinerary as well as she. The only surprise would be her wedding dress, which she had insisted on shopping for by herself, not anticipating the pummeling overwhelm she'd feel stepping into Kleinfeld's alone. Around the shop, other brides-to-be stood flanked by their army of mothers, sisters, and bridesmaids. It struck her that she might have asked Linnie to come, but the idea of tiptoeing around Benji's mother, catering to her fragile joy, was unbearable. Even now, Morgan struggled to meet Linnie's eyes for shame of how she'd handled herself at Alice's memorial service twelve years before. *You were just a child*, a voice in her head comforted. *But you were not as young as you like to believe*, an opposing one chided.

Over the course of their friendship, Morgan had frequently wished hardship on Alice. Not agony per se, but a bit of adversity. It goaded her how handily Alice had attained everything she strove for: a seat in the National Youth Orchestra, a spotless report card, a fellowship to the Aspen Music Festival – appurtenances of success for which Morgan too had vied. The worst part was that even when Morgan *did* win, she didn't feel gratified. She felt instead that she'd won by default, that Alice hadn't tried in earnest to compete.

Had she felt more secure in her talent, she might have seen that the stage was large enough to accommodate them both. But at fourteen, fifteen, she couldn't reconcile herself to such understanding. The restricted view of youth allowed her to comprehend only what was immediately apparent, like a driver swerving up a mountain at night, each bend revealed in the instant her headlights struck it.

In the center console, Nick's phone dinged. He swiped up, a jagged stock chart filling the screen. He quickly closed the app. 'Pavlovian instinct,' he said. Then, to Benji: 'Well, all this wedding stuff sounds exciting.'

'If only everyone thought so,' Morgan muttered, recalling her father's disapproval.

'Ah, well, it's our duty to worry about you kids. It didn't help that you caught us by surprise – but I'm sure you'll get enough grief about that from everyone else.'

In a calculated act, Morgan and Benji had chosen to cloister their relationship from the outside world. No sense in inviting parental scrutiny until the nature of their entwining became clear. What if they separated tomorrow, or next week? What benefit could come from exposing their love, tender as it was, to the harsh elements of their parents' judgment?

But soon, the days of *casual dating* had turned into months of *serious dating*, and the secret of their romance became burdensome. The summer after Benji graduated from Syracuse, he and Morgan moved into a shoebox apartment on Atlantic Avenue. They thrifted furniture from Craigslist and Facebook Marketplace. The eclectic items imbued the space with a whimsy charm that came, in time, to seem deliberate. They constructed their life together with the well-intentioned but sloppy ardor of children decorating the house for their mother's birthday, eagerly waiting to pop out and yell, 'Surprise!' Their justifications for concealment became increasingly thorny. 'I'm sure our folks won't even mind,' Benji said. It was a grave miscalculation. After three years together, he dropped down on one knee, offering Morgan a temporary ring he'd found in a pawnshop on Grand Street, and eliciting anguish from both sets.

'The main thing is that we're all here together celebrating,' Nick said. 'But don't be surprised if not everyone is as supportive as me. You know your mother, Benj, and Peter ...'

'Can we let in some air?' Morgan asked. 'I'm feeling sick.'

'Need me to pull over?'

'No, that's okay.'

She craned her head out the window and shut her eyes, recalling her last conversation with her father. It had ended with Peter accusing her of purposely blindsiding him. 'I just didn't think you were the marrying type,' he said.

'What type is that?' she asked.

'A person like Benji, who's been through what those poor people have been through ...' Her father paused, formulating his thoughts. 'You think he's past it, but he's not. None of them are. Their hearts are too swamped with rage to make room for anything else.'

Tears welled behind Morgan's eyes, and she willed herself to glance away, an iron barricade descending between them. Peter schooled his face into placidity, as if even a single drop of emotion would cause the gaseous material inside him to detonate. 'What you do is your prerogative,' he said, 'but there are more people involved in a marriage than just you and him. There're families to consider. Histories.'

In the car, the shrapnel of these words pierced Morgan anew. She watched Benji from behind, waving his hands as he spoke. He had his mother's complexion but his father's mannerisms. How had she not noticed that before? Look at me, Benj, she silently pleaded. Give me that goofy smile. Tell me this isn't a mistake. Tell me this car isn't about to drive off a cliff.

Say it again.

4

After Linnie Olsen finished packing, rechecking her list, and packing some more, she left to meet Ezra Newman outside his classroom at NYU, where he was teaching a six-week course on the history of modern philosophy. It was the same course where she'd met him the previous summer. Ezra greeted her at the doorway with a kiss.

They meandered through the maze of eccentric shops, bookstores, and farm-to-table restaurants that colonized Greenwich Village. Each storefront self-consciously embodied the beatnik atmosphere of a long-departed era, true bohemianism exchanged for the polished imitation. Linnie was struck, as she often was, by how willfully contained her former life had been; rarely had she ventured beyond the Upper West Side. Now the entire city lay at her fingertips. She could ride the subway at 11:00 p.m., and who would stop her?

'How was class?' she asked Ezra.

He transferred his shoulder bag from one side to the other, revealing a blue ink stain on his collar. He was constantly marking himself with the tip of his pen, which he liked to twirl in absentminded contemplation. Linnie's attraction to him transcended reason or explanation, a supernatural pull, a molecular connection. He was cast neither in the mold of the suave Nick nor the geeky Peter, but rather in that of the armchair philosopher – a vaguely artsy persona that spoke to the dancer manquée within her.

'We just started on Leibniz,' he said. 'Always a hit.'

'Leibniz,' she repeated.

'The Principle of Sufficient Reason – that every event, even the most seemingly inexplicable, has a cause. Which then leads us to the problem of evil and the Perfect World Theory.'

Linnie vaguely recalled this theory. Something about our universe being the best possible one, since God had plucked it from an infinity of universes. She imagined alternate versions of herself, Linnie Olsens who were independently successful, who were right now in Vienna or Moscow, preparing to dance the Firebird in theaters resembling enormous jewel boxes. In how many of those worlds had she stayed in Minnesota, never to meet Nick or mother their children?

She and Ezra entered Washington Square Park. A folk-dancing event was taking place, couples weaving together and apart. The skunky odor of marijuana permeated the air. Weathered figures sat hunched over chessboards in the southwest corner, daring opponents to approach. Chalk-drawn circles adorned the ground, each bearing the same three words: YOU ARE HERE.

When Peter Hensley had first suggested Linnie matriculate as a continuing ed student, she had laughed, claiming she was too old and dense to keep up. Peter refused to partake in her self-mockery. 'You mean to tell me a woman of your capabilities is satisfied picking out paint swatches and volunteering at the community garden?'

'One class,' she agreed, more stung by his critique than she let on.

The first day, she showed up with the course catalog in her back pocket, having spent the previous evening poring over it, circling lectures in medicine, literature, anthropology. She envisioned a stream of knowledge funneling into her with each pen stroke. Peter was right – the courses revitalized her. All those doors shut to her because she lacked a college degree; the way she'd suspected Nick's friends at Soho House mocked her when she copped to not knowing certain politicians; how she'd avoided lavish restaurants because she feared invoking the servers' belittlement if she incorrectly pronounced *boeuf bourguignon* – such insecurities were, although not entirely vanquished, at least diminished.

Attending college was the first thing Linnie had done for herself in a long time. As she accumulated days in the library, a hidden knowledge began to flow inside her like water beneath a glacier's surface. She was carrying out an existence her daughter would never know: sleeping until noon, collaborating on group projects, renting a one-bedroom on Perry Street. It was as if the vitality that had evaporated from Alice's body had regenerated itself in her own; as if she were an insect growing engorged on Alice's lifeblood – a poignant reversal of their roles as mother and daughter, nurturer and nourished. It wasn't living again, but it was a start.

The most important lessons, however, came outside the classroom, where she relinquished her married mindset for that of a single woman. She learned to change the light bulbs, kill the crawling bugs, investigate the creaks and sighs that frightened her after dark. She learned to store every object on a reachable shelf. She mastered all the tasks she'd once outsourced to Nick, growing independent to the point of impregnability, jettisoning love in favor of survival. What use was a husband when she alone could tackle every obstacle?

YOU ARE HERE.

If only she and Ezra could stay here, far away from the upcoming weekend. Had Benji revealed his wedding plans to her sooner, she would've leapt into preparations with fervor: arranging seating charts, calling caterers, choosing floral combinations. But he had withheld every detail until it was absolutely necessary to call, on Memorial Day Weekend, when the invitations were stamped to go out, and say, 'I've got news, Mom. You better sit down.'

Linnie hadn't reacted with the enthusiasm she would've liked in retrospect to say she had exhibited. He had caught her unawares, making her feel like a cornered animal.

'Christ,' she said. 'I always knew you were a wild card, but this?'

'We've been dating for three years,' Benji said, with barely suppressed annoyance.

Oh, that did it. The apartment walls collapsed, all of Perry Street rushing toward her. *Three years?* He hadn't

37

even mentioned he was *seeing* someone, let alone thinking of marriage. And that this someone was Morgan – Morgan Hensley, Peter's daughter? A distant pounding filled her head. Benji, with his covert manipulations – just like his father.

'How did you *expect* me to take it, Benj?' she asked.

'You don't have to come if you don't want to.'

'Did Morgan pressure you into this?'

'No, we decided together.'

She detected the lie at once. Her sweet-tempered Benji. His secrecy had a woman's touch written all over it. *A daughter's a daughter for life, a son till he takes a wife.*

'Well, good luck, then,' she said.

'Have a little faith in me,' Benji replied, his subtext impossible to miss: How typical of you to make some-one else's happiness about your own unhappiness.

How much else had he withheld? She remembered the edibles she'd discovered in the freezer one Christmas when he returned from boarding school. When she questioned him about the candied cubes, he shrugged and said, 'Cold keeps them fresh.' He was skating the limits of authority, behaving cavalierly because he could, because he knew she would not challenge him.

They had spent so little time with each other since he'd left for boarding school, followed by summers at the all-boys camp in Maine and college upstate. She had ceded Family Weekend to Nick and Caro, unable to imagine the three of them traipsing between Syracuse's buildings, affecting closeness during the university's Potemkin tour (as if the parents of college students were under any illusions about what their children got up to). Whenever he returned to the city for holidays or summers, he seemed sharper, as if someone had refined his boyish edges with a scalpel.

Linnie didn't worry about Benji as she had Alice. He exhibited none of her own depressive traits, the shadows she'd feared her children might inherit. His native constitution was one of ineradicable cheer. Nonetheless, she'd felt obliged to warn him about the blue streak that coursed through her family. One Saturday when he was home from college, she sat him down and said they needed to talk. As she recounted the tragedy of her uncle Clyde ('A shotgun blast to the head in Grandpop's barn — absolutely horrible, the wood permanently stained'), relief smoothed Benji's features. It occurred to her that he'd been bracing against some far worse secret.

'Are you all packed?' she asked Ezra.

'Everything except my toiletries. And the tick repellent, which should arrive tonight.'

'You don't hate me for dragging you into this, do you? I promise I'll make it up to you.'

'Happy to support you, babe.'

Babe – it had been so long since anyone had called her that; since she'd felt young enough to be called that. Would she ever tire of it?

Ezra retrieved a cigarette from his pocket and lit up. The ribboning smoke transported her back to a time when she was underweight, her shoulder blades pressed against the indiscriminate wall of a rehearsal space, her fingers paring strips of dead skin from the soles of her

39

feet. Odd, wasn't it, that bitter seasons could appear so sweet in reverie?

'It should be fun,' she said. 'Though it might also be awful – my ex is a real piece of you-know-what – so don't get too excited.'

'Minimal excitement, got it.'

Now that the weekend had arrived, Linnie's plan to bring Ezra as her date seemed poorly conceived. She was terrified to introduce him to the guests. None of them had been there through the long years when each hour was tendrilled by an ache so strong, she feared it would strangle her in her sleep. Hadn't seen her chest cave inward when she stepped into the shower to cry. The time Benji accidentally set down four place mats instead of three. The scrutiny she applied to the girls who constellated by the fountain in Washington Square Park, expecting to glimpse her daughter among them. For years, she had been unable to hear a single note of music without weeping.

She joined a bereavement group. These were her companions now, the pietàs. One man's wife had died, leaving him with twin boys. At least he still had them, Linnie thought. He may not have had his wife, but fragments of her still floated about the world. Whereas she, what did she have? Nothing remained of Alice but the overwhelming weight of guilt. Her own hatred repulsed her. Did she wish for everyone to suffer as she had? Surely not. But she couldn't help placing herself at the top of the victim totem pole, to assume her pain cut deepest. Death made you acutely aware of every inequity, every way in which you'd lost the coin toss, drawn the two of hearts while someone else got a jack.

This was her bitter fate – or so she'd thought. But then, a few years ago, a window appeared where there had previously been only wall. In springtime, she discovered she could breathe more easily. She smelled the flowers, the sewage churning through the city's intestines, fresh brioche. Above, the sky shone marvelous and clear. The pall of her grief was lifting. Now, she yearned to laugh; to dance at her son's wedding and be flippant, breezy, fun. Above all, she wanted not to feel ashamed for abandoning herself to such possibilities.

She turned to Ezra, who was watching two pigeons spar over a crumb on the subway grate. 'Everyone can't wait to meet you.'

He smiled. 'And I them.'

5

The day Linnie Olsen first entered Ezra Newman's classroom, she was as unfamiliar to him as the other students: adult learners, sophomores striving to graduate early, delinquents who'd flunked their way into summer school. After her divorce, she had reverted to her maiden name, lost twenty pounds, allowed her hair to silver. In class, she spoke her mind in a way her daughter never had – offering reflections, contributing to group discussions, voicing questions without trepidation. One day she and Ezra bumped into each other in the student center, and she said, 'Professor, there's something I've been meaning to ask you. What's your take on the afterlife?'

'I'm a scholar, Ms Olsen. Not a preacher.'

'As a *scholar*, then,' she pressed, 'you must have some hypothesis.'

He set his hand on his chin. 'Well, Nietzsche posits a theory of eternal return. He uses the analogy of an hourglass. When the grains run out, the hourglass is flipped over. Everything we've done, we're fated to do again.'

'That's preposterous. How would anyone know that?'

His eyes twinkled, charmed by her outrage. 'It's not so much about the premise than what the premise tasks you with: to live your life as if you were destined to relive it forever.'

Linnie invited him up to her apartment to continue their conversation. It was there, in the overheated foyer decorated with Franz Kline prints, that Ezra saw the photograph of Alice. She was standing on a stage in a pink dress, her hair combed back, blonder than he remembered. A hickey-like bruise marred her neck where the chin rest of her violin had dug in. Her smile exuded joy, but her gaze seemed troubled, like that of the two-headed Janus, presiding over past and future.

'My daughter,' Linnie said.

The floodwaters of understanding deluged him: Linnie Olsen, Alice's mother. The odds of this connection were astronomical, even impossible. Some force greater than chance — fate, perhaps — must have intervened. How else to make sense of the fact that Ezra had unwittingly reentered the orbit of the very family he had struggled to forget? Before he could explain, he groped for his coat and hurried out, descending the stairs two at a time. Linnie caught up to him on the sidewalk, halting him with a firm hand.

'So, you've lost someone close to you too,' she said.

'Not someone. *Her.* I knew your daughter years ago, when I was still teaching at Manhattan Tech. It sounds unbelievable, but I truly didn't know you were related. The coincidence of that, I mean . . .'

Had Alice known about Nietzsche's theory of eternal return? Had it been in the book she'd borrowed from his apartment all those years ago? He pictured her

43

leaping off the George Washington Bridge ad infinitum, suspended between ground and water, being and what comes after. The flipbook of her life turned over, thumbed through again.

Linnie smoothed her hands over her skirt and fastened the top button of her blouse, restoring order. She conjured a bored expression to conceal her shock. 'But you only saw her once a week, right? How well could you really have known her?'

Her meaning was plain: I don't want to entertain this; don't make me. He remembered the weeks following Alice's death with granular clarity – the circling vultures of grief counselors, eager to feast on the slightest morsel of sorrow; the school's flag flying at half-mast; the hallways closing in around him. Anti-bullying seminars. Self-dramatizing faculty meetings where the principal urged the staff to report any student exhibiting signs of withdrawal. This time, the principal said with mannered graveness, only one life had been taken; for that, they should count themselves lucky.

Halfway down the sidewalk now, where Ninth Street merged into Christopher and the scrum of NYU students receded, Ezra stalled. 'About this weekend—'

Linnie's phone rang. 'Hold that thought.' She rifled through her bag. 'Hello? Oh, hi, bunny . . . Yeah, the bridal suite, a room for you, one for me . . . Well, I don't know how many your dad . . . Okay, well just say the reservations are under my name . . . All right, honeybunch, see you very soon . . . Love you too. Buh-bye.'

'Room mix-up?'

'Usual hijinks. You sure you don't want to back out? Heck, I wouldn't blame you. In your shoes, I'd probably do the same.'

He placed a hand on her arm. 'It'll be great. You said the bride – Morgan, was it?'

'That's right. Morgan Hensley.' A pause. 'Your paths didn't cross, did they?'

'Alas. It was a big school.'

Another lie. Ezra had studied the wedding website, the photographs of Benji and his soon-to-be bride posing in front of a waterfall, canoodling on the Brooklyn Bridge, facing their inverted reflections in Chicago's metallic bean. A stutter, and his mind located her: she, a teenager, strutting through the hallways with Alice, their movements marked by a jerky adolescent blend of both hoping to be seen and fearing to be.

That Ezra had stretched his excitement for this weekend seemed the most innocuous of the falsehoods he'd perpetuated in recent weeks. Yet some uneasy part of him wondered if he wasn't being lured into a trap. Maybe Morgan and the others had devised this elaborate ruse to expose him. You've done nothing wrong, he reassured himself. And he hadn't, not on paper. But he was aware of his hidden desires, the seed of ill will nestled in his heart. It was this seed – the brother of curiosity, dropped straight down from the verboten Tree of Knowledge – that galvanized him to tell Linnie that he would be thrilled to accompany her to her son's wedding. Whyever not.

What did Ezra see in Linnie? A desire to right his past misdeeds, or something more insidious, an urge to steal from her the missing pieces he needed to complete the puzzle he'd long fixated on? He did like her, that was true. And the sex was undeniably good. Yet it was Alice he kept coming back to; Alice he kept hoping Linnie would mention.

He was delighted when she granted him this wish. Last December, she recounted to him her experience visiting a psychic in Alphabet City. Before Linnie had even taken her seat at the table, the psychic shuddered and remarked that a child had entered the room behind her, clutching a rectangular object.

'An instrument case?' Linnie suggested, a tinge of skepticism blunting her belief.

'Perhaps. She's young – four or five. Often spirits, even those of the elderly, present themselves in the state they were happiest. Her teeth are chattering. It was cold when she died, and deep.'

A cry flew from Linnie's lips.

'Should we stop?'

'No, please, go on. What's she saying?'

The psychic's eyes, hemmed by neon liner, flitted from one end of the room to the other. 'You're seeing someone, a scholar.'

'Sorry?'

'Your daughter says to tell him that he'd love it where she is. Anything she wants to know, she just holds out her hand, and knowledge spreads over it like light. From her vantage, all the world makes sense.'

46

Linnie attempted to laugh while relaying this to Ezra – the brittle, preemptive laughter one uses to forestall another's judgment. 'I know it's silly, a medium and all.'

A tremor of awareness passed through him. They were in his apartment, where Alice had, unbeknownst to her mother, once sat. Out the window, two men were shuttling a Christmas tree to their car, each gripping an end. Ezra filled a water glass at the sink and tried to focus on the sensation of the liquid sliding down his throat.

'Don't you think it's odd?' Linnie prompted.

'That Alice mentioned me? No, I—'

'We never buried her. There was no body to . . . The Coast Guard wondered if she hadn't gotten caught on something. So, when the medium said she's floating around out there, I feared – I mean . . . who's to say there's anything anchoring her down?'

Disappointment touched the corners of Ezra's mouth. For a moment he'd believed that he and Linnie were swimming in parallel. But each time they approached a buoy, the rip current of denial jerked her away.

Now, outside her building, he paused. 'I have to finish packing. See you later?'

'Sounds good.'

They parted, as they'd joined, with a kiss. On the subway uptown, Ezra recalled what the psychic had said about Alice, her vantage. Maybe Leibniz was right. Maybe to explain the problem of evil, one only needed to zoom out far enough.

6

By Friday afternoon, most of the guests had checked into their rooms at Elizabeth Cottage, a summer estate perched on a hill. For over a century, the cottage had stood secluded as a monastery, overseeing the passage of families and time. Hidden within its ornamental grasses and the concentric rings of its tree trunks lay the land's rich history — the long-gone tracks of moose and caribou, the blood spilled in the Anglo-Abenaki wars, the artifacts abandoned by the explorers who'd claimed this far corner of the New World. Arrowheads. Beaver pelts. Fragments of bone. Every pebble and clod of soil told a story of glaciation and formation. Against this backdrop the wedding guests gathered, oblivious in their Cynthia Rowley tops and Vineyard Vines chinos.

Dr Peter Hensley, father of the bride, waited on the settee in the lobby, prepared to welcome the guests. His 'hellos' and 'how do you dos' were marked by an English accent — a vestige of his years attending grade school abroad. He moved with precision, a trait that had served him well throughout his three decades of pediatric surgery at Mount Sinai. At fifty-eight, he still retained the aura of geekiness he'd assumed as high school hall monitor and captain of the chess team. So formidable were those years of orthodontia and untimely boners that even now when a pretty woman regarded him, his imagination couldn't help but etch a trace of derision into her gaze. The guests would doubtless startle to learn how often the winds of insecurity battered him; they saw only the esteemed single father, the world-renowned physician.

The guests smiled at Peter, and he responded in kind. Yet the one person he wished to see – the very person for whom he'd planted himself in the lobby – had evaded him.

'I'm looking for Linnie Olsen,' he told the receptionist.

The computer screen was reflected in the clerk's glasses, two white squares. 'She and her guest checked in about an hour ago.'

At the word *guest*, Peter's heart gave a swift thunk.

Since Alice's passing, Peter had become a support beam for Linnie, providing succor in the form of a West Elm sofa where she fled twice a week. There, she toiled through the viscera of her gangrenous marriage, divulging truths she could never tell Nick, about how she caught glimpses of Alice everywhere she went. One day, she rang Peter at work to say she'd spotted Alice in a café, chatting with friends about a scuba instructor she'd met in Thailand. The next, she manifested as a German girl who required assistance decoding the subway map. Linnie held her breath for an enchanted moment – could it be . . . ? Then some instinct of rationality prevailed.

Peter listened, seldom pushing Linnie further than she was capable. While she reclined on his couch, he

49

claimed the club chair across from her, not wanting to take advantage (but also wanting very much to). He stood by her side through the long nights and still longer days. A year after Alice's passing, when Linnie's divorce was finalized, he accompanied her apartment hunting, preparing a list of questions for the broker. He agreed that the Perry Street place was perfect, a space whose very immaculateness advertised child-free living. Who could fault him if he imagined one day moving in his belongings beside hers, commingling their shoes on the rack?

Oh ... if only he could cork the flow of memories there. But no, there was that fateful day last August when Linnie called him, her voice atremble. She had met someone – a professor at the university where she was taking classes, the very classes Peter had encouraged her to try. The revelation devastated him. Though they'd never articulated their feelings for each other, he thought they had an implicit compact that they'd be together as soon as she was ready. For almost a decade, he had embraced other women only fleetingly, not bothering to correct them when they mistook his hesitance for lingering heartbreak over his ex-wife, Sequoia.

Only once, on a particularly grim night after an endless hospital shift, did Peter permit himself to wallow in his unrequited love. Self-pity struck him as a quintessentially American sentiment. Only Americans could be so arrogant as to believe life owed them a happy ending. (Having spent his formative years abroad, he considered himself only peripherally American.) For a drink or two, he languished in his sorrow. Then he folded it up and stowed it away, never to retrieve it again.

Now, in the cottage lobby, Peter set pen to paper. He intended to compose a letter to Morgan, assuring her that he hadn't meant what he'd said about the wedding being too hasty, that he'd merely been playing the part of a protective father. But his mind was too preoccupied with Linnie, so he found himself writing a letter to her instead:

> *My dearest Lin,*
>
> *There is so much to say, so little time to say it! Since today is my last opportunity to tell you this, here it is: I love you. Every single part of you. I love how your nostrils flutter when you laugh, your lopsided smile, the coconut smell of your hair. Would it be too forward to admit I've spent endless evenings imagining our life together? Forgive my boldness. If any part of this note sounds appealing, come find me in room 304. Don't worry about waking me – I'll be up waiting!*

Peter set down his pen and read the odious sentences back to himself. He winced at each exclamation point, those painfully conspicuous attempts at enthusiasm. He tore off the page and began afresh, forcing himself to focus on Morgan. Within minutes, he had drafted a letter to his satisfaction, expressing his paternal pride and unwavering belief in his daughter. If Benji was whom she wanted, who was he to stand in her way?

Before he could sign it, an old med school friend who'd flown in from Winnetka slapped him on the back.

'Pete, my dude,' he said. The men slipped into an easy banter, digging up memories of anatomy labs and sleepless residency nights. The joy of this past fell like a curtain over Peter's plight, concealing it from view. So thoroughly was it concealed, in fact, that when he reached for the folded papers on the settee, he tucked both into his pocket, forgetting the former was meant to have been discarded.

7

At noon, while the others busied themselves in the lobby, Benji retreated to the solitude of his suite on the second floor. Striving for what a fashion catalog might generously label 'Hamptons Casual,' he traded his polo for a linen shirt and stood before the bathroom mirror, examining his shave. He pumped a copious amount of gel into his palm, trying to exercise his restlessness through the quick patter of his hands. No amount of grooming, however, could rid him of the urge to escape the cottage and bolt into the Maine woods.

The problem was not Morgan, whom Benji loved beyond compare and was confident he wanted to spend the rest of his life with, but marriage itself – viz., the lack of successful reference models he had for it. He'd scored a front-row seat to the fallout of his parents' relation-ship, the hurts they'd inflicted on each other following his sister's death. He had been only thirteen when they split, too young to comprehend the complexities of love. The world had been easily parsed then, classifiable. He recalled those games of Twenty Questions he and Alice used to play on car rides: *Is it a person? Place? Animal, vegetable, mineral?*

Boarding school had opened his eyes to a new galaxy, college to the universe beyond that. He read Marx (well, skimmed; well, SparkNoted) and procured an old Occupy Wall Street poster of a bull in chains. He nibbled this, puffed that. He attended a frat party where a pig was roasted whole on a spit, prompting him to go vegetarian. And then there was sex. Until then, the furthest Benji had gone was third base – a feat he'd accomplished in his boarding school dorm, when brace-faced Shelby-Ann Grinker undid his Hyperlite pants and fellated him with sensational zeal. He'd kept her from going further, fearful that he smelled of hockey practice, that he'd come too soon, that her clunky orthodontia would shred his delicate privates (as Brent Harbach claimed they would). Only in the shower afterward did he kick himself for cutting it short.

Redemption was not long to follow. During a Syracuse mixer his freshman fall, a chick from Oswego named Natalie asked him if he wanted to *go upstairs*. In his desire not to seem too eager, and to dutifully employ the rules of consent that his liberal education had drilled into him, he asked whether that was what *she* wanted. She shrugged, her sweater slipping from her shoulder. Was that . . . body glitter? Panting, he followed her, and praise be the deed was done, on someone else's XL twin-size bed, beneath a Tarantino poster.

Natalie, or Natalya, as she'd introduced herself at orientation, was a Russian lit major. She waxed poetic to Benji about the ill-fated Oblonskys and Karenins, showing him that the Weils were not unique in their dysfunction but part of a long legacy of screwed-up families.

Under Natalie/Natalya's sway, he attempted to reconcile with his parents, but his efforts proved one-sided. His father was bitter with him for quitting hockey, while his mother asked empty questions that revealed her preoccupation with Alice's death. Nothing he did could ever measure up to his sister. It was no wonder, then, that he'd kept his relationship with Morgan a secret. Why subject her to the chaos of a family whose fibers were on the verge of disintegration?

Part of Benji didn't want Nick to attend the wedding – didn't want either parent to be there – but he couldn't deny them the opportunity to see their only son walk down the aisle. Always, he was caught in between, weighing their desires against his own. When he called to tell them of his plans, each suspected some ulterior motive. Why marriage? they asked. Why not continue to date, explore his options. They didn't understand. They saw him as a boy, a twenty-four-year-old just starting out. He should take his time, they encouraged; not be rash. He knew they took his declaration of marriage personally, as if he were saying: *Watch me succeed where you could not.*

The only hindrance to Benji's romantic plans was financial. Despite being raised in one of the most progressive cities in the country, he couldn't shake the societal expectation that the man ought to provide – a burden he could never shoulder on a social worker's salary. If he couldn't hack it on his own, he'd forever be tied to his father, forced to ask him for loans and endure his misguided doubts on whether 'helping

55

others' was a viable career choice for someone who wanted a family.

Morgan dismissed these worries. There was shame in not having money, yes, but there was shame in having it too, in living in abundance while so many lacked. Benji had a trust from his parents, half of which he'd come into three months from now on his twenty-fifth birthday, and the other half when he turned thirty; Morgan had received a small windfall when her Granny Rose died. They discussed disbursing these inheritances with the same seriousness they applied to all topics, spending entire evenings swapping idealisms across the table. Morgan spoke fervently about class warfare and the widening wealth gap, her face luminous as if she'd upturned it to a firework display. Benji loved how she challenged him – loved everything about her. On nights when her arm fell across the bed onto his chest, or when he arrived home to find her humming to herself as she pored over a music score, he'd think, Here. Let's stay here forever.

A lawn mower roared to life outside the cottage, calling him back. He assessed his reflection in the bathroom mirror. Too much gel. Too little sleep. Love was the right thing – how could it not be? This thought infused him as he walked down the hall to find his mother. He knocked on the door and waited. A man in wrinkled slacks and an ink-stained button-down answered.

'Sorry,' Benji said, his eyes darting to check the number. 'The front desk must've mixed up the room.'

Linnie hurried forward. 'Bunny, this is my friend Ezra.'

56

She stumbled over the word *friend*. Both men turned to regard her.

'Congrats on the wedding, man,' Ezra said.

A shade of mistrust came over Benji's eyes. 'Nice digs you got here.'

He surveyed the suite – the twin suitcases open on the floor, the domestic accoutrements organized on the nightstands. On the trousseau chest near the bed was the gift basket Morgan had stayed up late preparing. It contained a list of nearby hikes, two Evian bottles, and a handwritten note thanking the guests for joining the celebration ('Our special day wouldn't be possible without Y-O-U!'). Above the stately mahogany bureau hung a map of Maine dating back to 1820 – the year of its statehood. Through the window, low-hanging mist marred what, on a clear day, would have been a verdant vista of tree-topped mountains.

'Are you coming down?' Benji asked. 'Morgan texted me that we're needed. Peter's been asking for you all morning.'

'I was just unpacking.'

'You can do that later.'

'I know, but . . .'

'Mom.'

'Sure, bunny. We'll come now.'

Benji led the way, his mother making polite conversation behind him. At the threshold of the lobby, Ezra paused and asked Linnie, 'Did you want to swing by the concierge desk to ask about those extra towels?'

She looked at him with confusion. He widened his

eyes at her. 'Ah,' she said, catching his meaning at once. She patted Benji on the shoulder. 'You run ahead, darling. We'll catch up in a minute.'

Score one for the new boyfriend.

Benji turned darkly to the lobby, where guests milled about, sipping cucumber-infused water from tiny plastic cups. Finely chiseled scrimshaw pieces adorned the wall above the Steinway. Clustered around the instrument's feet were an assortment of tropical bamboo plants in chinoiserie vases – the spoils of some seafarer's voyage across the globe. A quote from Thoreau hung above the mantel: *I suspect that, if you should go to the end of the world, you would find somebody there going farther.*

Benji's friends, a mixture of yuppie tech bros and high-functioning stoners (though these were not mutually exclusive), huddled around the davenport. They sported docksiders and polos in beachy colors: aqua, coral, salmon. A group of men Benji didn't recognize were assembled in a semicircle around Morgan. Statuesque in a white sheath dress, she evoked the image of a sea nymph twisting sailors' fates in her palm. The men listened as she shared details of their upcoming honeymoon. Italy, she said, to courteous nods. A luxe villa in the north, with Calacatta floors and a dining terrace jutting over the Riviera.

'*Ciao, bella*,' Benji interrupted, wrapping his arms around her from behind.

She wriggled out of his grasp. 'Hi, you. Come meet my dad's coworkers.'

'A pleasure,' Benji said, shaking hands with each.

58

Peter held firm at the end of the line, a few steps behind the others. He appeared impeccably put together – an air of orderliness that originated within and radiated outward in waves, making even a single uncombed hair seem purposeful.

'Mr Limelight,' Peter said. 'Mind if I steal you a moment?'

Without waiting for a response, he steered Benji to the side. They stood with several inches between them. Benji smoothed his hands along the sides of his pants, wishing he might once more retreat to his hotel room. He hadn't sought Peter's blessing before the proposal, which he hadn't considered any grave iniquity – asking for the blessing was an antiquated tradition, wasn't it? But a displeased glint in Peter's eye told him he'd erred.

Once, Morgan had explained to Benji that Peter held two selves. There was Peter the doctor, serene and composed, and Peter the father, protective and prone to outrage where his daughter was concerned. Side by side these dual identities coexisted like sparring roommates. Benji sensed he must now be speaking with Peter the father.

'So,' Peter said, his lips curling tightly around the 'o.' 'My daughter, she's something else, isn't she?'

'No argument there.'

In exuberant tones, Peter trotted out Morgan's achievements – academic excellence (top of her class), musical talent (first chair in orchestra), and a promising career as a rising conductor. Benji registered each accomplishment as a demerit against himself: *See how much better she is than you?* She was, Peter continued, the Most Important Person in his universe, bar none. He ended this speech with a stern warning: 'Should you, for any reason, break my baby's heart, I swear I'll – Let's not find out, yes?'

Benji glanced off to his fiancée. She was talking to Ezra by the concierge desk, a pained expression on her face. Had she been close by, she would have no doubt chastised her father, his mere presence catalyzing her regression into a moody teen. *Can't you see, Dad, that you alone are causing trouble; you alone are hell-bent on ensuring my unhappiness?* she'd have said, her courage dwarfing Benji's own pathetic attempts to confront Linnie and Nick. He pictured the map of Maine hanging in his mother's room upstairs, the newly drawn borders marked in a bold hand. How trying, the process of asserting one's autonomy.

With a surge of compassion, he nodded. 'You have my word.'

'Glad to hear,' Peter said. 'I know your heart's in the right place. You've got that smitten look about you. I've been there too.'

'Oh?'

Benji had never heard Morgan speak of her parents' love. He had difficulty imagining it – the mismatched partnership of Sequoia, the self-professed hippie, and Peter, who organized his ties by color.

He closed his eyes, allowing Morgan's earlier depiction of their honeymoon to fill his mind: pastel houses sewn into the hillside, trattorias cambered around a port's edge. Into this vision he implanted future versions of himself and his bride, strolling arm in arm on a cobblestone street, drunk and giddy. If only they could get there, to that place where it was just the two of them again, everything would be all right.

8

A thud sounded on the grand staircase at the center of the lobby. Linnie turned in time to witness what at first appeared to be a silent comedy reel – a slapstick bit of a dog scampering through the hall, his leash trailing behind him. The dog collided with a pedestal table, crashing a vase to the floor. A man hurried by in pursuit, his shirt-tail flapping. 'Matisse!' he called. 'Drop it. *Drop. It. Now.*' On cue the dog lay down, belly heaving with gleeful pants. An attractive woman and a young girl gave chase close behind. On the landing, the girl stopped, opened her mouth, and let out a roar.

'Scary zombie,' the man said.

'I'm a *tiger*,' she corrected.

The girl roared again to show him.

'Scary tiger,' he said.

Only then did Linnie recognize this man as Nick – *her* Nick. Seeing him back in his family man persona disarmed her.

'Ahoy, the light brigade,' she called.

Nick looked up and smiled, exaggerating his sheepishness with a mock shrug. Linnie knew this performance well. During their marriage, she had watched him charm his way through many a dinner party, working his talents on one distinguished guest after another. He could handle the spotlight just fine, the bastard. He thrived on it.

'All copacetic?' Nick asked, drawing closer.

'We just got here,' she said.

'Not too dreadful, I hope. I know how you get with flying.'

Was he trying to impress her with how much he remembered, trying to show her he still cared? Should she likewise embed some obscure fact about him into their conversation as evidence of her own proof of memory? No, that was a puerile game with no end, no victor.

'It's good to see you,' he said.

'Good to be seen. Don't I get a proper hello?'

They embraced clumsily, remembering only mid-embrace that they didn't do this anymore – didn't touch or treat each other with niceties or pretend the carcass of their marriage wasn't smeared in each other's blood.

'I brought you a little something,' Nick said. 'Remind me to give it to you later.'

'What is it?'

'If I told you, it wouldn't be a surprise.'

Classic Nick. Long ago, he used to come home from work each Friday with a bouquet of roses, and Linnie would call herself lucky for having a husband who still aimed to romance her after so many years. Their intimacy had seen an upward tick too. She cringed at the memory of those steamy nights when Benji was at hockey practice, Alice at violin. It was obvious now that Nick had been trying to cover his tracks. A middle-aged man couldn't have enough stamina to satisfy *two* women . . . could he?

Linnie angled to address Caro, who exuded an earthy allure in a tea-length frock that Linnie suspected cost three times more than it appeared. Her hair was set in loose waves, her eyelids varnished with shadow. Linnie admired and even took a degree of pride in the younger woman's beauty, as if she herself had inspired Nick's good taste. Still, her throat constricted as she imagined Caro selecting each piece from a wardrobe – perhaps a his-and-hers closet she shared with Nick.

'Is your mother here?' Linnie asked Nick. 'How's she doing?'

'Decent,' he answered, at the same time Caro replied: 'Sad.'

Caro frowned. 'I found being at her place sad, didn't you? I keep picturing her at Benji's old matches, carrying herself through the crowd like some general, a real force.'

Linnie flinched, certain Caro had supplied this memory merely to flaunt her participation in their shared family history. That Nick remained blind to this covert form of feminine warfare made its casualties all the more damning. When he had called Linnie to inform her that Caro had proposed naming their daughter after Alice, he'd done so with pride. As if she'd be touched! Oh, no. She was no dolt. She saw straight through the gesture to its mealy core. By aligning the two girls' names (Avery, Alice), Caro had managed to seal her place in the dynastic line and usurp Linnie's.

64

The women's showdown was broken by Peter, who entered the circle under the pretense of arranging transport to this evening's rehearsal dinner. 'Nick,' he said. 'Good to see you again.' Then, addressing the rest of the group: 'We had a little run-in at Starbucks last month.'

'Oh?' Caro turned to Nick. 'You never said.'

'Didn't I?'

'I think I'd remember. Where was this?'

'Near my office,' Peter said. 'Fifth Ave, wasn't it?'

'I was there for a meeting,' Nick mumbled, removing his phone and thumbing through with determined swipes.

'Darling,' Caro said reprovingly, with a small smile to show the others she wasn't a nag. 'What could be so urgent?'

Peter's gaze flickered to Linnie. A brief moment passed between them.

'Everything okay, Pete?' she asked.

'That's an odd question,' he snapped.

She shrank back, chagrined. He'd never spoken to her that way before.

'Can you believe the kids are getting married?' Nick asked.

The parents considered one another. To admit none of them had known about Morgan and Benji's relationship was to admit they'd allowed their own tunnel vision to restrict the view of their children. The kids, in love – how had they missed it?

'Where are those rascals, anyhow?' Linnie asked.

Nick pointed outside, where Benji's friends had tossed

him into the pool fully clothed. He was scowling, lamenting the ruin of his wristwatch. His upset only stoked the boys' laughter. Set against the overcast sky, they resembled satyrs carousing across the bronze face of an urn. It struck Linnie that she didn't know a single one of those boys' names.

'It's certainly a shock,' Peter agreed.

When Morgan had told him she was moving apartments two years back – coincidentally the same weekend Benji had planned to move to the city – he hadn't pried (so he'd confessed to Linnie). Why would he? Morgan parceled out what she told him, but such was the nature of their relationship.

Linnie had received a similar lack of information from Benji, who'd assured her that he'd enlisted some buddies to assist with the transition from Syracuse to Brooklyn. She'd been more focused on the location of his move – the *where* – than the who. Brooklyn, of all places. Why not Wichita? Why not Timbuktu? Brooklyn wasn't even *that* economical – $3,100 for a one-bedroom walk-up. Linnie was sure he could find a cheaper place in Chinatown or Hell's Kitchen if he wanted. But he hadn't wanted to, obviously. All he wanted was to get as far away from her as possible. Her only inquiry to him had been 'Are you sure you have enough pillowcases?'

She refused to accept that she'd been too absorbed to delve further, that her unflagging pursuit to decipher Alice (*why, why, why*) had impeded her relationship with her one living child. Armageddon, doomsday, the apocalypse – her world had plainly ended the day her

66

daughter died. Where others saw progress and efficiency, she saw collapse. She couldn't describe this image without coming across as unhinged, a Cassandra soothsaying society's demise.

'Anyway,' Caro said, as if she'd been speaking for some time rather than standing silent as a sentry by Nick's side. 'I, for one, think they make a dashing pair.'

9

The owner of Alibi, the Brooklyn bar where Morgan and Benji first chanced upon each other as adults, had modeled his establishment on the Florida Panhandle dive bars of his youth. An outline of a palm tree glowed against the wall. The cocktails slid across the countertop came adorned with tiny paper umbrellas. Fairy lights latticed the back patio, where plastic flamingos in flaming colors balanced on hairpin legs.

Morgan, then twenty-five, had come to the bar at the cajoling of her roommates, who wanted to meet new people but spent the hour chatting solely among themselves. Whenever a lull arose in conversation, the roommates would each gaze off longingly toward the other patrons, suspecting everyone must be having more fun than they. The music was loud and bouncy, the tackiness of the interior obfuscated by dark wood paneling. A climate of sulkiness lingered among the trio, each blaming the others for keeping them shackled to their group personas. After an excruciating silence, Morgan said, 'I'm gonna see what's out back.'

She stood on the patio beside a set of planters spilling over with artificial foliage and shut her eyes, her body indistinct from its surroundings. In the order of things, she was utterly unremarkable. Someone brushed her side. She glanced over. The figure that met her was strong, handsome; his shoulders were cloaked in a chambray button-down.

'Holy shit,' she said. 'Benji Weil.'

Benji turned. The overhead lights imprinted a strange pattern on his cheek. Whatever stamp life's struggles left on a person appeared to have missed him, or he had transcended them. The gleam in his eyes, unguarded as ever, filled her with wonder.

'It's Morgan,' she said. 'Hensley. Alice's old—'

He cut her off, leaning in for a hug. His embrace seemed to say: *How could I ever forget you?*

They conversed for an hour. Benji had just wrapped up his third year at Syracuse and was staying with Linnie on summer break. Nick had helped him secure an internship at a consulting firm, which he despised. As he spoke, Morgan thought about how she loved this city. Loved how it could usher into your life a person you hadn't seen for years. Loved feeling that the world was small enough to hold you, like a paperweight in the palm.

'I've been coming here after work,' Benji said. 'They serve coffee during the day.'

She didn't know if he was inviting her to join him, and he made no effort to clarify. When had they last met? The evening of her high school graduation, possibly, amid the sultry haze of some karaoke bar in Koreatown. She'd invited him at the last minute, not expecting him to show. Yet he was the first one there, his body matured and his face hardened. They sang a duet, and Morgan felt oddly liberated from her usual need to impress. Now, that same memory was accompanied by a sharp twinge of desire.

The next afternoon, she boarded the G train and rode the thirty minutes to Williamsburg and Alibi. Benji was in the back on his laptop. She sat down across from him and said, 'Just so happens I was meeting a friend nearby.'

'Can I get you something?' he asked. 'I seem to remember you going feral for a hot chocolate when we were kids.'

Carefully, achingly, they exchanged a smile.

She set down her bag. 'I wasn't actually meeting a friend.'

He laughed. 'This was the fifth shirt I tried on this morning. Also, I haven't come here during the day – not once. The coffee thing was total BS. But I guess it worked.'

'I guess it did,' she said.

Morgan slid the spare key card Benji had given her into the door. The lock clicked. Benji stood Adonis-like in a white towel, facing the window. The mass of him sent a thrill down her spine. With his normcore fashion sensibilities and unaffected sincerity, he was refreshingly far from those hipster rails she'd been with in Poughkeepsie. She wrapped her arms around his waist, entrusting herself to his familiarity. The tang of the hotel soap on his skin brought to mind those bohemian apothecaries where her mother shopped. He firmed his stomach reflexively. 'Hey, aren't we supposed to wait for tomorrow?'

She clung to him tighter. He read the unease in her

grip. He was attuned to her in this way, knew the instant she walked into a room how she was feeling, whether someone at work or on the train had tipped the lever of her calm. He led her to the bed. They lay entwined atop the floral comforter. Benji's heart boomed beneath her ear.

'How are we?' he asked.

'Hanging in there.'

'Top five worries. Spill.'

She elbowed him gently. 'Promise me we'll be nothing like our parents.'

'At least your dad is better than mine, with his jerk-off, I'm-so-supportive-of-you-kids act.'

'I hate that you defend Peter. "Yes, sir; I promise, sir,"' she parroted in a mock-subservient tone that sounded hardly like Benji. 'My dad's friendship with your mom is so weird.'

'Weird in what way?'

'Just unexpected.'

'I don't follow.'

'Like, when we were teens, I'm pretty sure my dad banned me from going to your parents' place. I don't think I ever told you that.' She tried to make this sound offhand, a throwaway tidbit from their youth, though her body went rigid when she said it.

'Why'd he do that?'

'Maybe "ban" is too strong a word. It was after Alice. He probably didn't want to overload your parents.'

'Yeah, or he didn't trust them to keep you safe.'

A recriminating look bounced between them, this

mention of Peter's edict setting off a redistricting of the borders that demarcated their overlapping worlds.

Morgan had initially worried that her shared past with Benji would prevent them from ceding to baser instincts. In a dark corner of her mind, he was still Alice's pesky kid brother, who belched out the alphabet at the kitchen table and planted a walkie-talkie in the closet to spy on them. She needn't have feared. One glance at the coarse hair dividing his middle proved enough to quell this inner voice of doubt.

'Tell me what's really eating you,' he said.

'Your mom's boyfriend – did you meet him?'

'Briefly. Seems harmless enough.'

'He used to teach at Manhattan Tech.'

'No kidding?'

'He skipped out right after Alice died, before the semester even ended. There were rumors too. About him and some of the girls.'

'Oh, come on. He's dating my mom. You really think he'd mess around with his students?'

'Wasn't your *mom* his student?'

'That's different.'

Morgan felt her wariness, ordinarily pointed elsewhere, swivel onto Benji, casting his features in an unflattering light. Her closeness to Alice in both age and interest had caused her to obsessively examine that final year, when Alice entered a tailspin from which she couldn't wrench herself free. The self-harm, the truancy, the drugs – what had been the tipping point? It seemed to Morgan that in another lifetime, she herself might have been the one to lose control; that only by sheer misfortune had Alice been the one to tumble off the edge instead.

'Obviously your mom's a grown woman who can do as she pleases,' she tried again.

'I sense a "but . . ." coming.'

'I'm just afraid she's gonna get hurt.'

'You act like I'm her keeper. Eventually, she'll have to learn to pick up after herself.'

Benji had always been fiercely protective of Linnie, a defensiveness that bordered on the Oedipal. In the year before he departed for boarding school, he'd regularly pick up dinner for them both from the dim sum restaurant on the corner, texting her if he ran late to avoid the dreaded tableau of her in the kitchen, her face drawn and quivering as she dialed his friends to inquire after his whereabouts – a reenactment of the events of That Day.

Early on in their courtship, Benji had confessed to Morgan that he'd believed he would eventually come to understand why Alice had jumped; that he suspected the adults around him all possessed this sacred knowledge, a secret code inaccessible to him as a child. If anything, though, the brume that enveloped Alice's fateful act had condensed rather than dispersed. His parents presented two opposing approaches for dealing with it. The first (his mother's): fear; to recognize grief's form advancing on the horizon and prostrate herself before it. The second (his father's): denial; to continue erecting his battlements in the hope that he might one day slay the Leviathan. ('There are many mysteries in a man's life,' Nick said, 'on which it doesn't behoove him to speculate.') Benji found both methods equally myopic, though he struggled to envisage an alternative.

'I'm not trying to upset you,' she said now.

'Oho, well. Count this as a failure.'

'C'mon.'

'C'mon *what*?'

'Don't be that way. I'm just trying to talk to you.'

He rose to pace, putting distance between them. 'Why are we discussing anything to do with my mother right now, let alone my sister? Can't we have just one weekend that isn't a goddamn memorial to her?'

'This coming from the guy who's still looking for her.'

Regret swept into Morgan as soon as the words left her. Benji spun, his jaw set, an engraving of physical rage intensifying his movements.

In the three years they had been together, he and Morgan had fought only once, when they were still long-distance – she in the city, he up in the Rust Belt. One evening, while they were on the phone, Morgan heard the clacking of a keyboard and asked if she was boring him. No, Benji said. He was on his monthly mission to find his sister.

'To . . . find her?' she repeated.

He explained. Once a month, he'd plug Alice's name into a search engine and wait for the pixels to cohere.

'But, why?'

'Do you ever talk to her?' he asked. 'Out loud, I mean.'

'No, Benj. You do?'

He did. Every night, he would recount the day's events into the air. He saw himself as one of those NASA technicians, loading up a ship with phonographs and launching them into the ether to await a response.

'Honestly,' he said, 'I still feel a bit in shock, like the finality of it hasn't hit me. When I pass a store, I think, *Oh, I should get that for her for when she returns. She'd like that.*'

'To be clear, though, you don't actually think she's out there.'

'I'm not delusional, Morgan. Don't make me sound like a head case.'

'I'm just trying to make sense of it. The surveillance video is . . . well, I'd imagine it's pretty damning.'

'I know how it looks.'

'Okay, fine, let's follow your logic. Say she is out there. What's she doing? Choosing not to see you? Choosing to stonewall your parents? You can't tell me it's better to believe that.'

'Never mind,' he said.

Morgan felt a dam give way inside her, sorrow rushing to the surface. In expecting her to be different, to discharge him from the miserable solitude of his yearning, Benji had saddled her with a weight she could not shoulder. Only four years separated them, but that time accounted for a fundamental difference in how they perceived Alice. Morgan knew things Benji didn't, injurious things – the promiscuous tales of his sister that had spread like creeping thistle through the eleventh grade upon her death. By the fall of senior year, every boy had a story about the mysterious Alice Weil and how she'd taken them behind the school to, well (here they'd bow their heads in affected bashfulness) – it wasn't polite to say.

Now, Benji took a few steps toward the cottage suite window and crouched down. He bounced on his toes, as if lowering his gravitational center might allow him to activate some untapped knowledge.

'Do you think this is a bad idea?' Morgan asked. 'The wedding with everyone here – it's not exactly some big kumbaya.'

'As opposed to what? Hiding it forever, then having kids and hiding them from our parents? Never inviting them to birthday parties or holidays? Eventually they'll have to suck it up, and if they can't, that's their loss. At least we can say we were the bigger people.'

'*Can* we say that?'

'Just tell me what you want, Morg. You want to cancel it, elope? Then fine, that's what we'll do. They all know about us now anyway, so the secret's out. It's not like we can put the genie back in the bottle.'

Morgan bit her thumbnail. The calluses on her fingers, formed through years of violin, had long softened, but she still ripped her nails out of habit. Again the old instinct to strike before stricken reared its head inside her. She reminded herself that this was Benji, her good-hearted Benji, who was neither her mother nor Alice; who possessed not a single duplicitous bone in his body.

'C'mere,' he said.

She slumped into him, the conversation sapping her of even the ability to stand upright. He wove her fingers between his own. 'Your hands are freezing,' he said.

'I'm sorry for saying all that. I'm not even sure why I did. Who cares if Mr Newman's here?'

'Exactly. It's a stressful weekend, but everyone'll be on their best behavior. This is about us, not them.'

Morgan shored herself up with an affirmative nod. All afternoon, she'd imagined enumerating her misgivings and having Benji dismiss them. 'You're just nervous, is all. Cold feet,' he'd say, and she'd sniffle, ornamenting her plight with a simpering cry before relenting that he was right; she *was* nervous. That he hadn't responded as anticipated, hadn't strong-armed her into going through with it but instead suggested calling off the affair altogether, was the true source of her distress.

Together, they gazed out at the bay. Geese sat cumulated in the water's center. The waves sent a ripple through Morgan's gut. She pictured those NASA phonographs, the ones Benji had described, hurtling through the vacuum of space. The disks contained musical selections from Bach, the sounds of laughter and footsteps, a recording of Carl Sagan's son saying, *Hello from the children of planet Earth*.

'Everyone's moved on,' Benji whispered. 'We should too.'

His hands roved up the sides of her body. Grateful for the distraction, she threaded her fingers through his hair. His scalp was still damp from his shower. In his eyes flared a flicker of lust. The medicinal scent had dissipated from his skin, leaving only the smell of the man she loved. How deeply lonely it was to love. She moved his hand down between her legs. For a few minutes, they spoke through urgent strokes alone, as best they knew how.

PART TWO

PART TWO

I

'Are you ready, bunny?' Benji heard his mother ask. 'Dad's waiting in the kitchen to help you with your tie.'

'I think the pants are too big,' he said, cracking the door. On his floor lay piles of discarded clothes, a plate containing the remnants of a grilled cheese, a cat's cradle of gaming cables.

'Well, there's nothing we can do about that now,' she said with a sigh. 'Didn't I tell you to try them on?'

'I forgot.'

A series of fine-tune adjustments transpired on Linnie's face, her expression modulating across a gradient of moods until it landed on resignation.

Contrary to what she might have believed, Benji was not put off by his mother's sternness. If anything, he considered it a relief from how she'd treated him since Alice went missing two weeks before, when she pulled him toward her with such force, it knocked the breath from his lungs. At age twelve, Benji was keenly attuned to any fluctuation in the emotional tenor of those around him. He sensed that his mother's austerity was the real thing, while her suffocating love was mere simulation.

In the kitchen, he found his father waiting with his legs crossed at the round table. The day's newspaper lay open before him, but his eyes stayed unmoving on a solitary breadcrumb. The entire house smelled unfamiliar, an amalgamation of all the people who'd trafficked in and out. Already the morning had been endless, each hour dragging as they did on the eve of Benji's birthday. In the corner, the fish tank burbled. Had anyone remembered to feed the guppies?

'Did you have breakfast?' Nick asked, positioning Benji before him. 'There's fresh bagels on the counter.'

Benji nodded, but his mind had already veered down memory's foreboding trail, back to the day his world was upended. There he was in the hockey rink two weeks prior, his stick thrust overhead. He'd scored the final goal. The cheer that followed suffused his body with gratifying warmth. The moisture on his fingers, the sting of ice on his cheeks – these were trifling deductions against the elation of victory. His eyes cut to Nick behind the plexiglass. *See, Dad? I'm making you proud.*

After the game, the team went out for ice cream cones, parents at one table, seventh graders at another, still in their sweaty pads. It was then, bathed in the unforgiving lights of the parlor, that Nick got the call from Linnie: Alice was missing.

'Did you see your sister today?' he asked Benji.

'Can't remember,' Benji lied, covering for her, just in case.

While the other boys and parents continued to rejoice, Nick thumbed furiously at his phone, fine lines creasing his forehead. Don't do that, Benji thought. He had reached that sensitive age when he perceived himself as an object of judgment. He loathed anything that might draw attention to him or his family, a fact that only amplified the torment of the two weeks that followed: the policemen giving him juice boxes; the questions at school; the guilt of craving his parents' attention, of needing to remind them that he was still here.

Nick finished knotting Benji's tie and smoothed down his collar.

'Dad?'

'What is it?'

'I . . . I . . . Do you think . . .'

'Come on, Benj. We don't have time for this.'

Nick glanced at the Superman watch Benji and Alice had given him for his birthday. He tapped the face twice. Today was Alice's memorial service, and they were going to be late.

2

Mid-forties and hirsute, Nick Weil had the thickset bearing of a workhorse, and the mentality of one too. Each morning he woke at sunrise to lift weights and absorb the market data from overseas. On clear days, he would walk the thirty blocks south to his office so that by half past seven, when he was seated at his rosewood desk on the thirty-first floor of a skyscraper overlooking the park, he could assure himself that he had accomplished more in a few hours than many did in a week. Toiling in the corporate world was, he'd come to believe, akin to partaking in a cultish circle jerk – one needed merely to convince others that his trauma was worse than theirs.

Nick wasn't the sort of man who harbored delusions about changing the tide of history. He knew men like that, had gone to school with men like that – ones who read a single biography of Robert Moses or watched a film about General Patton and grew rabid with the notion that they were playing life too tamely, betting on Baltic rather than Boardwalk. Nick termed this the Great Man Complex, which consisted of two fundamental components: (a) the desire to accomplish a feat that would dazzle the world, and (b) the knowledge that they never would, a failure for which they oscillated between blaming others ('If only I hadn't needed to provide for my family . . .') and themselves ('If only I hadn't been such a lazy fool . . .').

Oh, sure, if pressed, he'd admit he too had once dreamed about puttering around the globe, amassing a stockpile of tales to make him a marvel at any dinner party. Well into his twenties, he envisioned himself carousing through the whitewashed streets of Mykonos, where he'd be thought charming and oh-so-American by a group of Aphrodites who desired, above all, to mother him. But if there'd been time for such excursions, he had missed it. There were the usual university escapades at Haverford, and then the business degree at Stern, and then Linnie and the kids. The mechanical arm of Progress had tossed him onto a carousel from which he couldn't disembark.

Leaving Benji to his bagel in the kitchen, Nick picked up his mug ('Who needs Google when you've got Dad?' it read) and walked stiffly through the brownstone to retrieve Linnie, passing macaroni art projects and staged family photographs. Past Benji's room, where the door was open, the lights on. Next, Alice's. He'd entered only once since that Tuesday, when he'd discovered a single thread of golden hair on her pillow. He'd held it taut for several minutes, unsure of what to do, his eyes drifting over the concert programs pinned to her corkboard. Shoes on her floor, an uncapped perfume bottle on the nightstand, a compact mirror on the desk – all these objects laid out as if she'd only just set them down. Had she stood in the room's doorway, contemplating how others would perceive it?

85

His phone buzzed in his pocket. He knew before he looked that it would be Caro, whose messages he'd ignored for the past week. He would erase this text later, just as he'd meticulously erased his call log and email inbox.

Nick and Caroline DeLuca (she preferred the diminutive; Caroline was too frilly for her taste) had flirted with each other for so many months that consummating the relationship had seemed the only logical terminus. Why, however, they'd continued to sleep together after that initial indiscretion, Nick couldn't say. Any answer he concocted – that he enjoyed the proximity to danger; that he and Linnie had operated on autopilot for so long, he'd forgotten how hectically his heart could stutter in a woman's presence – sounded trite. And the true reason, that he'd fallen in love with Caro, was unbearable.

Love – good grief. Twenty years his junior, Caro had at first seemed too great a cliché to entertain. Her age was evident in her choice of perfume, a fruity scent like the inside of a Victoria's Secret store that would have been nauseating in larger quantities but which Nick enjoyed when they passed each other in the hall. To enhance their conversational landscape, he memorized the names of the members of the royal family, studying them as if for a quiz. He splurged on expensive Air Jordans to wear on casual Fridays. The total effect of these choices made him feel pathetic. All through his thirties and early forties, he'd considered himself a perennial twenty-two-year-old. But embedded in Caro's youthful flesh was a mirror so that he couldn't help seeing himself as he was, sketched by the hand of Age.

In college, Caro had spent a semester abroad at Trinity College. This brief period on the Emerald Isle, a formative blip in the course of her otherwise uneventful life, proved the source of her sophomoric tendency to adorn her speech with antiquated turns of phrase, as if she were perpetually auditioning for a George Bernard Shaw play. ('Would it suit you to . . .'; 'Shall I collect the papers from . . .'; 'Do you fancy a drink . . .') She showed no inclination toward mercantilism, that practice driven by pure efficiency. Instead, each sentence emerged a perfectly composed structure devoid of utilitarian purpose, much like an upside-down house. They were the linguistic choices of a woman without offspring, a woman who had time to spare.

Their affair followed the usual stages of development, moving from youths teasing each other on the playground to teenagers passing notes in class to adults probing each other's bodies and minds. And what a mind Caro's was: engaged, witty, and just contrarian enough to excite him yet not enough to make him feel threatened. Culturally, they understood each other. Catholicism, Judaism – two sides of the same dogmatic coin. Both were well-versed in motherly guilt. (A joke: What's the difference between an Italian mother and a Jewish mother? The Italian mother says, *You've disappointed God.* The Jewish mother says, *You've disappointed your mother.*) Nick didn't worry about offending Caro like he did Linnie, whose Scandinavian roots made her taciturn, tense. To be with Linnie, he'd needed to plane down his edges. But those edges had grown back more jagged with time, and he could no longer embrace her without lacerating her.

Nick had deliberated coming clean to his wife many times but feared the consequences. Inside her lurked a serpent of vulnerability and rage, its V-shaped snout hovering just beneath the surface. The only reason to tell her would be to absolve himself of his guilt, and wasn't that ultimately more selfish – to shatter some-one's entire Weltanschauung just to make oneself feel better? No, he couldn't do it. In the bathroom mirror, he practiced smoothing the deceit from his features with the precision of a baker frosting a cake. Who would ever have thought that he, garrulous Nicky, known to spoil surprise parties well in advance, could withhold a secret so massive?

Nick wondered if Linnie had ever strayed herself. He remembered a game of Scruples they'd played in their twenties, when he erred in answering yes to a dilemma card that asked whether she'd pose nude for $10,000. Their friends whooped at his response. 'What?' he said. 'Dancers monetize their bodies all the time.' Linnie laughed along with the others, but when Nick glanced at her, he caught in her face an unanticipated spark of malignity, bright and eerie as radium. Right then, he vowed that should it ever come to it, he would be the first to walk.

For all his musings, though, Nick knew deep down that his wife had remained faithful. This was the most brutal truth to accept of all. She was a better person than he, her every action fueled by some sort of proletariat moral imperative. She believed in doing what was best for their family, even if it came at the expense of her own pleasure (*especially* if it did, for then she could play the martyr), while he considered the distinction between *self* and *other* a spurious binary – a palliative means for people like Linnie and his mother to justify why they'd forsaken their own vanities for some illusory familial good.

He reached the master bedroom. Linnie was inside, holding the eulogy she'd typed the night before. Her lithe figure, which once lent her an ethereal air onstage, imbued her now with a severity Nick found off-putting. She was twirling her ankle, tracing the alphabet. The morning light fell in abstract smudges over the furniture. He set the mug on her nightstand. 'Want some?'

'What is it? Coffee?'

'Scotch.'

He slung an arm around her shoulders. She flinched, a reflex they both ignored. He stayed touching her, though their contact was obstructed by the cloak of grief between them. Red rimmed her eyes. They were blue, like Alice's; pale enough that the sun could pass through them unimpeded. The ophthalmologist had recommended she wear shades even on cloudy days to slow the development of spidery blood vessels along her retinas. Her gaze was slightly narcotized. She must have taken something. Her face betrayed only vague traces of emotion, rising from some inner, hard-to-reach zone.

Her wispy blond hair, which she processed every four

weeks to keep away the grays, was slicked into a neat bun, whetting the cheekbones below. She hadn't eaten in days, and only evaporation could account for the diminishment in the drinking glass on the dresser. She had been the one to view the CCTV tape the police had collected from the bodega near the bridge, the one to journey down to the school to clear out Alice's locker. She had volunteered to do these tasks, and he had let her, terrified of doing them himself.

'Is that what you're wearing?' he asked, his mind yawing into a bewildering gulf of numbness.

'Yes, why?'

'No, nothing. It looks – you look – nice.'

She exhaled forcefully. It was the wrong thing to say. Twenty-one years of marriage, and they'd never been so unmoored. When she regarded him, he swore he could see a trace of contempt behind her eyes. They each needed someone to blame, but why had she targeted him? If they were pointing fingers, it was her family tree that was blighted by melancholia, not his.

We both should have viewed the tapes, he thought, then swiftly comforted himself remembering that he'd been the one to wait on the frigid banks of the Hudson while the dive team strapped on their gear. Hours he'd stood there shivering until the detective came over to say they'd notify him if any remains were discovered, and he should head home.

'This is the worst day of my life,' Linnie whispered. 'I wish we could skip ahead to when it all feels distant.'

'Mhm.'

She looked at him suddenly and asked, 'How do you feel?'

'Me? Fine.'

'Bully for you.'

'Obviously not fine, but—'

'How does someone survive this?'

'I suppose they don't.'

'Every time I walk, I can hear pieces of my heart rattling around inside me, like I'm a bag of metal tools someone is shaking. I can't live like this.'

'You must. For our son.'

'How?'

'Eventually, the old you will die, and you'll become someone else.'

'I dozed off just now. Sitting here. I dreamed of her.'

Her hands fretted the paper in her lap, twisting it into a scroll. She had long, delicate fingers – a magician's grasp, suited for holding cards, making them disappear. Her whole body trembled. He hugged her to make it stop. She pulled away, her eyebrows coming together in a question; she hadn't realized she was shaking at all.

'What happened in your dream?' he asked.

'We were at the beach—'

'Which?'

'I don't know.'

'Rockaway? Riis? Long Beach?'

'Any of the above. Pick one.'

'I'm just trying to get the full picture.'

'Christ, Nick, it was just a beach. Does it matter?'

'I suppose not.'

When the kids were younger, they had taken family trips to the shore in Maine where Nick had spent his own boyhood summers. Alice had loved Judith's house. How easily he could visualize her as a girl, fulfilling the picket-fence vision of fatherhood he'd once venerated: fishing tadpoles from the estuary, tossing a Frisbee in the yard, carving her name into the night sky with a sparkler. A person got only so many opportunities to make an impression on a child before they calcified into a being all their own.

'Okay, so what were we doing in this dream?' Nick asked.

Linnie lapsed away from him into memory. The spout in his chest released a stream of compassion. His sweet, aching Linnie. All the resentment he'd felt over the past few years as the scope of her ambitions seized up around them receded. Hate, love – two states of the same element, like ice and water vapor. He longed to sidle closer to her and smell the citrus of her Jo Malone perfume, to knead her cold feet in his hands (poor circulation – a result of years spent compressing her toes into pointe shoes), but her posture gave him pause. He was frightened of her, as one is frightened of a feral animal that might lash out without warning.

He was frightened too of himself; he should not be functioning so well. He crossed to the walk-in closet, pretending doubt over his choice of tie. The space was neat as a military barracks. He held up two options for Linnie to choose between.

'You were with Benji,' she said, selecting the one on

the left. 'He needed help with fractions. Alice was on a towel, reading. She was happy.'

'*Happy*, happy?'

'Yeah, why?'

'Nothing. Good – I'm glad.'

Oh, Linnie – you liar. In recent years, Alice had avoided sharing with her parents any detail of her life. Those who met her often commented on this clandestine quality, this aura of elusiveness. She radiated an energy that wasn't quite sadness, although Nick suspected, with a flash of shame, that in the aftermath of her suicide, those who'd known her would misremember it as one.

'Well,' he said, 'Benji's downstairs waiting. We should get going.'

'It really happened,' Linnie insisted. 'My dream.'

He nodded as if to sift this vision of Alice into the heap of other memories he had of her. He too wanted to think of their daughter this way: happy.

3

From the street, Linnie watched Nick secure the door. He twisted the knob once for certainty before tucking the keys into his pocket, where they left an unseemly bulge.

To enter the family home, a historic Anglo-Italianate brownstone she and Nick had acquired during the housing bubble burst, one had first to ascend the sandy stoop, which led to a turquoise entryway – an abridged pilgrimage from desert to sea. Four avenues to Central Park, the Hudson to the west. A farmer's market nearby every Sunday where vendors hawked greens grown in kinder soils. The brownstone, its neighborhood – what safe places these had once seemed to raise a family.

'All set?' Nick asked from the stoop, his face careworn beneath the cool February sun.

'I can't remember if I turned off the stove,' she said.

'I'm sure you did.'

'Maybe I should go back and double-check.'

'Lin, it's fine. Let's go.'

The sidewalk undulated before her. Trees, buildings, telephone lines – the entire world seemed unreal, as if covered in protective film. Only Alice, and the world Alice inhabited, could be real. Linnie didn't know how to step or speak in this foreign place. Between her throbbing temples, words shriveled and grew gangly offshoots. *Let's go*, Nick had said, or was it *Let go*? *Go let. Goblet. Gobble.*

She saw now that the most terrible fact of mourning was the indifference of routine. After today, Benji would return to school and Nick to work, and she'd be left swimming in the gulch of hours alone, wishing for a freak accident to claim both her husband's and son's lives. Only then could she swallow down the bottle of Xanax stored in her nightstand drawer without guilt. This would be ideal – if the whole family could be obliterated in one fell swoop.

To resist the temptation of death, she focused on performing chores – dusting the blinds, aligning the coffee table books – as if by cleaning every surface, she could remake the world, coat its edges in sealant so that no unbidden feeling could slip in.

Linnie was one of those rare Upper West Side mothers who'd always resisted hiring a maid. She'd brought one on when the children were small, a woman named Magda, who'd arrived the first day with a baby strapped to her. For hours, she mopped, swept, and scrubbed with the baby attached. She soothed him hurriedly when he fussed, her eyes full of fright. She swore to Linnie she wouldn't bring him again. Please, she begged, she needed this job.

'It's all right,' Linnie said, but it was not.

Housekeepers were, to her, a disquieting signifier of wealth. Did everyone in her and Nick's enclave carry this same compunction? Doubtful. A couple they knew from the kids' school confessed to paying their house-keeper an exorbitant sum merely so that she could reprimand them for their mess. So accustomed was this couple to having money and the ease it offered, they needed to pay someone to create a little friction in their lives. 'She's like a dominatrix,' the wife said with a collusive smile. 'But without the added strings of a ruined marriage.'

Linnie, Nick, and Benji walked on Broadway toward the synagogue, passing the same grocer, the same ventilation duct, the same bookstore they passed every day. None of it was familiar. Curls of mist rose from a steam stack nearby.

'Look out, Mom,' Benji called.

Linnie startled, realizing she'd stepped off the curb into the bus lane.

Nick placed a hand on her shoulder and delivered a gentle squeeze.

Born and reared in Little Falls, Minnesota (hometown of aviator Charles Lindbergh), Linnie Olsen had moved to Manhattan as a wide-eyed eighteen-year-old, with dreams of dancing Aurora in *The Sleeping Beauty* at Lincoln Center. At the coercion of her company's repertory director, she changed her name from Linnie to Lynette and consumed only clear liquids for an entire month.

The ballet dream had ended abruptly, when Linnie plunged ten feet into the orchestra pit during a grueling tech rehearsal. The doctors said she was lucky to have only broken a few ribs. But something inside her had shattered as well. She'd been drawn to ballet for its order, symmetry, discipline – all the qualities an artist's erratic lifestyle lacked. She wanted to dance, but she did not want to be a dancer. As she lay convalescing, she realized this city had exhausted the fumes of ambition and youth that once propelled her forward.

And so, on the eve of her twenty-second birthday, she packed her suitcase and took a cab to Penn Station, with every intention of returning home. She was in the terminal when a man approached her. He introduced himself as Nicholas Weil – Nick, for short. He was off to a business meeting in Pittsburgh but promised to take her out when he returned. Confident, courtly, attractive. She heard 'finance' and thought: *Stable*. How differently her life might have played out had she boarded that train back to Minnesota.

Ahead of her now, Nick and Benji walked in lockstep. Father and son. Both their gaits remarkably wide, as if straddling stones amid a rushing river.

The Weils had never been religious, never belonged to a congregation. One time, while on the way to a theater in Times Square, she and Nick were stopped by a bearded man in a black hat who was trying to engage Jews in the Shabbat rituals. 'Are you Jewish?' he asked (only, pointedly, to Nick). Linnie smiled and said no, and they continued on their way. For the subsequent few blocks, Nick seethed. He wasn't annoyed by having been stopped; he was actively offended by it. When Linnie tried to prod him, he brushed her off. Seldom did he speak of his father's relatives who'd been gassed in the camps; relatives whose genes were within him, and within their children, who cared more about Christmas than Hanukkah. When the holiday season arrived, Benji insisted on acquiring a tree from one of the many stands on Broadway. That past fall, Alice had enrolled in a philosophy seminar and returned home each Wednesday (the only day she'd willingly engage in the family dinner conversation) brimming with theories to disprove the existence of God. *How about this, Mama: Can God create a stone so heavy he can't lift it?*

How worldly she was. How cynical. Linnie could imagine her daughter scoffing at the idea of a temple service held in her name. But death required rituals – a crucible in which to soften the heart before grief mutilated it into its new shape.

The dream from that morning, the one Linnie hadn't shared with Nick, resurfaced: Alice, her fingers tightening her bow, her eyes skimming a sheet of music. Motes of rosin eddied in the sunlight through the picture window. Such an ordinary scene, one Linnie had witnessed thousands of times. Alice's feet were turned out, her face assuming its usual industrious expression. The silver necklace she wore, a dainty treble clef given to her by Judith, swayed as she moved. Linnie had merely listened, not wishing to disturb the girl. If only she had done more. What significance could she glean from such a mundane vision?

Alice and her violin had long been a marital sore spot. Nick accused Linnie of pushing their daughter too hard, depriving her of the joys of a normal childhood. What joys? she wanted to ask. She, who wished her own parents had pushed her harder, further. She, who'd needed to claw her way to the top.

Despite the cold, the city streets bustled with people. An airplane soared overhead, its sleek back unzipping the blue. On the corner, a man was caught in a tug-of-war with a giant mastiff. Nick watched them pass, fascinated in spite of himself. His preference for dogs over people baffled Linnie. She'd grown up with dogs on her family farm, but those were viewed as instruments of labor rather than as beloved family members. What saddened her most about dogs was how little they asked in exchange for their loyalty – some treats, a few scratches behind the ears. A dog gave you its whole heart, and what did you do? You broke that heart, and brutally, every time you walked out the door.

Every now and again, Nick would proclaim they should adopt a puppy. Linnie, forced as usual to play bad cop, said no, absolutely not. Nick was seldom home, so the burden of tending to the beast would fall on her. Besides, a home congested with Waterford glassware was no place for a pet. 'You're right,' he agreed. But still, he wanted one.

Surely their wanting must have a limit. Even if Nick retired tomorrow, they'd be fine. They could take lavish holidays, see Benji off to college, live comfortably in their brownstone (albeit within the confines of their suffering). Yet it was not enough; not for her husband and, if Linnie were honest, not for her. At some point along the way, she had subscribed to the insidious mindset of urban merit-ocracy, where complacency meant sliding backward.

Her materialism horrified her. Before Nick, she hadn't been able to name the schools that composed the Ivy League, had never attended a film premiere or gala. Nested into her gut was a flint of shame waiting to ignite whenever one of his Haverford buddies made a snide remark about the waitstaff at a restaurant. For a long time, she'd felt more tethered to the waitstaff's class than her supposed own.

'Here we are,' Nick said.

The three of them stood taking in the Reform synagogue, a formidable structure of red brick with the Star of David etched into the doors.

For the past two weeks, before the video footage emerged, before it became clear that Alice would not return, Linnie had watched Nick pray for their daughter's safety, placing his right hand over his eyes in the middle of the night when he assumed she was asleep and mouthing the words he'd learned in Hebrew school as a boy. He must have felt guilty praying, because he began each time with an apology to God, in whom he'd never believed.

She had sought comfort in her own rituals, using the mahogany prayer beads she'd received as a girl. She did this in the privacy of her closet, believing it gauche to openly broadcast one's need. She was not devout in any traditional sense – she couldn't stand institutionalized religion, which she felt tried too hard to lure people in using pyrotechnics (water into wine, bushes aflame) – but she couldn't abide the notion that no higher power existed at all.

Back when they were young, Nick used to share with

her stories about his father, Victor, who'd flown fighter jets in the war, unveiling each tale with the unabashed delight of a child unearthing matryoshka dolls. Her favorite story was about the time Victor decided to take a plane out over the swath of forestland extending across western Massachusetts. Midway through his journey, the fuel gauge suddenly dropped to empty. Victor nosed the plane down so that he could scan the dense pine groves for a patch of open field below. Everywhere he looked, though, he saw only dispiriting swales of trees. Sensing death was upon him, he released control of the yoke. A thud, the plane striking earth, the putrid smell of burning rubber. In disbelief, he opened his eyes to find that a clearing had opened right where he'd needed it.

After ensuring he was indeed alive, Victor abandoned the plane to walk toward safety. He combed through the brush for hours until he finally stumbled upon the lights of a lookout tower. He relayed to the guard inside what had happened. The guard said he'd like to see the plane for himself — he knew of no clearing in these woods, and boy, did he know these woods well. The two men set out. After many miles, it became apparent there was no clearing and, furthermore, no plane. The earth had yawned open momentarily and then stitched itself back up. By every account, what had occurred was a miracle, as awe-inspiring as the parting of the Red Sea.

A miracle — that was precisely what Linnie had wished for leading up to today. Maybe the police were right and Alice *had* jumped, but when she did, the river gelled into a trampoline that bounced her back to land. It sounded impossible, yet Linnie lived in a world of impossibilities. As a dancer, she'd defied the laws of gravity, standing on one toe and flying through the air. Pierina Legnani had performed thirty-two fouettés in a row; Alicia Alonso danced the role of Giselle until she was seventy. The world was full of lunacy. Who said that a girl couldn't come back to life? What proof did they have? It felt perverse to hold a memorial service when no remains had been recovered; no vessel into which Linnie might pour her mania; no child for her to point to and declare: That fragment of me that I birthed, which for sixteen years has floated outside me, is no more.

She hesitated before the synagogue doors. If she didn't open them, the service would not take place. If the service didn't take place, her daughter could not be dead. What if, what if, what if. Maybe Alice had kept walking and was right now in Delaware or Ohio or some other place, calling out for her mother's help. How easily this might all be a mistake. Schrödinger's cat, with the box's lid eternally taped shut.

Linnie felt the fabric of time warp beneath her. Today might well be the day two weeks before, when she marched herself down to the police station, a gnawing presentiment in her gut. The officer on duty, a stocky man named Ernesto, indulged her with the usual questions: Had Alice run away before? Was she doing drugs? Hanging with the wrong crowd? Were there adults she'd been speaking to – older men, perhaps? Had anything transpired at home to set her off?

No, no, no, Linnie said, growing more uncertain with each declination. A mentholated feeling filled her veins. When the policeman asked her to follow him to another room, she couldn't bring herself to move. To take even a single step forward was to travel away from Alice, away from the fact of their lives together. She sensed, as a mother did, that some cataclysm was occurring in the cosmos. The only time she'd felt that sense of metamorphosis before was when she'd given birth. The officer proffered a form requesting the release of Alice's dental records. As Linnie signed, she forced herself not to consider the cases in which such records would be consulted. But her subconscious could not easily be tricked. The present was a harsh light lancing through the mists of her hope.

'Nick,' she said, turning to him. 'Slap me.'

'What?'

'You have to, please. I need to know this is happening, that I exist.'

'Oh, Lin.'

'What if?'

'What if *what*?'

She raised a hand to her forehead, feeling for fever. Her thoughts each bore a serrated edge. What if she's still alive. What if I'd done it all differently. What if . . . what if . . . what if . . .

Linnie had always felt that one's fear must always be measured in proportion to the Worst Possible Outcome. The more ambiguous the threat, the more you could torture yourself dreaming up possible conclusions. So it was with Alice. There was the chance (unlikely) that she'd been drugged or sex trafficked or struck dead in the street. Linnie tormented herself by enacting each of these scenarios in her mind. Was it better to believe her daughter had taken her own life, or that she was off in a cellar somewhere, held against her will?

'It'll be over soon, promise,' Nick said.

Then he stretched forth a hand and seized the door handle, the edge of Schrödinger's box. With a tug, he opened it, extinguishing her hopes with a single gesture.

4

The synagogue's interior pink walls evoked the lime-stone of the Judean Hills. A chandelier dangled from the ceiling like a tarantula on a thread. As the Weils entered, the room's atmosphere shifted to rearrange itself around them. The guests had organized themselves according to domain of Alice's life (violin, school, family) – the like-minded seeking one another out. In their starched attire, they resembled participants at a conference, each waiting for someone else to take the lead. These were the same people who had formed search parties, troop-ing through the city and pinning up flyers bearing Alice's photograph.

Collectively, the guests had visited all seven continents. They had endowed university chairs, donated hospital wings, contributed to political campaigns, attended inaugural balls. Two Marshall Scholars, a Rhodes Scholar, four attorneys from Kirkland & Ellis. Their photographs regularly graced the pages of *Barron's*, *The Wall Street Jour-nal*, and *Forbes*. Several owned boats, jets, artwork by Rothko and Koons. A few stashed their wealth in undis-closed offshore accounts. Some had gotten burned when the last major Ponzi scheme unraveled. For a horrifying instant, Nick indulged the thought that if he were richer – say, on par with his college buddy Gavin Keifer (heir to the Keifer meatpacking fortune) – there might have been paparazzi from the *Post* here, clamoring to capture him at this nadir.

Wealth in Manhattan was divided by neighborhood (to say nothing of those so-called outer boroughs), and within these neighborhoods, by street, and within these streets, by building, and within these buildings, by apartment. No one would contest that a two-bedroom on Seventy-Second and Madison was more desirable than one on Ninety-Third and Second Ave., although both were considered the Upper East Side. To belong to the city was to recognize where you fit within the system, as some students obsessively tracked their class rank and knew precisely what grade was needed to overthrow the next pupil in line.

'Nicky, there you are,' Judith exclaimed, emerging from the throng. In one hand she'd tucked a tissue, which she used to blot her forehead. 'I'm schvitzing. If only *someone* would turn down the heat.'

'Please, Mom. Can we not.'

Nick had seen his mother every day over the past two weeks, though an onlooker might presume otherwise by how she clutched him. Her theatrical display would have rankled Nick under other circumstances. Today, though, he welcomed her oversize personality, which he prayed might momentarily subsume him.

Like her son and the forebears whose intransigent genes he'd inherited, Judith was of durable stock, driven by a set of convictions that ranged from proper table manners to politics. On a typical day, she could be found wandering the aisles of Hannaford supermarket in a loud-patterned frock, her comportment recollecting that of a street peddler as she phoned friends to announce the latest health scare within their circle. ('The town crier,' Nick called her. Also, 'Paul Revere.')

'Look at me,' Judith said, wiping her eyes. 'A leaky faucet already.'

Benji stepped forward to greet his grandmother. She tousled his hair, kissed his *keppie*, remarked on how tall he'd grown overnight.

'Linnele,' Judith gushed. 'My darling girl.'

The women shared a searching look, mother to mother. For years Judith had disparaged Linnie, whose lack of a college degree and Aryan countenance stigmatized her as distinctly *other*. Nick had to bite back the reminder that she'd treated his ex, one Rachel Epstein, copresident of the Haverford Hillel, no more warmly. Rachel had been *too* Jewish for Judith's taste, though at least she was the right religion.

Lynette Olsen, Judith liked to say, what kind of *fakakta* Wasp name was that? (As if Nicholas Pierson Weil, a name so self-consciously anglicized as to befit a Rockefeller or DuPont, were any better.) And Linnie's looks – the emaciated arms, the refined nose a girl from Riverdale would pay a pretty penny for. Lynette Olsen, who might look like a Wasp but was assertively *not* one, as her hometown would attest. There was nothing *wrong* with Little Falls, but it was far from the likes of Camp Androscoggin and Choate. Her childhood home was one of those Gothic Revival farmhouses that sent a chill

through your bones just looking at it. Nick hadn't antici-
pated that, because she was poise personified. But she'd
worked at it, boy had she worked at it.

Now, in the synagogue lobby, Nick perceived an
unusual warmth coloring his wife's and mother's expres-
sions, a closeness born of necessity. Linnie sought a
mother's solace in Judith's critical gaze, and Judith was
more than eager to oblige.

Of her own mother, Linnie had revealed little, only
that she'd possessed a weak spirit she herself vowed
never to inherit. Mabel Olsen had been a salt-of-the-
earth Midwesterner, slender as a wheat stalk, with flaxen
hair that mirrored the plains on which she'd spent her
life. This description sounded like the opposite of Judith,
who was as steadfast as they came, belonging to that ilk
of immigrants for whom intermarriage poses a direct
threat to the survival of the Jewish race. When Nick had
brought Linnie home to Maine twenty-odd years before,
Linnie had asked whether her Protestant background
would bother his parents. Not in the least, he'd lied.
Because the matter of her religion wouldn't *bother* Judith
and Victor Weil – it would crush them. That Linnie's
piety was greater than that of either parent was irrele-
vant. Privately, each would wonder where they'd gone
astray. Had they failed to instill in their only son, their
sole source of *naches*, the importance of continuing his
sacred lineage? 'Why not spit on your ancestors' graves
and save us all the trouble?' Judith had said to Nick on
the eve of his wedding.

The older he grew, the more it occurred to Nick that

his mother was not a happy person. When he showed her pictures from his travels, she'd sigh and say, 'Ah, Europe, how I miss it' – not out of genuine nostalgia, but out of some need to assert her own worldliness. Her inquiries over the phone maintained a frosty distance. She referred to his friends she hadn't met as *those people* – as if their absence from her life negated their value in his. Oh, his mother – his petty, smothering mother, who viewed his leaving the nest as a betrayal, him turning his back on the woman who'd given him everything, everything, everything. No amount of gratitude would suffice.

'You remember little Jacob Goldfarb from day camp, *nu*?' Judith asked, shoving the aforementioned forward.

In a rush of condolences, Jacob Goldfarb, the funeral director-cum-synagogue president (no longer so little), ushered the Weils to a room off the lobby where the rabbi waited, sheathed in a black overcoat.

In Nick's experience with rabbis, they tended to fall into two categories. The first was the brainiac, drawn to their profession out of a need to quench some unnamable thirst. Such men sought comfort in esoteric books, reviewing the teachings of rabbinical scholars. They were akin to transactional attorneys in their fealty to technicalities. The other was the sociable kind, the trial litigators, who lived for the Friday-night dinners, where they could revel in the congregants' adoration over a bottle of Manischewitz. Their bravado might not win them any Talmudic awards, but it played well to a crowd of upper-class strivers who craved a commercialized, even Christianized, version of faith – spirituality for the suburban yoga mom.

Rabbi Friedman fell into this latter category. Not top of his high school class at Ramaz, but proud awardee of the 'Best to Bring Home to the Parents' superlative. He styled his russet beard with artful dishevelment so that it read more hipster than religious leader. His sonorous baritone thrummed inside Nick's chest as he instructed him to safety-pin a torn black ribbon to his shirt. He passed similar ribbons to Linnie and Benji, explaining that the tear in the ribbon signified the rending of the mourner's heart.

Nick stole a glance at his wife. A wrinkle had shoe-horned itself between her brows. The pin would not cooperate with her fingers; thrice she pricked herself. If he tried to assist her, she would resist. Or maybe she wouldn't, and would that not be worse – her yielding, expecting him to withstand the crushing pressure for them both?

'I wish I had the right words to offer,' Friedman said. 'With time, the ache will grow fainter; your distance from it greater. But this' – he pointed to the torn ribbon – 'will never go away, I'm afraid.'

'Can I ask you a question, Rabbi?' Linnie said.

'That's what I'm here for.'

'You believe in God, right? So what's your explanation?'

'My explanation?'

'Why do *you* think He did this?'

Contempt was gaining in her voice. Nick winced. She was wasting her breath, tormenting the rabbi because she couldn't bear to work the knife over herself any longer.

Friedman was patient. 'At one point in Exodus, Moses requests to see the Lord's face. He asks this of Hashem, and do you know what Hashem says? He says no. "No man shall see my face and live."'

'Great, more riddles,' Linnie muttered.

Friedman scratched his beard. In his eyes was the resigned look of a man twice his age. 'Sometimes, Mrs Weil, understanding is beyond man. When God wishes it so, the truth can be so powerful, it would kill us even to look it in the eye.'

The fact of the matter was that Linnie Weil had few friends. Other mothers considered her an odd duck. At playdates, her solitary inquiry to them – *What do you do all day?* – elicited dismay, as if she'd asked after their sexual fetishes or their husbands' salaries. Their responses were a refrain on the same few tasks: ensure the upkeep of the city and summer homes, manage their child's intense calendar, frequent workout classes at luxury studios. Some had siphoned their privilege into quaint business ventures: bespoke wooden jewelry, twee bath products in the molds of desserts, a line of angora apparel. The mothers listed these activities defensively, as if to say: *See? We are fulfilled.*

Linnie identified the boundary separating her from these women as the integument of her judgment, conceived the moment she was handed an audition number to pin to her leotard. She couldn't gravitate toward the median if she wished to stand out. The only way to ascend was by pitting her talents against those of her peers, using them as stepping stones.

She reflected on this as she sat beside Benji and Nick in the shiva chapel, accepting condolences. Many of the mourners were young, classmates of Alice's who were unschooled in funeral etiquette. They studied their shoes as they stumbled over the words rehearsed in the cab ride over. The teenagers huddled in groups, eager to distribute the responsibility among them. Some giggled nervously as they spoke; others wept. The adults were more adept at harnessing their urges, though Linnie sensed their scorn sweeping over her from across the room.

It was evident the congregants grieved more for her husband than they did for her. In every social circle, Nick was well regarded. He was amiable but not gratingly so; enthusiastic but not servile. When he wanted a task executed, he declared it so – a trait that others, imprisoned in their own need to be liked, found commendable. They lined up before him as though he were their homecoming king.

'I'm *bored*,' Benji whispered. 'When can we go home?'

It was precisely the wrong thing to say, and Linnie cherished him for it. Before her eyes, he transformed from a boy of twelve into one decidedly younger. As a kindergartner, he used to take his pillow each night and curl up on the floor beside Alice's bed. Linnie only learned of this one morning when she went to wake the children for school. That bond between the siblings, what would become of it? Where would Benji direct his displaced love?

She again tried to survey the snaking queue of mourners, but a sense of detachment pulled her from the room. In her mind, she was once more sixteen years old – Alice's age – on the precipice of a glorious future. That summer, she'd honed her dance skills to the point of expertise, yet she felt neither joy nor satisfaction when the teacher singled her out for praise. Only the teacher's criticisms stirred in her any feeling. In this, she realized that her yearning was not for success, but rather its pursuit. She was inflicted by a brand of masochism wherein she craved only more ache, was tantalized by only her failures. Ballet, an art form focused on perfection, provided the ideal veil for this affliction. In choosing this path, Linnie all but guaranteed that she'd forever remain apprenticed to her hunger, in thrall to the interminable *almost*.

A hand grazed her shoulder. A face hovered above her, alight with expectation. High cheekbones, unplucked brows, hypermobile arms that bent inward at the elbow. Morgan Hensley.

'Hi, Linnie,' Morgan said. 'I'm really sorry. For everything.'

Linnie nodded. 'I heard you spoke well at the assembly. Thanks for that. You're a good friend.'

It was a generous lie. From the start, Alice and Morgan's relationship had been defined by competition and jealousy, Alice pouting on the Saturday walks home after conservatory, complaining that Morgan had insisted on showing off her triple stops each time the studio teacher came around. Both had been hailed as young prodigies, peerlessly talented. Each was featured as a performer on NPR's *From the Top*. In encountering each other, they were forced to confront the reality that neither was as unique as she believed, sensing a threat to the identity she had dutifully carved out for herself.

Not until high school did they manage to resolve their

differences. Both were accepted into the same specialized magnet school and agreed to put aside their rivalry to form an alliance. Linnie suspected that the loathing between them had not dissipated but merely been spackled over. Teenage girls could maintain such rapports, capable of accommodating love and enmity in equal proportion.

Linnie turned to Morgan's father. Agony had seeped into every crevice of Peter's face, hardening the kindly features. 'You as well, Doctor. Your family meant so much to her.'

Peter smiled, a smile that managed to convey both intimacy and reserve. 'I've been holding you in my prayers.'

'Oh, Pete. It's been so hard. I feel—'

Devastated, adrift, bereft – each word skated only the surface of Linnie's emotion, an anchor dangling thousands of feet above sea bottom. She didn't know what to do with herself, how and who to be. Just last week, she'd gone down to the school, walked the hallways her daughter had walked, opened Alice's locker as if it were a portal to the past. What evidence did she expect to find inside – a note laying everything out? The contents had disappointed her, the debris of any teenage girl: a mirror Linnie vaguely remembered purchasing at Staples, a book of essays by Camus. She opened the cover. *Property of E. Newman*, it read. A clementine wilting in its Ziploc. Photos of Alice and her friends, tacked up with clothespins.

'It's all right,' Peter said. 'You don't have to explain.'

His eyes, the same brown as Morgan's though more benevolent, touched in her a nerve so deep that she shivered. She felt a twinge of being seen and understood – a sensation she'd long consigned to the past.

'Allie was one of the good ones,' he went on. 'I always thought that. If there's anything we can do . . .'

He reached for her hand. She forced herself to inhale, exhale – staccato bursts of oxygen that left her light-headed. (Do not cry, do not cry.) To stanch her tears, she turned her head and met, there, Nick's eyes. A barb of embarrassment spiked her chest.

She withdrew from Peter's touch and thanked him again for his words. He held her gaze for what seemed an unbearably long time. She imagined Nick, seated only two chairs away, distancing himself enough from his waiting line of devotees to admire the subtlety with which her emotions bloomed on her skin.

6

Morgan cleared her throat. To her father and Linnie, she said, 'I never imagined that Allie was . . .'

Linnie looked up. 'Suicidal?'

In the mother's frown, Morgan caught a flicker of compassion, the assumption that they were both impaneled on the same grand jury, struggling to assert their innocence.

'Did she say anything to you?' Linnie asked.

'I wish.'

But Morgan had suspected *something*, hadn't she? Over the past few months, Alice had missed more violin rehearsals than the other students combined. When she did show, she was unprepared. Maestro Keller called her out for dragging in the measures. Such a critique, which would once have brought Alice to tears, was met with only a defiant shrug, a half-hearted mea culpa.

'I don't want you to apologize,' Maestro Keller said. 'I want you to fix it. Count the measure aloud, please.'

Alice counted while the ensemble waited in charged silence. In an orchestra of fifty, seeing one of your peers called out was both thrilling and humiliating. Beneath your schadenfreude was the awareness that the conductor might next turn his temper on you.

'Now sing it,' Maestro Keller ordered.

Unfazed, she did.

Where did Alice go on those days when she didn't attend rehearsal? And where did she go on those days when she *did* attend but might as well not have, as she kept messing up the bowings and shifting her hand too early along the fingerboard? When Morgan tried to broach the subject, Alice grew steely, as if she believed Morgan was trying to sabotage her by encouraging her to quit. 'Are you that jealous of me?' she asked.

'Of course not,' Morgan replied, offended by the insinuation that even after all these years, she would seize any opportunity to dethrone her friend as concertmistress. Yet wasn't it only last month she'd sped up the accompaniment beneath Alice's runs to throw her off tempo? Just a few weeks before that she'd purposely turned the page a quarter-beat too late?

'It just doesn't seem to make you happy anymore,' she mumbled.

'You think I need to be happy to be the best?'

'No, you're right. Imagine how terrible we'd be if *you* weren't there.'

Alice scoffed, seeing right through Morgan's sarcasm to the root of her shame.

That final Tuesday, Morgan had arrived at school early and was by her locker when Alice entered the hallway. Alice didn't saunter like the popular girls in their year, but her presence – grave and shimmering as light on water – arrested Morgan's gaze all the same.

Every junior had their locker on the ground floor. Alice's and Morgan's were tucked beside the weight training room. The girls had memorized each other's combinations, though Morgan wouldn't dare open Alice's locker when she wasn't around. She had learned to suppress this urge to snoop when, at age eight, she'd gotten caught rifling through her mother's bedside drawer, discovering the love letters between Sequoia and a man named Bodhi. Morgan hadn't been digging for anything in particular and couldn't explain what had prompted her search. Every closed door she came upon seemed merely to glow with temptation, the possibility of finding that the person behind it wasn't who they purported.

Alice yanked open her locker and brusquely shoved her jacket inside. She wore a corduroy skirt and a light blue sweater, the sleeves rolled to her forearms. None of the other girls wore skirts or dresses save for on Valentine's Day, opting instead for leggings or jeans. On anyone else, Alice's fashion choices might have seemed snobby or desperate; on her, they simply read as Alice.

'Where were you yesterday?' Morgan asked. 'You missed rehearsal.'

'Yeah, well. Forgot my violin.'

'Let me guess: Your mom again?'

'Another fight. Stupid bitch.'

'Fuck, dude. I'm sorry.'

Alice reached into her locker and removed a pack of gum. She shook it, dispensing two pills into her hand. 'Want?'

'I'm good.'

Each school in the city could be measured by the strain of drugs circulating its hallways. Cocaine and

119

Molly were for the wealthy private school kids; amphetamines and SSRIs for the try-hards and overachievers; alcohol and weed for everyone else. Alice's substance of choice was Adderall, though Morgan didn't know what else she'd tried since she'd begun hanging around with guys like Mike Mitchell (whom everyone called Mike Mischief), and Grant Lawrence (Grand Larceny). Morgan didn't pry, terrified of having her care met with further stoniness.

Knapsacks slung over their shoulders, the girls began the journey to homeroom, negotiating around the detritus of folders, pencils, and coats that littered the ground. The impending bell charged the hallway with frenzy, as friends hurried to relay the latest gossip – who'd spoken to whom; who had posted what on which social media platform.

Alice appeared oblivious to all this, distracted by whatever had transpired between her and Linnie that morning. Insofar as Morgan could tell, the recurrent disputes between mother and daughter all concerned Linnie's lofty aspirations for her daughter: the SATs, college applications, violin. Morgan wanted to shake her and say: Don't you know how lucky you are to have a mother who cares? Her own mother, Sequoia, was a California-style hippie who had fallen for Peter when he, as a student at Caltech, became entrenched in a free-love cult inspired by Osho's teachings. For Peter, enlightenment was a passing craze; for Sequoia, it was a worthy telos toward which to anchor her life. When Morgan was ten, Sequoia packed a suitcase and announced she was headed out West, back to the ranch, back to Bodhi.

Morgan clung to her mother's leg and begged her not to leave. 'Sweet butterfly,' Sequoia said, 'don't you want Mommy to have dreams too?'

Morgan and Alice ascended the stairs to homeroom, where they'd soon be forced to part. The stairwell window overlooked the football field, lassoed by a red running track. Frost glistened on the Astroturf. Above the goalposts, two gray birds surged up and down, trapeze artists on a swing.

'Did you hear Gretchen Rothman's party got busted?' Morgan asked.

'By the police?'

'Yeah. Max was there. He told me the whole story.'

Alice looked out vacantly, as if the words *police, party, there* held no meaning.

Out onto the football field dashed a regiment of shirtless senior boys with white letters painted across their chests.

'Idiots,' Morgan snorted.

When she received no reply, she turned and was dismayed to find that Alice's cheeks were damp, tears cutting two neat tracks through her makeup. What was more unsettling: Alice herself didn't seem to notice. 'Dude, what's wrong? Is it the thing with your mom? Is it, y'know, trouble in paradise?'

'God,' Alice said, 'why do you have to make everything so prurient?'

'Prurient? Who are you, my SAT tutor?' Morgan was aiming for humor, but the quip failed to elicit even an eye roll.

'If you must know, he and I don't talk anymore.'

'What happened?'

Alice shook her head, a veil of blond ringlets falling to obscure her profile. Even like this, Morgan could picture her perfectly. The exact spray of freckles along her chin. The birthmark on her left ear. The indent on her nose where she once banged it while playing with Benji. One day, some man would graze his finger over her face and feel that break. The thought sent a cool jolt down Morgan's spine.

Rarely did Alice mention boys. The only man of whom she spoke highly was her philosophy teacher, Mr Newman. Morgan visualized him: unruly chestnut hair, a prominent nose, eyes that stared out from a sunken plane in his face as if from the topmost story of a watchtower. They were the eyes of an emperor, accustomed to perceiving the affairs of others from a convenient distance. Though Morgan hadn't spoken to him – had only ever glimpsed him through the glass panel of his door – she felt toward him a keen sense of animosity. One time, when she and Alice strolled past his door, he looked up through that glass panel and winked. The moment unfolded both instantly and frame by frame, and Morgan sensed that he'd *wanted* her, Morgan, to witness this gesture; that she, not Alice, was the intended recipient of that wink. Watch me, he was saying. Watch me closer than that.

The warning bell rang. Morgan and Alice were perched on the stairwell landing. Students jostled around them. Morgan gripped the handrail to bolster herself against the crush of bodies. 'I'll see you in seventh period, 'kay? We'll discuss it then.'

Alice opened her mouth but didn't respond. She shook her head, allowing herself to be carried forth with the swarm. Hours later, when seventh period finally arrived, she did not show.

Now, Morgan peered into Linnie's face. What had been the subject of mother and daughter's quarrel that morning?

To her dismay, Morgan realized that she'd not asked this in her mind as intended but instead aloud, the words leaving her like those in a fugue: 'Why were you and Alice fighting?'

Linnie retched out a sound that landed somewhere between a sob and a snort. Questions, evidently, didn't fall on the list of courtesies for which she'd thusly prepared herself.

'You and Alice,' Morgan pressed. 'You fought that last morning. Alice told me so.'

'I'm sorry,' Linnie said, her voice glossed with insincere care. 'I don't know why she'd say that. Yes, we had our fair share of disagreements, as mothers and daughters do, but we had a nice conversation that morning over breakfast. Odd that she felt compelled to tell you otherwise.'

'You're lying. It was you, the pressure you put on her with that stupid orchestra. She *hated* that. You knew, but you didn't care.'

Peter cut in, waving to the chapel around them. 'I

apologize, Linnie. This is a bit overwhelming.' Then, to Morgan: 'Cool it. You're behaving like a child.'

His voice, typically firm and authoritative, held a note of impotence – more a plea than a command – as if he'd already calculated his loss. On a typical day, Morgan might have left the conversation there. Today, though, the world's order had shattered, collapsing her inhibitions with it. Already beyond what she believed herself capable, she was now wandering through uncharted territory.

'You did this to her,' she spat, her volume rising.

Linnie bowed her head, a sinner accepting a blow of penance. No one stepped forward to rescue her. By now, Morgan's diatribe had caught the crowd's attention. Even Rabbi Friedman was leaning forward, his elbows on his knees.

'Do you even hear yourself?' Morgan cried. 'She's dead. Your daughter is dead. And you're sitting here like some fucking Stepford wife—'

A hand landed on her shoulder. 'Okay, that's far enough.'

For an instant, Morgan mistook the hand for her father's. Her gaze traveled up the arm to Mr Newman's face. Close up, he looked younger and more elegant than the man she'd glimpsed through the classroom door. His dark eyes and hair struck her with the effect of an underexposed photograph. 'Don't,' he warned. 'This isn't what she would've wanted.'

She – Alice. On the spectrum of closeness to her, nobody was further along than Mr N., making him the de facto arbiter of what did and did not dishonor her memory.

Mortified, Morgan wheeled from the chapel, her father tailing her. She darted into the coat closet, where she sank to the floor, enveloped in the murk of old furs. She braced for Peter's reproach, readying a retort: *I only spoke the truth.* But he didn't scold her. Instead, he hitched his pants and settled beside her.

'The bad thing about suits is they aren't conducive for floor-sitting,' he joked.

Morgan offered a weak smile. Tears were in her eyes and throat, and she allowed them to pour out. The emotion was real for a minute and required no thought. Then she became aware of the wetness on her cheeks, aware of the fact that such a display might excuse her tantrum, and conscientiously supplemented her crying with a sob.

Around them in the coat closet, snow was melting, slipping off hems and sleeves. Morgan felt its chill enter her. The emotion that had animated her heart only moments before ebbed. When she shut her eyes, no tears – not even fake ones – came.

Peter patted her leg. 'I'm going inside. Meet you there.'

He rose and crossed to the door.

'Dad?' she called, sounding far younger than her sixteen years. 'Am I in trouble?'

'We'll discuss that later.'

Once he was gone, Morgan buried her head in one of the furs, waiting for the bass drum of her grief to kick in. For a few moments, she imagined that the coat was not empty but filled with the warm body of a person who loved her. When she lifted her face, she was startled to catch a glimpse of Benji Weil, peering at her from the other side of the door, his eyes brimming with concern.

'What do you want?' she asked, resenting the sharpness in her voice.

'Are you okay?'

'Do I look okay?'

Benji stood wavering in the doorway, soft and amenable to her moods. She wished he'd see past her bitterness and come sit beside her, but he'd already turned and scurried back to the chapel, to the safety of the others.

7

Nick had assumed the first occasion for which their family and friends would gather would be Alice's wedding. She'd meet a Yalie (a lawyer or doctor, God willing), and they'd marry at the Waldorf Astoria or the Botanical Garden, beneath a fragrant ornamental canopy.

'Ready to go in?' Friedman asked.

The chapel had emptied. Nick was standing alone, crushing a plastic water bottle in one hand.

'Come,' he said to his family.

They crossed back into the lobby, where the heater was on full blast. Framed photographs of Alice sat propped on the entryway table beside a guest book. A red handkerchief lay on the ground. Nick was mid-stoop to pick it up when someone called his name.

Caroline DeLuca hurried toward him, her face ruddy with cold. Clumps of mascara sat beaded on her lashes like raindrops on nettles. The faux-fur collar of her coat tickled his chin as she barreled into him. Her skin shone with underlit warmth. Around her neck hung a tiny gold cross. He pictured her beneath him, gilt in custardy afternoon light . . . her hands grasping at the edge of the couch . . . the asymmetrical circles of her nipples . . .

flecks of eyeshadow already drifted onto her cheeks . . . her astonishing firmness and youth . . .

As if reading his thoughts, Caro stiffened, newly aware of herself. She pulled away, her lips drawing downward in a neat arc. Her eyes bore their usual alertness, a readiness to assist at a minute's notice. Her unrelenting quest for his approval made him weak at the knees. During moments of intimacy, she thrived on his validation: *There you go, it's okay, slow and steady now*. It was as if she sought his permission for her pleasure – or at least gathered that playing into such vulnerability could spur his own arousal.

'Linnie,' Caro said, looking beyond Nick. 'I'm so, so sorry.'

Nick spun. Linnie's face was drained of all color. Side by side with Caro, she appeared insubstantial, a wisp of cloud against an electric blue sky.

8

Caro slipped into the rearmost pew, beside a man who looked as out of place as she felt, with his ill-fitting blazer and nicotine-stained fingers. They exchanged a nod as he made room. She glanced around with faint unease, relieved not to know anyone. The idea of being observed in her shame was intolerable. Shame was like a fire; each witness, the oxygen that intensified that fire's blaze.

Two weeks had passed since she and Nick last spoke. He'd called her upon learning of Alice's disappearance. He couldn't get the words out. She offered to come to him, but he turned her down. Too much was happening. She remained calm, steady and collected. 'I should come,' she insisted. Nick grew cross. Under no circumstances, he said. 'All right, darling,' she replied. She stayed on with him for half an hour, distracting him with mundane work talk. No one else would do that for him, talk about themselves; they'd all want to know how *he* was doing. She spoke of nothing, feeding him inconsequential stories, and didn't let up until he said he had to go. If he'd wanted, she would have stayed on the phone all night.

Their relationship had begun the previous June, on the afternoon Nick pinged her to ask whether she could work late. He'd been doing this with ever more frequency. Caro wondered if he was testing her, trying to gauge her willingness to please him.

Michelle, the office manager who manned the desk opposite Caro's, peered up from her screen. Caro tried to relay the request casually – 'Guess who wants me to work late again?' – but a quiver in her voice betrayed her.

Michelle lifted a skeptical brow. 'Just tell him no.'

'I can't.' *I don't want to.*

From the moment Caro met Nick, she felt pulled toward him. She was hyperaware of his movements throughout the office, as if a cable connected them. In his presence, she seldom got the impression he was thinking about the time, or what to order for lunch, or any other of the ten thousand thoughts that darted through a person's mind on a given day. Nick *saw* her, and in seeing her, made her visible to herself. How infrequently she'd felt noticed, vulnerable beneath another's gaze.

'Really,' Michelle said. 'What nerve.'

The cursor flashed expectantly on Caro's screen. The summer heat fogged her mind and made her irritable. She suppressed the urge to snap at Michelle, an urge that manifested in the impatient bouncing of her knee. 'It's no big deal. The only plans I had tonight were with Alex Trebek.'

'But it's the principle of it – the principle of *expecting* you to stay late because he knows you'll feel like you're letting him down if you say no. That's psychological warfare.'

'Well, let's not be dramatic about it.'

'Emotional nukes. Manipulative WMDs. Ka-BOOM.'

A proud feminist, Michelle seemed better suited for the latte-art milieu of Greenpoint than the glass-towered one of Midtown, where her primary function was confined to replenishing the mini oatmeal containers for the suits. She carried a tote bag with doodles of misshapen breasts on the front, and every morning she retreated to the bathroom to outline her gaze in kohl. Each workplace infraction she processed through those lined eyes became fodder for her campaign against the Patriarchy. Like the time she heard Caro refer to herself as Nick's secretary. 'Don't demean yourself,' she said. 'You're an *administrative assistant.*'

At twenty-six, Caro was plagued by an awareness that she too ought to get fired up about gender equity and the wage gap. Each time she tried, though, she could only parrot the rhetoric she saw in the comments section of the *Times*. Humiliating.

'It's fine, I don't mind,' she said, straightening her keyboard and replying to Nick's message with succinct confirmation.

'Whatever floats your boat,' Michelle said, removing her blazer from the back of her chair. She put it on, sweeping her assortment of chain necklaces out from beneath the collar. The sound of her heels thinned against the linoleum as she departed.

In her absence, the office transformed into a simulacrum of itself, eerily still, like a diorama at the Museum of Natural History. Caro stood and strode to Nick's door.

Inside, he was seated at his desk, a sheaf of papers in

one hand. Gauzy light filtered through the blinds behind him. Soon darkness would fall, and Caro would be able to see her reflection on the pane. She lifted a sweating can of Coca-Cola in greeting. 'Need a pick-me-up?'

Nick's office was sizable, indistinct: a couch; an oak bookshelf; several vertical filing cabinets, neatly labeled. Walls papered in diplomas from Haverford and NYU Stern. In the center of the room stood a large silver telescope, aimed at Central Park across the way. Each totem had been carefully selected to give off an impression of a fine family man, properly credentialed. In the corner rested a violin case: Alice's.

'It's not her good violin,' Nick said, following Caro's gaze. 'She stores this here in case she forgets her other one at home. Easier for her to catch the express train from school to the office . . .' He trailed off. 'Did you want to come in?'

'Kerr?' she asked.

'Ducked out early. Doctor's appointment.'

Nick harbored a particular dislike for his boss, a man with the ridiculous moniker of Wayne Kerr, who'd wanted him gone since the day he was hired. Wayne Kerr had no doubt brooked a lifetime of playground bullying for his name ('Wanker') and been left meaner for it. Quick to sniff out any former popular boys, he'd immediately seized on Nick, who, through a brew of witty comments and fraternity-style jabs, had managed to convince his superiors it was they who required *his* approval, rather than the other way round.

Caro closed the door, her eyes roaming the contents

of Nick's desk, seeking a conversational focal point. Several photo frames stood arranged in haphazard rows. Though they faced away from her, she could picture them – professional portraits of Alice and Benji in matching linens; a shot of Linnie in her pointe shoes, one slender leg lifted into an arabesque; the entire family huddled beneath a towel by the gleaming lip of Penobscot Bay.

'Does she have a recital coming up?' she asked at last. 'Alice, that is.'

Nick rubbed his chin. 'Possibly? Her mother keeps track of the dates. She could tell you every recital a year out.'

Her mother. You mean your wife, Caro thought.

'I bet you're a great dad,' she said, blushing.

'Did you speak to Chennai?' he asked.

'Their offices were closed. I left a message.'

Nick walked around the desk and plucked the soda can from Caro's hand, spinning it in his palm. His movements were indecipherably slow. He studied each letter of the Coca-Cola logo as if memorizing the countries on a globe. 'Thanks for this.'

'Mad weather, isn't it?'

'Mad,' he repeated, smiling to himself.

He extended the can to her arm, rolling it along her shoulder to the contour of her neck, drawing out the pleasure. Caro's vision blurred until Nick was no longer Nick, but some idealized version of a man who happened to share Nick's features. She had never felt his touch before, not even a friendly pat when both reached for the elevator panel at the same time. He traced his finger over a crease in her brow. 'Stress, stress, stress,' he tsked.

'Do I seem stressed? I'm not.'

A sharp honk outside, the city trying to bust its way in. Nick moved nearer, accidentally stepping on her toes. His gaze broke through the enamel of their pretenses to summon in her an honest longing. The pressure built between them. She leaned in and set her mouth against his. In the fraction of an instant before she shut her eyes, she saw tiny reflections of herself mirrored in his pupils. A few seconds later, he pulled away.

'Oh, Lord,' she whispered.

Nick shook his head. 'Fuck. That was a mistake.'

'Was it?'

'Was it? *Was it?* I'm married, Caro. I have a wife. *A wife.*' He wagged his ring finger at her.

'That's usually what married means, yes.'

'It's Alice's birthday tomorrow. I'm supposed to pick up candles for her cake.'

A mixture of panic and confusion crested inside Caro. Had she misread his cues? If they walked out of here now, would he claim she had come on to him, kissed him against his will? To frame it that way would be to ignore months of flirtation: compliments on her appearance, the occasional late-night text, an eyebrow cocked in her direction when no one else could see . . .

'How could I be so stupid?' Nick asked. He was still holding her, the heat of his hand contradicting his words. He spoke in the canned manner one did when they suspected they were being wiretapped.

'If I misinterpreted—'

'Shh.'

She smiled diffidently, wishing they might do it again, and more. The vision was implanting itself in the folds of her imagination: their bodies toppled on the couch, ignited with desire. Perhaps they'd pause to review the risks of the path ahead. So irresistible was the pull between them, though, that in the end they'd have no choice but to surrender to Eros.

Nick withdrew behind the desk, using it as a shield. Skyscrapers glistened like the fangs of a great animal behind him.

'You said you had that portfolio for me?' he asked.

'I'll shoot it to your inbox.'

'Good. I don't want to keep you.'

Now, as she sat in the synagogue, Caro felt the humiliation of that day rise inside her. She had permitted herself a daydream of arriving at today's funeral and boldly kissing Nick in front of everybody. But such a notion was unthinkable. Their relationship was like some rotten vegetable neglected in the fridge, exuding a vile green liquid. It had been good once. It had been good that first day, when she went to switch off the lamp on her desk and a new ping popped up on her monitor. Nick Weil: *Monday, same time?*

PART THREE

I

To understand Maine's rugged spirit, one must look to its origins, how the grind of glacial sheets left a jagged scar along America's uppermost eastern corner. Peaks jimmied their way up through bedrock. Erosion scoured the land, deepening the labyrinthine valleys, like a child carving his initials on a school desk. For centuries, the Wabanaki people were the sole inhabitants of this land. Then settlers arrived with their axes and dreams of enterprise. Before long, sawmills had sprouted up along the rivers. The sulfurous scent of coal tainted the sweet pine air. Logging sounds stabbed the night – the heralding cries of industry. New Yorkers and Bostonians in search of summer hideaways recognized the state's untapped beauty. In they poured like ants through a wall. Estates, retreats, and hotels colonized Maine's coastal towns.

Morgan and Benji had arranged to host their rehearsal dinner in one of these famed towns, in the Sugar Hill Boathouse. Niched within a grove of hemlock at the end of a serpentine road, the Boathouse stood undifferentiated from the quaint New England houses that surrounded it. Only by passing through a modest corridor could one reach the striking rear – a glass-floored restaurant that jutted out on stilts over the water. Pontoons and cruisers sat docked in the marina below, creaking with each gust of wind.

Like most restaurants in the area, the Boathouse was renowned for its seafood-heavy fare: crab cakes, clam chowder, baked haddock. The décor was simple but effective: a wooden bar that extended over two wine barrels, lanterns strung from the ceiling, flowers numerous and blue. Upon entering, several guests were accosted by memories of childhood summers spent at camps in the Poconos or Berkshires, developing first crushes and weaving lanyard bracelets in the arts and crafts barn.

Tonight's dinner was an informal affair, a low-stress opportunity for the families to intermingle before the big day. The guests naturally cordoned themselves off, with the Hensleys on one side and the Weils on the other. Within these halves lay a complex series of microdivisions: which friends had cast their lots with Linnie during the divorce, which with Nick.

A self-mythologized changeling, Linnie despised when people from disparate parts of her life were made to converge. Nick had been steady since college, the same man with the same shortcomings, and thus never felt the need to obscure himself from others. She, however, had shape-shifted from Minnesota Linnie to Ballerina Linnie to Mother Linnie to Scholar Linnie. A chasm gaped between each of these personas; one couldn't leap from one to the next without falling. Worse, if they could, they'd only reveal to her the artifice of her transformations – that none were as complete as she'd presumed.

The crowd thickened. Linnie sought out Judith. The two women had grown close in the wake of Nick's affair, speaking by phone once a month. With her old-world mores, Judith was the one person who despised Caroline DeLuca more than Linnie herself. Judith's perfect Nishenka, shacking up with a Catholic girl from Nassau County. ('You can marry all the gentiles you want,' Linnie had once heard her tell Nick, 'but when the Gestapo comes knocking, they'll still call you Jew.')

Linnie had even ventured to Maine's rugged shores last summer, where she and Judith sat together in the glassed-in sunroom, sipping lemonade. Fog hung in the air, a single cloud without end. Judith rested her hand on Linnie's and whispered, 'Oh, my Linnele. I always liked you.' Linnie knew it was a lie, spun from the yarn of forgetfulness. Still, she'd welcomed the comfort it offered.

Now, Judith was reminiscing about her own summers in the Borscht Belt. During the week, she said, her father (*Berthold*, Linnie remembered; they'd named Benji after him) would depart for his factory in the Garment District, leaving his wife and children behind to swim, play tennis, and attend theater productions on the property. On Friday afternoons, he and the other husbands would carpool back into the mountains for a leisurely Sabbath.

Had Nick been present, his mother's account would've dumbfounded him. Seldom could Judith keep straight the names of her grandchildren, never mind the names of those past. But Nick was still back at Elizabeth

Cottage, where Matisse had vomited on the room's Aubusson carpet. While most of the dinner guests barely noticed his absence, it was glaring to Linnie, who'd plowed through her first blueberry mojito and was now nursing a second. She rang him twice. Both times her call went straight to voicemail.

'He'll be here,' Ezra said.

'Don't be so sure,' she replied.

If anyone should agree that her ex-husband lacked human decency, it ought to be Ezra. She had tried over the past few months to impress on him the severity of the damage Nick had wrought, taking perverse pleasure in depicting each deceit. She framed Nick's infidelity as an entity separate from their wintry seasons of marital strife – the arguments, the withering looks, the tension born from every unanswered question that hovered over the dinner table. Theirs had been a fragile existence, where feelings were conveyed indirectly, through silences and insinuations alone.

On the eve of Nick and Caro's wedding, Linnie had phoned her old dance partner Ricardo, who arrived at the brownstone bearing two pints of Ben & Jerry's Half Baked. He folded her in his muscular arms and said, 'That bastard doesn't even know what he's missing.' She was glad he stopped at that, because her instinct, honed over twenty-one years of marriage, would have been to defend Nick.

'C'mon,' Ezra said. 'Let's go eat.'

As they retreated into the amber glow of the Boat-house, a pair of headlights kindled the grass behind them. Linnie turned to see Nick and Caro exit the car. Behind them, Avery prattled on about whales: the blue whale is bigger than a dinosaur; its heart is the size of a grand piano; its aorta is so wide, a child could swim through it. 'Aorta,' she repeated, her lips tumbling over the staircase of vowels.

Seeking sympathy, Linnie crossed to Peter at the hors d'oeuvres table. He did not address her, instead focusing his attention on the cetacean-obsessed child, who'd dashed straight to the food table for a plate of mozza-rella sticks.

'Benji told me you won the spelling bee,' he said. 'Is that true?'

Avery flicked her tongue against a loose tooth. 'I can spell lots of words.'

'I bet you can.'

'Quiz me. If I get it right, I get a dollar.'

'And if you get it wrong? Then do I get a dollar?'

She frowned at this proposition.

Linnie tapped Peter's arm. 'Pete, can we—'

'I'm busy,' he said, waving her away.

Oh, his plunging coldness – what had she done to incur it? Maybe he didn't know how to address her in this formal setting. Usually when they went for dinner or to the movies, they were alone, and he was more than willing to indulge her black moods. Now, he had flipped a switch. Chop chop, back to the old routine, no more of this, no more of you. A lump formed in her throat. Not Peter; anyone but him.

Linnie was no dummy. She knew full well that Peter

had feelings for her, and she even relished the zing of validation that his desire gave her. Lately, however, she'd begun to regard their friendship with a mingled feeling of guilt and dread. It pained her to be around him, to witness his blatant need. She blew off his dinner invitations, declined his calls. Yet she couldn't bring herself to end things entirely. She wanted to keep Peter waiting in the wings in case her relationship with Ezra crumbled. It was wrong, manipulative. As her father would say, *Play with matches, don't be surprised when you get burned.*

She grazed Peter's arm, fixing him with that doe-eyed look she knew drove him mad. A cheap trick, but it worked. He turned his full attention on her. In his eyes, she searched for something, and yes, despite his best attempts at concealment, there it was: a glimmer of hope.

2

At the rear of the Boathouse, Caro threaded her way to the bar, catching sight of her liverish face in the mirrored wall behind the bottles. Her cheeks were flushed, her forehead clammy. She'd felt ill all evening. 'I'm commiserating with Matisse,' she had jested to Nick back at the cottage. On an ordinary day, the mere hint of indigestion would've sent her rushing into the bathroom for a pregnancy test. The number of sticks bearing traces of her urine had likely filled a small landfill by now. Given the hectic day, though, the idea of taking a test wouldn't occur to her until the following morning, when the illness was still there, as pronounced as if someone were probing her guts with a stick.

The bar smelled of cinnamon and cloves. Caro inhaled. She needed to take the edge off this evening. When the bartender passed her a glass, she thanked him and hurried away to sip in privacy, allowing the wine to linger in her mouth for several long seconds until the snap of the tannins had dissipated. She didn't consider herself a drinker, and certainly not a drunk, though sometimes her craving for alcohol sliced into her with a knife's edge.

'Looks like you could use a topping up,' a voice said.

Caro wheeled around to see Linnie's boyfriend, his eyes clasping hers with a knowing look.

'Can I help you?' she asked.

Ezra was holding his own drink, his hand idly swirling the glass. 'Hiding from someone in particular?'

'Taking a moment for myself, or do I need permission to do that too.'

He lifted his eyebrows. 'No offense intended.'

If she'd wanted to be charitable, Caro might've recognized that both she and Ezra were outsiders to the Weil clan and shared more in common than not. But the day's events had conspired to bring out her surliness, and Ezra's association with Linnie positioned him squarely behind enemy lines.

'These events can be taxing on us plus-ones,' he said.

Caro frowned. 'I'm the groom's stepmother. I hardly qualify as a plus-one.'

'Of course not. I didn't mean it that way. I'm just thinking of that other time you and I were together, the last time, at the service for Alice. Do you remember? You asked me then if I'd ever done something I regretted.'

'And what did you answer?'

'I can't recall.'

'Well, if it makes you feel better, I probably assumed you were lying. Want to get another drink?'

Back to the bar they went. With a fresh cure in hand, Caro felt a glowy carelessness luminate her. She scanned the room for Avery and found her across the way, talking to Peter. Her precious girl.

Before having a child herself, Caro had beheld other mothers with a potent blend of envy and awe. She maintained some cockeyed sense that these were women of a higher order; that they had their shit figured out and sorted into neat piles; that their shit wasn't shit at all, but fertile compost that nourished the most exquisite little flower beds. Then her friends started popping out babies, and since she knew these women and their flaws, she realized that no one was an adult when it came down to it, merely an expanding heap of choices and consequences.

She fished for an excuse to offer Ezra her earlier rudeness, but when she turned toward him, he seemed removed from the scene, his face troubled and faraway.

'Funny, isn't it,' she said, nudging him. 'How the past can sneak up to tap you on the shoulder when you least expect it.'

3

It was November, three months to the day before her death, when Ezra first spotted Alice on the subway. She'd been in his class since September, though she seldom participated. Sometimes, when the rest of the students were absorbed in their assignments, he'd find his eyes drifting to her. His inner monologue regarded her severely, with a disdain intended to redress whatever feelings of inadequacy her presence stirred in him. He'd never applied such scrutiny to any student before. Yet the more he indulged his desire to study Alice, the stronger his fascination grew.

Attired in a slick, slate-colored raincoat, she seemed to hover inches above the other passengers. Two loose curls clung damply to her forehead. As the train careened around a bend, she gripped the metal handrail, her weight tipping her onto the balls of her feet.

'Alice,' he called, juking straphangers to approach her.

She looked up, unsurprised, as if she'd already clocked him. 'Mr N.'

'How are you?'

'Fine.' She gestured to the case on her back. 'On my way to rehearsal.'

'I didn't know you played.'

'Huh,' she said, not without a touch of pride. 'What are you up to?'

He held up his grocery bags. The contents shifted. 'Errands. It's nasty out. "For the rain it raineth every day." I might put up some tea, get a head start on grading your essays.'

'Sounds fun.'

'That's one word for it.'

His eyes glossed over the passengers. He saw them not as people but rather as guards, present merely to enforce upon him the rules of public civility. The train screeched to a halt. The doors clicked open, admitting a blast of icy air. A few people funneled out to catch the local. The temporary mise-en-scène of the subway car emboldened Ezra, who felt any action he took in this confined space would exert no bearing on the realm of school.

'You could join me,' he said.

Alice gave a small, nervous laugh. He regretted his words instantly. What business had he inviting a student to his place? He wasn't *that* sort of guy. Yet the longer his offer hung between them, the more he enjoyed having extended it. He wanted to be someone who strayed from expectations, who could surprise even himself. Anyway, what did it matter what he did, what anyone did? He lifted his shoulders as if to shrug away the world and its puritanical morality.

On the other side of the car, a group of teenage boys in red sweatpants and shirtsleeves clapped. 'Showtime,' they hollered.

One pressed a button on a boom box. Bass-heavy music rolled through the car. The tallest teen, with close-cropped hair and a boxer's streamlined physique, grabbed hold of the pole splicing the car's center. He hoisted himself into the air and executed a perfect backflip. 'Ohhhh, shit,' his friends cheered.

'I have a riddle for you, Mr N.,' Alice said, a ghost of confidence (or was it the opposite?) haunting her expression. 'What's light as a feather but becomes harder to keep the longer you hold it?'

Ezra paused, wondering if the other passengers had overheard his invitation, if they were judging him.

'Dunno. I give up.'

'Can I ask you something else?'

'Fire away.'

'How old are you?'

'I'll be thirty-nine in March.'

Alice registered his answer without alarm. What did this number mean to her, if anything? To Ezra's ears, it sounded unbearably old. He ran back the years in his mind. For a while in his twenties, he'd been able to plead aimlessness, to say that teaching high school was a stepping stone to more considerable achievements. With time, these words lost their ballast and became embarrassing even to think, never mind utter.

They rode together the rest of the way in a silence punctuated every few minutes by the ding of the subway doors. The train deposited them at 135th Street. They strolled in the rain at the languorous pace of two people with nowhere else to be. The street was wide as a boulevard in a French painting, the sidewalk flanked by historic Harlem brownstones. Ezra could feel himself dawdling, taking an indirect route home. At least if someone spotted them out here, he'd have plausible deniability: they'd run into each other on the train and happened to get off at the same stop.

They came upon St Nicholas Park, a sprawling vista of trees. A gentle rise of lawn and a cluster of blunt rocks were visible through the trees' lace.

'It's so green here,' Alice marveled.

'You don't get up north much?'

'Not past 125th – that's where my rehearsals are.'

Ezra withdrew a cigarette from his pocket.

'Can I have one?'

'Is that a joke?'

He held her gaze. She was not joking.

'Absolutely not,' he said. 'It's a terrible habit.'

'Hey—'

She stopped and bent down. With delicate motions, she tied his undone shoe. He forced his eyes to trace the outline of a tower in the distance. 'Ta-da,' she said, standing. As if on cue, the sun pierced the cloud cover above, whitening the windows of the buildings around them. Ezra thought of how birds crash into glass, mistaking the reflection of sky for the genuine expanse.

Alice smiled, a smile that thinned as it reached his bloodstream. He paused in front of his building. It was a Queen Anne-style row house, with a dogleg stoop and a stucco facade. 'I'm on the third floor,' he said.

He ascended first, glancing back every few seconds to

151

check whether Alice had fled. Her breathing closed the gap between them. At his door, he fumbled for his keys. She asked if he needed assistance with the groceries, but no, he was fine, he'd already unlocked it. He stowed the keys between his teeth and nudged the door open with his foot.

The apartment was a one-bedroom with hardwood floors and exposed brick. The temperature inside hovered in the eighties from October to May and in the sixties the rest of the year. Too hot in winter, bitterly frigid in summer.

'Lived here long?' Alice asked from the doorway.

'A few years,' he said. 'It's rent stabilized, so I'll probably die here.'

Adult humor. She didn't rise to the quip.

The apartment was small, the furniture joined by only a shared palette of earthy tones – an olive futon in the living room, a few brass industrial lamps, an S-shaped bookshelf crammed with tomes. Several unread issues of *The New Yorker* sat piled on the breakfast bar. Ezra swore he'd get to them eventually, though he'd likely end up tossing them unread. Under Alice's gaze, each object radiated a cold detachment that he deplored. He wished he could take her to his childhood home, show her the memorabilia of his youth – the posters on the walls, the academic awards, the comic books. He wanted her to know him, the real him, and felt at once trapped by the bland identity he'd assumed.

'These are nice,' Alice said of the three windows on the

far-side wall that gazed onto the street below. The sky behind her shone pewter, the hammered surface of a dish.

She divested herself of her violin case and coat. The hems of her jeans had yet to dry. On her feet was a pair of canvas tennis shoes, remarkably white, as if she'd only ever worn them indoors.

'Allow me.' He hung the coat on a hook beside the door. 'I'll put up the tea.'

While he filled the kettle, Alice scavenged the bookshelf. She removed a volume from its place.

'You'd like that,' he said.

She glanced at him with an unreadable expression and replaced the book on the shelf. From next door floated voices, his neighbors – a man and a woman. They sounded underwater.

Ezra produced a pair of mismatched mugs from the cupboard and dropped a teabag into each. He was jittery; his fingers shook. As a teenager, he used to sneak into renovated spec houses after dark, boilerplate units with staged living rooms and kitchens. He always felt a low-level jolt of anxiety sneaking around the homes. More than fear of being caught, he feared his own potential as an agent of chaos, a force of uncontained ill. The frisson of peril Alice's presence elicited in him now was akin to what he'd felt then.

'Do you do this often?' She waved her hand to encompass the apartment. 'Invite students over?'

'Not exactly.'

He almost added, *You're the first,* but was afraid this

would unnecessarily freight the moment. 'If you're uncomfortable—'

On the stove, the kettle climbed to a falsetto. He poured the water into the mugs.

'And this?'

From the S-shaped shelf, Alice withdrew a weathered volume.

'What about it?'

'Would I like it?'

'I think so. You liked the excerpt of his I shared in class, didn't you?'

With a hum of assent, she riffled through the book's pages, which bore marginalia from Ezra's days at university, scribbled commentary about the nature of ethics. He had been so full of convictions then; he would sketch the world in black and white and wait for it to bend to his biases.

He set the mugs on the table. 'Here we are.'

Alice installed herself across from him, absorbing his stare. She sipped the tea, her lips barely parting. What was she thinking?

'So. You live alone,' she said at last.

'My preference. Gives me time to do what I please.'

'Which is?'

'Read. Think. Order takeout from wherever I want.'

'You don't date?'

'Sometimes. When I'm not busy. Teaching's a full-time gig.'

'What about sex?'

Jesus. He drew back. The colossal magnitude of his

predicament was becoming clear. In inviting Alice over, he had relinquished the safety of solid ground. He gulped his tea, scalding the roof of his mouth. His face must have been the reification of shock itself because Alice added, 'What? Discussing life and death is on the table, but the stuff that *makes* life is off-limits?'

'Alice, come on. It isn't appropriate. We both know that.'

Across from him, Alice drew her knees into her chest, looking chastised. All her earlier boldness was like a mask he'd knocked out of place. With a single motion, he might dislodge that mask permanently. She was not a girl who had done much of anything. She wanted to act like she had, but she was as innocent as they came.

She returned her attention to the book, pretending to read, or maybe she really was reading. It was hard to tell.

'I'm just trying to understand you better,' she said, not glancing up.

Her voice was plaintive. Oh, please don't cry. He didn't know what he'd do if she started crying. He worried he'd get angry.

'What do you mean?' he said.

'Well, what it is you're after.'

Ezra had raised this very question to himself nearly every day. What did he want? What did *anyone*? And how could you be sure that once you attained those wants, you wouldn't find further ones lurking behind them? Perhaps it was true, what the philosophers said – maybe it really was turtles all the way down.

Most teachers Ezra knew had side gigs. The English teachers were chipping away at novels; the Spanish teacher played dulcimer for a New Age band; the theater teacher spent his summers at a youth camp, directing productions of *The Mikado* and *Into the Woods*. The only ones who viewed their jobs as ends unto themselves were the older women who'd managed to satisfy their external cravings through the act of motherhood. Ezra didn't possess a secondary interest, a side passion. He didn't have the stomach for public intellectualism as certain of his graduate classmates had; he was too terrified by the prospect of critique for such exposure.

In some sorry attempt at carving out a spot for himself upon the intellectual dais, he chose to spend his weekends in the library, reading the most abstruse texts he could find. Such practices left him dissatisfied and cut off. When he did go out to experience Real Life, he grew disillusioned with the banality of others' concerns and saw no choice but to retreat back into the shell of his seclusion. Like this, he entered a sorrowful holding pattern. That Alice viewed him as some respectable scholar pained him. Soon she'd depart for college, where she'd be surrounded by thousands more fascinating than he. Her world had just begun to widen, while his was closing up, vines of regret latticing the once-open overhead.

'Alice,' he said.

'Hm?'

'You're quiet in class. Why is that?'

'I don't know.'

'But you have such insightful things to say. It doesn't upset you not to talk?'

'Would it be upsetting to you?'

'Absolutely. In school, I hated how little I participated.'

'Why didn't you?'

'I don't know. I was afraid of taking up space, I guess, being labeled a know-it-all. In college, I had this notion that one earned the right to speak by saying the most erudite things, so I'd spend the class period trying to package my thoughts into pithy statements. Sometimes, I'd spend fifteen minutes crafting a single sentence, and we'd move on before I could share it.'

'You still could've said it. Harry does that.'

'Harry?'

'O'Neill. In our class.'

Why had she mentioned Harry? Was she giving him a warning, a kick under the table to remind him she was his student? He pictured her at her desk, concealed behind her tangle of curls. Before and after class, while the others clumped by cohesive force, she stayed apart. Her peers reacted warily to this isolation, as if afraid she'd hex anyone who came too near.

She turned back to the book in her hands. 'What did you say about Nietzsche again?'

'He came up in our discussion about morality. Here, gimme that.'

Ezra flipped through the book until he came upon the desired passage. Alice scooted her chair beside his. The heady scent of her soap filled the space between them.

'For Nietzsche, every action humans undertake is driven by the will to power. What is it we want? he asks. Simple: to control others. And morality is one of the mechanisms by which we do this. Does this sound familiar?'

A tentative nod.

'Great. So, morality is invented by the lowest of the low, who are teeming with hatred for their impotence. To combat this, they construct a Trojan horse, which they call virtue. They say those in authority are wicked, corrupt, and they themselves are good. They extol weakness as some kind of holy ideal. Think of it as a very effective rebrand. By framing their meekness as a moral choice, the oppressed are able to flip the power hierarchy on its head, positioning themselves at the top. And voilà, we have the birth of morality.'

Alice skimmed the page. 'Can I keep this?'

'Of course.'

The tea in their mugs had cooled, its color now sunset orange. It seemed a thousand years had passed since they'd entered the apartment. She carried the book to her violin case and zipped it into the front pocket.

'Will you play me a song?' Ezra asked.

Alice paused. And then, reluctantly, she opened the case, peeling back the velvet flap. She removed her violin and considered it, an archaeologist turning over a fossil. Ezra wanted to say he'd only been kidding, but now he was intrigued. He folded his hands in his lap.

She looked over at him and lifted the violin to her shoulder, sawing the bow over each string and adjusting the fine tuners. Satisfied, she took a sharp inhale and began.

The initial chords emerged rich and full, as though

from an entire orchestra. Alice bent her knees, driving herself into the music. A second became a minute, which turned into two. The longer she played, the more she seemed to slip away, crossing over the threshold into some remote portal. An expression of deep concentration settled on her features. It was her and the notes, with nothing in between. To his astonishment and discomfort, Ezra felt tears prick his eyes. He looked away, afraid he was self-dramatizing, but it was hopeless. The sound was a kind of sorcery, pulling feelings out of him he didn't know he had.

Alice's own eyes were shut, her breathing heavy. She was transfiguring the nature of time itself, molding each second to her will. When the piece finally broke off – she'd played only a quarter of it – her eyes fluttered open, but the look in them remained distant. Only when Ezra began clapping did the spell break, returning her to herself.

'That was beautiful,' he said. 'What's it called?'

'It's Bach's Chaconne, from his collection *Sei Solo*. He wrote it after his wife died.'

She retreated to her case, drawing the velvet flap with the obeisance of one pulling a sheet over a body.

They stood, taking each other in, reassessing. Something had swept into them, replacing the earlier sensuousness.

'I should go,' Alice said. 'Rehearsal.'

'Do you need me to walk you to the train?'

'That's okay. I remember the way.'

He moved to help her with her coat, but she'd already

retrieved it. She opened the door. He followed her into the hallway, surprised to find it in its usual drab state. Moments earlier, Alice's music had varnished the bookshelves and table, revitalizing them. Now, by increments, everything reverted to its previous appearance, the dullness glaringly intensified.

'Maybe I'll run into you on the subway next week,' she said, fiddling with her coat.

Ezra studied her face. Some spirit inside her was teetering before his eyes, dipping in and out of shadow. With each blink, a new impulse enlivened her gaze. It was hypnotic, terrifying.

'You're welcome here anytime,' he said. 'You know where to find me.'

4

Nick surveyed the crowd of rehearsal dinner guests like a general studying a battlefield, classifying them into two categories: those who could offer him a job, and those who might expose him. As he appraised the room, he found himself resenting the value of every embellishment – the flowers, the booze, even the luxurious scent of the air freshener wafting toward him. What an utter waste.

He spotted his old buddy Shack (full name Oswald Shackleton V, of rumored relation to the Arctic explorer), who dealt in securities at Wells Fargo. Nick approached and struck up a conversation. Soon enough, Shack had steered their talk headfirst into the foreboding gulf of Pleasantries, lamenting the costly renovation of his Sag Harbor manse. Nick foraged his mind for any excuse to dovetail into career talk but emerged empty-handed; work was the last thing anyone wanted to discuss on vacation.

Having exhausted the usual points, Shack said, 'So, Mr Finance, is our economy doomed?'

Tiny darts of awareness prickled Nick's neck. The comment struck him as eerily prescient. Was Shack mocking him? No, all anybody could talk about these days was the sordid state of the economy. Late-stage capitalism was on its deathbed, choked by the emerald fumes of its own greed. The Great American Experiment was banking toward a second Dark Age – the overturn of *Roe*, the mass shootings, the Fed hiking interest rates at record pace. The market was in free fall, portfolios reduced to rubble. The prospects for the next generation were bleaker than for those who'd come before. This wasn't how it was supposed to go.

'Sorry, excuse me a minute,' Nick said.

It was all too much. He couldn't get away fast enough. He headed toward the chafing dishes, where Linnie stood tweezing a few limp leaves of lettuce from the salad bowl. 'Rabbit food?' he asked, cocking his beer bottle toward her plate. Her dress billowed loosely, her shoulders hardly more than a coat hanger. She looked as gracile as she had in her ballerina days, but with a striking lack of tone. He imagined her lost weight had been displaced onto his figure, that they were fused forever in equipoise.

She looked older too, weary about the eyes. Not any less beautiful, but it was a beauty of a different sort, an acquired refinement. Only he could see the younger, uncertain woman lurking behind her expression. She had on an eyelet dress in periwinkle, with a boat neckline and smocked waistband. If he tugged down her collar, he'd find on her clavicle the two beauty marks he used to kiss, distinct as Castor and Pollux. Every one of her features – her lips, her knees, the bones of her wrist – was pinned on the corkboard of his mind.

'I've forgotten how you look at me,' Linnie said, not lifting her eyes from the tiny blue flames.

'How's that?'

'Like I'm a fish in a bowl.'

'You're prettier.'

She smiled distantly.

He recalled the week they'd cleared out the brownstone, which had swiftly transformed into an austere, unfamiliar place. No longer a family home – simply a building they all happened to inhabit simultaneously. In short order, he and Linnie managed to disassemble what they'd pledged years to constructing: breaking down the furniture, spackling the nail holes, packing up the cookware. It was as if they'd suddenly shifted into reverse, unwoven the tapestry. They might have been confused for teenagers were it not for the streaks of grief their bodies trailed in space, blinding as the light stains transiting cars leave on long-exposure film.

That final week of packing, Nick had offered to tackle Alice's room, spare Linnie that pain. After she left, he phoned a maid service. There was a hefty surcharge for same-day cleanings, but he didn't care. (Oh, to be so flippant with money.) He directed the two Polish women who appeared on the doorstep to dispose of everything: the condolence notes, the stuffed animals, the prayer candles. He had enough keepsakes as it was. He never told Linnie about the maids. He thought she'd object to them, as she had most of his actions then. A few days later, when sorting through the toiletries, Linnie discovered Alice's sundries in the bathroom cupboard; the maids had forgotten to pack them. Her sobs – shattering, as if a fishing line had yanked them directly from her solar plexus – ricocheted through the empty rooms. In small ways, she always managed to remind him that he'd failed.

'Having a good time?' he asked.

She shrugged. 'Me and parties, like oil and water. I hear you have the first toast.'

'Saving the best for first, naturally.'

'Did you prepare something?'

'I did. Want to hear?'

Nick patted his breast pocket, feeling for his speech. He continued to pat, then peered down the front of his shirt. With a climbing sense of dread, he realized that in his hurry to depart the cottage, he must have left his speech behind. He pictured the three yellow pages, torn from his trusty legal pad, folded on the bureau.

'You're joking,' Linnie said. 'Tell me you're joking.'

'Un-friggin'-believable.'

'I have a pen in my bag if you want to . . .'

'Nah, screw it.'

'What're you gonna do?'

His eyes twinkled conspiratorially. 'What do you say we smoke some weed?'

At first he was kidding, and then he wasn't. He'd procured a joint from a friend earlier in the day. Why he'd brought it with him tonight, he couldn't say, but he suddenly had the urge to smoke it, so he stepped outside behind the Boathouse and was amazed when Linnie followed, holding her dress off the ground. The sounds of bossa nova music, and of guests attempting to heft their voices over it, pared away. For an instant, they might have been anywhere – Maine, New York – it didn't matter; they were the only two people in the world.

5

Nick passed Linnie the joint. 'Ladies first.'

Many years had elapsed since they'd last done this. When they were younger, they used to sneak off at parties, finding a quiet room to silo themselves, like birds sheltering from a downpour. Now here they were, adults at a dinner party, one they were technically throwing, doing the same.

'Good?' he asked.

'Absolutely terrible.'

'Terrible in a good way.'

'I don't feel a thing.'

'Give it a second.'

Linnie tipped her head back against the wood, catching her hair on a nail. The stars, those ancient lights, were clustered as if for warmth. She studied them, seeking patterns, poetry. Far off sounded the plangent cry of a loon. After a moment, a second loon answered.

The rehearsal dinner was going smoothly so far, and though this ought to gladden her, it left her feeling only depleted. How could their friends and family go on so blithely, as if things had always been as they were right now?

'So,' Nick said. 'Our boy's getting hitched. Who'd a thunk?'

'Honestly, not much could surprise me these days.'

'Everything in order for tomorrow – flowers, photographer, the whole shebang?'

'Who knows. It's all the kids' doing. I'm not involved.'

'Color me skeptical.'

Once, Linnie's dinner parties had been spoken of with awe. How could she rear two children *and* find time to prepare a four-course meal? Only after Alice's death had her elaborate meals signaled her as someone who cared too much, who put tremendous effort into events the rest attended merely out of obligation.

'I've never seen Morgan so serene before,' she said.

'That's good. It means she's doing the right thing. Holy moly, this stuff is strong.'

'*Does* it mean they're doing the right thing?'

'My little doubting Thomas. What? You think it's too soon?'

'Look at him,' she said to a fictive audience. 'Trying to get me in trouble. They're adults. So long as they're happy, I'm happy.'

She meant this, though a leaden feeling came over her at the idea of someone else's daughter walking down the aisle. The calendar had morphed into a minefield – holidays, birthdays, and anniversaries were all shaded by loss. When Mother's Day arrived, she'd hide beneath the covers, praying for sweet annihilation.

She looked up at Nick, suddenly unsure of what to say. Had he read these thoughts on her face? Even after all this time, she felt transparent to him. She steadied her breathing, timing it to the lapping of the harbor's waves.

The water itself was pitch-black; it looked as if it had leached the darkness from the sky. From inside spilled the milonga drums of Paolo Conte's 'Via Con Me.' Nick flung out his arms and spun until he collapsed. There were critters beside him, their bellies pulsing. Linnie felt there was no separation between her and those bugs, that she was throbbing too.

'Join me,' he said.

Paying little heed to her dress, she lay down and fanned out her hair behind her. She slid off her shoes and pressed her heels into the forgiving earth.

'Oh, love,' Nick sighed, rolling into her. 'Love, love. What is it?'

She giggled, the syllables jumbling in her ears. It *was* wonderful, she thought, the lyrics fusing with her senses, to lie beside a man whose breath patterns you knew as well as your own. She pinched a piece of dog fur from Nick's lapel. Her hand lingered. He curled toward her, their knees bending at complementary angles. The grass tickled the backs of her shoulders; she swore she could feel each individual blade. She leaned closer and whispered, 'There's moonbeams in your eyes.'

'Are you gonna ignore my question?' Nick said.

'What question?'

'About capital-L love. Remember my friend George Proctor?'

'Princeton guy.'

'You sat beside his wife at the Central Park Conservancy dinner.'

'Sure, I remember.'

'They divorced last year.'

Linnie snorted; she couldn't help it. There seemed a no-soap-radio absurdity to the hurt humans insisted on inflicting upon one another.

Nick, who'd been lying snow-angel with arms and legs outspread, gathered his limbs and went on.

A month earlier, he and George had met for drinks at the Oyster Bar. George confessed then that he'd been a real bastard to Ingrid throughout their marriage. He regularly pushed her away, proclaiming himself undeserving of her love. While he may have believed this on the surface, a deeper part of him didn't want to be loved, because to be loved meant that you were mediocre enough for someone else to comprehend.

George discovered in Ingrid an acquiescent target for his anger. He mocked her for going vegan and for offering unsolicited advice on his work. Every one of her words, each anodyne remark, he twisted back at her as proof of her womanly inability to follow logic through to its conclusion. He wished to provoke her to grapple with her compassion and naïveté, which he held in contempt, as one holds in contempt anything they fear themselves to lack. Poor Ingrid couldn't help but persist. She was like a kicked dog, full of learned helplessness. For decades they contested each other. It became a war of attrition – George trying to prove his unworthiness of Ingrid's love, and she maintaining to uphold the vow she'd taken on their wedding day.

'We were at their wedding,' Linnie said. 'I wore a red dress, satin. Remember?'

'Dress, yes. Wedding, no. Was that the one where Geneviève St Cloud hit on me?'

'Geneviève St Cloud – God, I haven't heard that name in forever. What a wackadoo. Is that the end of the story?'

'Almost.'

Eventually, George accepted that maybe Ingrid *did* love him, and he stopped trying to argue it out of her. Only then did Ingrid realize that what she loved was not George himself but the challenge of their conflict. Once she figured that out, she left.

'When we met at the Oyster Bar,' Nick concluded, 'George had reverted to full-blown misanthropy.'

'I suppose that story was meant to tell me about love.'

'Maybe there's no such thing.'

'And you call me the doubting Thomas.'

Quiet lapsed between them. Linnie envisioned herself back in the brownstone, passing Benji's room, a pair of mud-spattered sneakers with the heels tamped down by the foot of his door. The portraits above the wainscoting. Alice's handprint set in clay. The hole above the chaise longue in the master, where Nick had driven his fist when she asked for a divorce.

'This old song,' he said now, humming a few bars.

Linnie grew aware of the music cresting from inside. A sudden paranoia came over her, a fight-or-flight instinct, fear screwing itself beneath her skin. She fished for her heels in the grass.

Nick rose too, his expression revealing itself in the glow of the Boathouse's lanterns. Time and fatigue had scored lines across his forehead. Silver sparkled in his hair. He had not switched his cologne in thirty years, and Linnie could smell it on his skin, a sharp but pleasant scent, wood wax mixed with vanilla. A foreign emotion ambushed her. A moment ago, she'd had such clarity. Now it was gone, a letter in a bottle ferried far away.

'I found a picture of us at my mom's house,' he said. 'From our honeymoon.'

'How'd we look?'

'Like handsome devils. It was quite irritating, actually.'

She smiled, the weed loosening from her tongue's grip the words she'd forbidden herself to say. 'Know what I wish? I wish Alice could be at her brother's wedding. I never get to talk about her anymore. There'll be entire weeks when I don't mention her to anyone. I go to type her name, and my phone autocorrects it to "Alive" – how twisted is that?'

Every time Linnie attempted to expand beyond the past, a vicious force yanked her back. Back to the sea chamber where her daughter was forever falling. Back to the river's sinister edge. The water slipping into both their lungs. The anchorage of the bridge crushing their chests. Only a thin partition separated her new self, the Reinvented Linnie, from the old. On one side of that partition sprawled the living world, unfathomably blue, and on the other, a formless void. Whenever she dared to step forward, the madwoman of her grief appeared, seizing her back down the rabbit hole of terrors.

'She wasn't a joyful kid, was she?' she asked. 'Did we not love her enough, is that it?'

'No, no, no. We loved her the most. *The most.*'

'Want to know something sick? Sometimes I find myself thinking, if only she'd been one of those girls who did it for attention – the half-hearted overdose, a stint at Bellevue, the therapy and meds. That's heinous, isn't it? But I really do think that. I think, What if she hadn't been set on completing everything she did on the first go-round? It's like I wished she'd suffered longer, so I could've had her here longer, so I could've changed the outcome. And when I start getting that way, I'm just so angry at whatever god would allow this.'

Nick gripped her shoulders. 'Listen to me. You cannot think that way. You can't rationalize what she did. It is not rational. Regardless of what your *boyfriend* might say, this isn't a matter of philosophy. She was sick, whether or not we knew it, whether or not *she* knew it.'

Sick – was that how he justified it? If Alice were sick, it would have been Linnie's job to aid her to health. Rarely had she felt so essential as when the school nurse phoned to say her child was running a fever and needed to be picked up. Myriad other tasks her own provincial upbringing had left her ill-equipped for: shuttling children between activities across the city, ensuring they got into the best schools and premier day camps, managing grocery trips without a car. But putting up a pot of consommé for a flu-ridden kid, playing one round of Uno or Yahtzee after another – that, she could do.

I should have grasped via a mother's intuition that Alice was hurting, she thought. Burn me at the stake;

flog me for not seeing, for passing on to her the cursed melancholia that runs through my family. Her uncle Clyde with the twelve-gauge, his brains spattered across Grandpop's barn, the pigs still squealing when the sheriff arrived. Once, as a teenager, Linnie herself had lifted a letter opener from the drawer and held it to her wrist, applying just enough pressure for a red line to appear. Her efforts hadn't been earnest; she'd merely wanted to see how her parents would react. Even in this, she couldn't compete with her daughter's conviction.

The fault was not hers alone, however. The psychic in Alphabet City had said as much when consulting her astrology chart. There was nothing particularly alarming in the mapping of her planets, nothing to forecast the amount of suffering that had befallen her.

'Will you do one more for me?' Linnie asked, removing the folded printout from her purse.

The psychic studied this second chart for a long time, her rings clinking metallically as she dragged her finger from one planet to another. When she reached the final point, she jerked back her hand as if scalded. Darkly, she said, 'Now, this is different.'

She pointed to the page. In this chart, the rising sign and moon were hemmed between malefic planets.

'In layman's terms, please,' Linnie said.

The psychic paused. Then she told her. In the olden days, the particular aspects of those planets indicated the death of a child – *Balarishta*. 'Of course, nowadays,' the psychic said, adopting a breezier tone, 'we tend to

173

consider the metaphorical implications instead of the physical ones.'

Though Linnie never revealed the analysis of that chart to anyone, the findings had flooded her with relief. It was not in her chart after all where the stars had been ill-fated, but Nick's.

6

Time stretched. The sea and sky were twin shades of burnished blue. Nick felt the earth spin beneath his feet, producing its strange music.

'We should've gotten a dog when the kids were little,' Linnie said.

'Too much hassle, remember?'

'I was wrong. Sorry for that.'

'You and the philosopher king could get one.'

She laughed, a golden sound, her face dimpling with a look of ecstasy unequal to the moment. She doubled over, a hand to her stomach. Her whole body quivered. 'I'm sorry. It's, oh, it's just—'

He laughed too, sinking his teeth into his lower lip to contain it. The threat of getting caught only amplified the hilarity. Adrenaline pumped through them in short, orgasmic bursts.

Eventually Linnie's laughter settled save for a smattering of red blotches on her upper arms. Nick badly desired to caress these. He recalled how she used to dance for him in the living room, using a chair as a barre. How lucky he'd felt to witness her in such a state of liberation, her face stripped of its usual guardedness. Now the memory made him horny – very horny. He imagined taking her in the pine needles, doing what he'd done many times before but was prohibited from doing ever again.

He tugged at his earlobe, fishing for a sensation to parry the one barraging his nether regions. The muffled voices of their loved ones floated from within. We should go back, he thought, but each directive his mind cast to his feet went disregarded. He reached out and ran a thumb over the cracks in Linnie's lip, his finger sticking to the gloss. He bent as if to kiss her. She tilted up her head and whispered, 'Do you think she's still alive?'

The words shattered the concupiscent undercurrent of his thoughts. Alice, alive? Hope was a dangerous lure — a rattlesnake camouflaged as a lifeline. Only certainty, or at least the illusion of it, could enable him to forgo his bargains with the universe and springboard into the next phase of living.

Linnie didn't agree. Some days, he'd arrive home to find her replaying videos of Alice's old recitals. Her face colored each time he caught her, as if he'd barged in on her doing Lord knows what. She had drawn her pain tightly around her to the exclusion of everyone, even him. They had turned into people who had forgotten how to behave around others. They couldn't be alone, and they couldn't be together.

Benji bore the brunt of this turmoil. Half a year after Alice's death, Nick and Linnie tried to throw him a slumber party. Only two boys showed. The other parents regarded the brownstone as a contaminated zone; heaven forbid their boys were irradiated. Nick rationalized their behavior, insisting they were merely being mindful of their family's predicament. 'It's amazing how quick you are to defend anyone who isn't your own flesh and blood,' Linnie said. A lonely expanse of empty mattress separated her from him, an unbreachable divide. It was, he told himself, an impulse of self-preservation that kept him from connecting.

'Alive?' he said. 'I don't . . .'

'Of course not. Good ol' Teflon Nicky – the world rolls right off him.'

He rubbed his Adam's apple. His high was souring. Why were they fighting? He hadn't wanted to fight.

'What do you want me to say?' he said.

Linnie tossed up her hands. 'Nothing. You don't ever want to talk about the things that matter, so.'

'Oh, for fuck's sake.' He pinched the bridge of his nose. Each word seemed to lack shape and definition, as if he'd sculpted them from Play-Doh. 'You're right. I don't want to talk about her. It's exhausting to tread the same waters only to come up empty. And sad. Holy moly – aren't you sad?'

'How could you even ask me that?'

'Well, so am I. Just because someone isn't grieving how you want them to doesn't mean they aren't doing it. It was like this with her too. You thought that if you kept pushing and pushing her, you could mold her into what you wanted her to be. You didn't even see how hard she was trying. The whole reason she tried as hard as she did for as long as she did was to make you proud.'

'That's a lie.'

'I wish it were.'

'I spent more time with her than you.'

'So? Did that make her less my kid than yours?'

In Linnie's silence, Nick located his answer. Of all the blows they'd exchanged, this was far and above the cruelest.

'Not a single day, Nick,' she said. 'Not a single day goes by that I don't think about her or wonder what she'd be doing, who she'd be dating, whether she'd have forgiven me.'

'And you think I don't?'

'Honestly? I have no idea what goes on in that brain of yours.'

'Fuck off. You don't know the hell I've been through. You always treated this like a competition, needed to make it clear that your hair shirt fit just a smidge snugger than the rest of ours. Congratulations, you win – is that what you want to hear?'

Linnie stepped back, the cords in her neck growing pronounced. Again Nick registered her frailty, the waxen pallor of her skin. He forced himself to slow down. Quietly, even tenderly, he said, 'You were miserable to be around, Lin. When we were younger, you'd been so vibrant, and I felt like I was the reason you weren't that way anymore. You wanted me to be the bad guy, so I became him. There was no winning with you.'

'My daughter died.'

'As did mine. It wasn't a cakewalk for either of us.'

'Oh, yes, I'm sure it was excruciating for you to jet off on your three-week-long honeymoon to – where was it again? Bali? I bet Caro had to twist your arm on that one.'

'Give me a break. You *made* me look elsewhere.'

'I made you? Well, that's quite the efficient shirking of responsibility.'

'I was perfectly happy with what we had. I never wanted more. But you poked holes in our life until all I could see were the flaws. You can go ahead and play innocent, but you were anything but – can we at least agree on that? You married me to get ahead, to catapult you out of your bumpkin life once and for all. Our marriage was a business arrangement to you.'

'How dare you.'

'I'm not saying it's a bad thing – just the opposite. You have more chutzpah and competitive edge than any city slicker I've ever met. But it's true: nothing was ever good enough – you're the one who taught me that. So, yes, you made me look elsewhere.'

'Did I drive your cock into Caro too?'

'Fine, I wanted some fun. I wanted to be playful. Hold it against me.'

'Playful? Is that some sexual euphemism?'

'I wanted excitement, Lin. Our lives were so . . . well, and our love—'

'Don't say it, whatever you're going to say.'

'—had become inert. We weren't growing. You were consumed by what could have been. I couldn't spend another minute tabulating all the things we were missing out on.'

'You *did* kill my spirit, Nick. Slowly, day after day. It would be eight o'clock, and I'd have been dealing with the kids all afternoon, and there'd be dinner on the table, and I'd think to myself, "Where is Nick? Where is my husband? Why did I give up my dancing career—"'

'Your career, is that what we're calling it now?' He let out a cruel laugh.

'Fuck you. You'd never have the balls to put yourself out there.'

'True, but at least I have enough fortitude to look reality in the eye.'

'Boy, are you filled with zingers tonight. You sure liked telling people I was a dancer. You went around saying it at cocktail parties long after I'd hung up my pointe shoes. You couldn't let it go.'

'Au contraire, madame. I was just catering to your fragile ego. What was I going to say: This is Linnie, my *housewife*? Stick around, maybe you'll catch her piddling with the drapes?'

'Go to hell, Nick. You got off on the erotica of it – admit it. Your leggy blond, your showgirl, a million miles from every other intellectual Jew on the Upper West Side. Because you hate yourself. You're such an open book, no mystery at all. All I ever was to you was a fantasy, a worn-out cliché. Then you had to twist the knife in deeper by making me even *more* of a cliché: the scorned woman. And now that I've broken free, now that I've experienced the world and properly educated myself – now that I'm more *interesting* than you – you're lost at sea.'

'You're right.'

'I am?'

'You are.'

She squinted at him, searching for the catch in his

words. He watched her anger short-circuit, unsure of how to process his resignation. She proceeded hesitantly, still inflamed by her earlier revelation.

'You wanted the fantasy, Nick, and I was all too happy to give it to you. With Caro too. What role did you cast her in, the sexy secretary? The hot young floozy? Yes, just another part in your play. Because you can't handle the real thing. You only want the figment.'

'Leave my wife out of this,' he said, an edge to his voice.

His use of the word *wife* stopped them both. He detested this side of Linnie, this world-weary woman. He wished he could summon back the girl she had once been, the one she was now so convinced had never existed.

'Hasn't it ever occurred to you that you might not be the only one who blames yourself for Alice's death?' he asked.

'As a matter of fact, no. I guess your smugness failed to lead me to the flashing "Guilt Resides Here" sign over your head.'

'Ahh, that's nice. That kind of sarcasm is really conducive to having an adult conversation. Remind me again why we divorced?'

Linnie flattened her hands against the wall behind her. 'We should go back in.'

'Wait.'

Tell me, he wanted to say, would our marriage have survived if Alice had lived? He rarely gave in to such speculation. Yet the wonder lingered in the back room of his mind, waiting to be unboxed: What had been the coup de grâce: the affair, or what Alice had done upon discovering it?

'It's too dangerous for us to stay here,' Linnie said.

'Dangerous – I like the sound of that.'

'I'm serious.'

'So am I.'

Hoping to recapture the vulgarity of his earlier thoughts, Nick reached for Linnie's hand but grasped her elbow instead. He stroked it a few times before she drew away, folding back in on herself. Her eyes were so utterly devoid of warmth, they resembled two dark stones. There was no meekness left in her. Her body was a hard carapace.

Just as he was contemplating running a hand up her thigh, the dire reality of his economic plight ambushed him, filling his vision with an oddly clinical image of stock returns – white graphs overlaid with squiggly blue lines. Once the sight had taken hold, he couldn't shake it. How had he let Linnie, Benji, and the wedding jockey for priority in his mind, when the stakes were so much graver than any of them could comprehend?

'It's so easy to get wrapped up when I'm around you,' Linnie said, oblivious to this change. 'For the past thirty minutes, I've been standing here feeling nostalgic, remembering what it's like to have you as my best friend. Then – *whoosh* – everything snaps into focus, and I think, Come on, Lin, have some integrity—'

'I was let go from work.'

She paused, recalibrating. 'What?'

'I. Was. Let. Go.'

This time, the words penetrated. He was grateful; he didn't have it in him to repeat it a third time.

'Tell me this isn't some ploy to keep me here.'

'If only.'

'Good grief, Nick.'

'You're telling me. Fucking Kerr. That son of a bitch has got such a chip on his shoulder, you can see it from outer space.'

'Oh, grow up.'

So quickly, their bitter jags had managed to scrape away the scar that years had formed around them. The wounds of the past pulsed hotly beneath their feet.

'Money-wise, though, you're okay?' Linnie asked. 'Because if you're not, I can – You'll let me know, won't you?'

Nick laughed. 'Don't tell me you're offering to give back the alimony I paid you.'

'Hey, now. We were partners, buddy. Fifty-fifty. I did just as much work as you to keep our home-ship sailing. And you – lawyering up before you even came to me. It was a shitty thing to do, all right?'

'If you remember, I was more than happy to stay in our marriage. You were the one who chose the other way.'

'Oh, Nick. Nick, Nick, Nick. That is such *bullshit*. There was no choice. None. Zilch. I had already lost you. You and Alice both. My whole world – gone, zap.' She snapped her fingers. 'Your son had too, by the way – lost you. Not that he'd ever tell you that. You were an asshole. A grade-A asshole. But y'know? Maybe this weed has got me a little sentimental, because I'm starting to feel a little sorry for you.'

The timbre of her voice, its unexpected care – how he resented it. Linnie, bless her heart, had never managed to unravel the intricacies that distinguished income from wealth. Wealth wasn't a flux identity but a fixed one, signifying a particular lineage. Income, by contrast, was merely the slips of paper that intimated that wealth. She hadn't grasped this, the gradations. How people like him went to Starbucks, while their more privileged acquaintances – the ones who gave their kids last names for first names (Thayer, Buckley, Parker) – employed private chefs to froth their cappuccinos; how he cruised down the Saw Mill River Parkway in a sensible Lexus, while others splurged on Rolls-Royces, Porsches, Aston Martins; how he owned but a solitary house in Westchester, while others paid cash up front for properties in the Hamptons, Miami, Majorca. There was New Money and there was Old Money, and Nick had spent his entire adult life trying to pass as the latter. The knowledge that he had played this part so convincingly to deceive even Linnie filled him with anguish. How badly he'd bungled everything . . .

'So, rough year,' she summarized dryly.

'Wait, it gets better. Caroline wants us to have another kid, and I haven't told her yet about the job. I mean, she must suspect something's up, given this market. But not *that*. No, I don't think she suspects that.'

Linnie stumbled back a few steps, her heel twisting awkwardly as she lost her footing in the pine needles.

Her expression veered toward a horrified frown. To Nick, each of these facial shifts appeared exaggerated: her lips lowering by degrees, creases of shock coursing across her forehead. Even once she'd released this tension, crinkles remained etched in her powder.

'I realize I'm old,' he said. 'I'll probably be dead by the time this kid hits college—'

'Don't even joke—'

'—but she wants it.'

'How about you? Is it what you want?'

'I shouldn't be telling you this. She'd kill me if she found out.'

Linnie extended a hand to his cheek. She stroked his stubble, wondering at its sandpaper quality. Her touch broadened outward to the neat arrangement of cartilage in his ear, the circular bone where his jaw attached to his skull.

'What're you gonna do?' she asked.

'Who knows. Move to Costa Rica – want to come?'

'About the baby, I mean.'

His eyes searched hers. 'Whaddya think? Should I have it, or what?'

'You don't need my permission.'

'I'm asking your opinion.'

'It won't be . . . It's not . . . I want you to be happy, I do. I want that badly for both of us.'

'I am happy,' he said, a little too forcefully.

Just then, the crunching sound of footsteps repelled them apart. In a minute, Benji rounded the bend and emerged, face shining with sweat.

7

'What the fuck,' Benji said.

Nick lifted a finger, watching its tip swell in a ballooning illusion. Oh, he was higher than high.

'Everyone's been looking for you, Dad. You're supposed to make the first toast.'

'My toast,' Nick exclaimed, glancing at Linnie. Laughter bubbled up inside him, and Linnie joined in, the mention of the toast igniting their private joke.

Benji narrowed his eyes. 'It reeks out here.'

'Damn waitstaff.' Nick clapped his son on the shoulder. 'All you, squirt. Lead the way.'

Inside, the guests were seated in Bosch-like clusters. Nick visualized a web between them, gossamer threads connecting one group to the next. The objects too seemed interrelated – the forks laid down beside lemon wedges whose juices glistened atop fragments of lobster shell. He took in the partially sipped glasses of Chardonnay, the half-eaten plates of food. There were still several portions' worth of fries at the buffet table. Each leftover transformed before his eyes into a lump of money, destined to be scraped into the garbage at the night's end. Ninety dollars a head . . . At that price point, each individual French fry cost how much? Think, Nick, think. No, he couldn't do the math. His mind had melted to goo. It was no wonder Kerr had fired him. Fired him before he lost his mind and turned into his goddamn mother.

Judith. She was seated by the microphone beside Caro. His pretty, young wife. (Not young. No longer young.) Wine had raised the color in her cheeks; she looked like a child who had played too long in the snow. His beautiful bride. He heard Avery's chime-like voice: 'Mama, my tummy hurts.'

His baby. She was tall enough now that if she stood on tiptoe, she could loop her arms around Caro's neck and jump onto her back monkey-style. Her days of no longer wanting to hold her parents' hands or be cradled in their arms were nigh. Self-consciousness could graft itself onto a child's psyche with alarming swiftness. Before you knew it, there was a last time for everything.

Nick tapped the microphone. 'Testing, testing.' An ungodly screech of feedback tore through the speakers. He cleared his throat, fumbling to locate the ideal distance between his lips and the mesh grille.

'Good evening, everyone,' he said. 'For those who don't recognize this dashing mug, I'm Nick, father of the groom. I want to start by saying that despite what my mother might have you believe, I'm not the best wordsmith, so bear with me.'

He licked his lips; his mouth was dry. He spotted a water glass in his periphery. Gratefully, he reached for it, the heat of the group's attention flaming his face. Sipping required immense concentration, so he shut his eyes and surrendered to a vision of himself at his bar mitzvah, drinking from his father's kiddush cup. Where was that cup? Stowed somewhere in a box in the attic, likely covered in mouse droppings. It was one of the few objects he'd kept when he and Linnie split. By the rule of separation, half their valuables should have gone to him, but he hadn't wanted them; not the oak curio cabinet nor the kitsch figurines purchased in Santorini. He could divorce these objects from their sentiment no more easily than he could divorce himself from the role he'd played as her husband.

'I know you're all eager to hear about the man of the hour,' he said. 'This kid has always been a little pisher. Back in the day, he scared the hell out of us by hiding in the closet, pretending it was Narnia. We thought he'd run away, so we rang up half the people in this room.' A few nods of recognition, a few cheeky smiles. 'I'll never forget the ecstatic look on his face when he popped out and yelled, "For Aslan!" And how badly he felt afterward, seeing how upset he'd made his mother. He was so distraught, he handed me his Nintendo as penance.'

Nick took another sip of water. Generosity radiated off his guests; they were enjoying his speech. See their posture, how they were leaning toward him? They loved him. He was their wise leader, their Solomon. Why shouldn't they cling to his every word?

He gripped the microphone and continued:

'The biggest surprise came when Benji rang me a few months back and said he and Morgan were tying the knot. I thought he was pulling my leg. My Benji, king of the kids' table? Jokes aside, Morgs, you're like a daughter to me. A second daughter? A third? I'm never quite sure how to figure it.'

He sought out Morgan's face in the crowd. Her lips were held in a purse. He felt a filigree of red blood vessels spread across his cheeks. Wrap it up, buddy.

'What more can I say? I'm proud of you, Benj. Proud of the man you are and continue to become. You're more levelheaded now than you used to be – is that fair? I wish you and Morgan all the happiness in the world. As they say here in Maine, "May you have fair winds and following seas." And some extra cash wouldn't hurt either. I guess the founders left that one out, huh.'

He could feel the guests' attention waning. A few were consulting their watches, the rest stealing furtive glances around the room. No one cared for Churchill-style oration anymore; they wanted tweet-size prosaisms. Nick buried his hands in his pockets, anxious to step away.

'Well, here comes the part where I'm supposed to impart some pearls of wisdom. Marriage – it's tough. It's like climbing a mountain. Just when you think you've reached the top, you realize it's a false summit, and you gotta keep trudging. But the view is worth it, trust me. Life is better with someone by your side. That said, give it up for my beautiful wife, Linnie, who helped put this evening together. She's the real MVP. Hear, hear.'

There was a murderous silence as his words sank in. The guests vacillated between horror and mirth, a scuffle that played itself out across their faces. Their applause – a pitiful trickle of it – came less from jubilation than relief at knowing the speech was over. Nick was too swept away in his maudlin sentiment to see the quiver of pain that torqued Caro's lips. He raised his glass and toasted the happy couple with a booming 'L'chaim!' Tepidly, the others joined in, though their attention had shifted to the back of the room where Linnie sat, a single tomato skewered on her fork, tears round and intact on her cheeks, like raindrops on a windowpane.

8

The fulcrum of Caroline DeLuca's life lay some thirteen years before, on the Independence Day weekend she agreed to meet Nick in his office. Everyone else had vacated the city, leaving the two of them alone. Still young enough to play the ingenue, Caro feigned surprise when Nick drew the blinds in a whirlwind of excitement.

He moved for her blouse. As he lifted it overhead, she caught an ill-masked whiff of sour perspiration. (Her roommate had, regrettably, convinced her to switch to an au naturel deodorant, whose boast about being 'microbiome-friendly' did little to offset its diminished efficacy.) She had selected her bra that morning with Nick in mind: a dusty-rose color, with semi-sheer cups that forced up her breasts. She wished he'd take a beat to admire it, but his hands were already on the hook, his wedding band a cool admonition between her shoulder blades.

The summer air was hot, their bodies coated in sweat. Caro swept up her hair. Nick's lips located a tendon in her neck and sucked. God, yes, she whimpered with a tinge of performance. Yes, yes, yes.

He knelt down and, pushing up her skirt, traced his tongue along her thigh. She squirmed. It was too intimate. 'Stand up,' she ordered with false confidence.

She reached down to grab hold of him. He was, to her surprise, soft. She glanced into his eyes only perfunctorily, afraid of what she'd find.

'Sorry,' he said. 'It's not you. It's just – it's been a while.'

The words passed through the membrane of her mind, where their essence was extracted through an expert process of feminine centrifugation. Had it been a while since he'd slept with anyone, or since he'd slept with someone who wasn't his wife?

Eventually, with steady coercion, the situation was remedied, and what they had spent months building toward culminated in a mere four and a half minutes of thrusting. Spent and reclothed, they lay curled together on the couch, their exhaustion born not from the physical toll but the emotional one. Her gaze followed the spinning fan blades above as pangs of panic – not dissimilar from the ones of excitement she'd felt earlier – drew tight her nerves. Nick reached into her blouse and clamped her nipple with his thumb and forefinger. 'Do you like this?' he asked.

'What do you think?'

'You're the most stunning woman in the world, is what I think.'

She removed his glasses from his nose. 'They're dirty,' she said, tilting them toward the light. He smiled peaceably, taking them back without comment.

That Caroline DeLuca, *administrative assistant*, would fall in love with her boss shortly thereafter was not as definitive as retrospect would make it seem. She had merely been having fun, following her whims. A twenty-six-year-old who did not fully grasp the consequences of her actions; who found it easy to view Linnie Olsen as *the other woman* rather than herself.

There was the matter of her and Nick's age discrepancy, though what were two decades when one considered the age of the earth, the span of humanity? Such was Caro's chosen method of aversion: to absent herself to a vantage so cosmic, it rendered every problem microscopic. This sort of sweeping view was not without its perils, though. If you manipulated timescales enough, pinched the screen so that the image grew smaller and smaller, you predisposed yourself to nihilism. To counter this, Caro forced herself to think everything mattered. It all mattered, and it was all good.

With a force that belied her inner doubts, she maintained that the age difference only contributed to their attraction. Nick had seen things, been places. He didn't worry about money, climbing the corporate ladder, establishing a family – goals he'd already put in the rearview. (Later, this would prove a source of tension between them: Caro felt cheated out of experiences Nick had gotten to enjoy. 'I missed my chance to figure out who I was,' she'd say.)

Nick informed her that she worried too much about such stressors; they'd sort themselves out. When she asked how he could be sure, he shrugged. 'People your age are so concerned that youth is their springtime, and it's all downhill from there. That's a load of bull. When you're young, you're too preoccupied with making something of yourself to enjoy it. It's freeing to discover you can't do it all.'

'That's sad.'

No, he said, he didn't think so. He got happier with each passing year and suspected others did as well. The only people who dreaded growing older were those stuck reliving the heydays of their past. 'I'm not saying I never get nostalgic for my twenty-year-old self – the vim he had, the vigor. Sure I do. But I wouldn't trade my current life to redo every second over again. No sane person would.'

With time, Caro and Nick grew bolder, winking at each other during meetings, sneaking off in the middle of the workday to the bathroom, where Nick would fold her over the porcelain sink, muttering phrases that were by turns erotic and disturbing: *You drive me mad; promise you'll never leave me; no, you will, you'll get sick of me and think I'm nothing but a wrinkly old man.*

The sheer audacity of the office as a stage for these encounters held its own perverse appeal. All the sex they had was tinted with danger; it was skirt-up, panties-aside kind of coitus; point A to point B; highways rather than the scenic route. By confining their intimacies to this space, Nick effectively secured a tourniquet around their affair, restricting it from bleeding into his other life – his real life. He and Caro were operating within a painstakingly crafted illusion, Eden before the fall.

'Any chance I can convince you to come with me to this art show on Gansevoort?' she asked him one day in August, a month into their affair. Outside, the sky was engorged with heat, clouds prowling slowly across the window glass.

'Why?' he asked.

'My friend – he writes for *The Village Voice* – he was saying this artist's the real deal.' She touched the delicate spray of Nick's eyelashes. 'Have I told you about my stint at Sotheby's in college?'

'Ah, so you wanna show off.'

'Jerk.'

'Why don't you pick a date and put it on my calendar.'

It was an empty gesture; they would not go.

'What's an art history major doing here, anyhow?' he asked.

'Art history *minor*. Economics major.' Caro shrugged. 'If I told you that my dream is to run my own gallery someday, would you fire me?'

'Doubtful, given your unique skill set.'

'Funny.'

'On a serious note, I'd encourage you to quit and chase the gallery thing if that's what you wanted.'

'Even if it meant I'd be broke?'

'Sure. At least you'd be happy.'

She rolled her eyes.

'What?' he said. 'You think you don't want to be happy? Bullshit. Everyone does. And happiness can only come when your actions and thoughts align. For instance, if you think to yourself, *I wish I traveled more*, but then stay in one place your whole life – that's a one-way ticket to regret. Believe me.'

The simmering intensity of his stare sent a watt of

anxiety through Caro's spine. She sensed that Nick had tucked his genuine feelings beneath these words, the ones he didn't dare say. He released his grip, and she grabbled for her jacket, a houndstooth tweed that lay puddled on the floor.

'Can I ask a question?' she said as he helped her with the cuffs.

'By all means.'

'If I got cancer, would you take care of me?'

He smiled as if she were being coy. 'Of course.'

She gave an uncertain nod. Was it only the gravity of cancer that had impelled him to say yes? What if she'd selected a minor ailment, like having her tonsils extracted? There seemed to be some boundary that delineated what level of commitment she ought to expect from him. But where this boundary lay, who had drawn it – such particulars remained obscured by a grove of half-truths.

'You know what my friend called this?' she asked, combing her fingers through her hair.

He froze at the word *this*.

'Psychological warfare. Emotional nukes. We're on a path of mutually assured destruction.'

'Nice to know you think of us so positively.'

'Us,' she mused, allowing the term to linger. 'Isn't it strange that we can be an "us," yet know so little about each other?'

'Oh, kid. You know me better than anyone.'

It was true that Caro, ever fastidious, had undertaken a study of her boss's behavior. She collected factoids about him and used these to endear him to her: how he took his coffee (two creams), which vegetables he omitted from his salad (onions and tomatoes), his pet peeves (slow walkers, people who were chronically late). Yet she was aware that these things did not a person make. You could know virtually everything about someone and still not know them at all.

The months went by. Melancholy swept in with the autumn air. Nick pulled away – not physically (for their rendezvous remained as frequent and carnal as ever) but emotionally. He withheld details about his life beyond the office. Under the guise of good-natured lampoons, he mocked Caro's suggestions during the weekly all-hands meeting. He could shunt his outward flow of affection from entirely present one moment to brutally apathetic the next.

'Woof. Wonder what you did to piss him off,' Michelle said one morning when he strode past Caro's desk without even a hello. 'Men – friggin' temperamental.'

Darkness saturated Caro's heart. She imagined storming into Kerr's office and laying out the entire affair for his perusal. But to what end? The only outcome she craved was for Nick to choose her, and there'd be no chance of that if she sold him out for a measly promotion.

Caro wondered if, in some concealed part of himself, Nick despised her. No; if he hated anyone, it must only be himself, whatever brute urge had allured him to her in the first place. Sensing this, she felt her own depraved longing amplified, an ice pick slipping deeper into her chest. She was abducted by dreams of the day he'd say he had served Linnie the divorce papers. Entire evenings she devoted to envisioning this – the two of them absconding into another story, dining beneath a lofty ceiling, sharing an immaculate king-size bed with Egyptian cotton sheets. More than once, she imagined them as the couple in that famous Chagall painting, soaring high above the rest of the city.

Seated in her and Nick's room in Elizabeth Cottage, Caro released this reverie, allowing it to slither back to whatever depth from which it had emerged. She cradled her wet face in her hands, regathering herself. She had put Avery to sleep in the other room and was painfully alone. The sound of revelers down the hall only magnified her desolate condition. She reached up and clutched the necklace Nick had given her for their tenth anniversary – a diamond heart that dangled from a white gold chain. Once, the necklace had brought her comfort. Now it was cold and heavy where it rested against her chest.

Nick, the speech, Linnie – how quickly the deluge overtook her. She felt like a clown.

For over a decade, Caro had been patient, knowing that the path of grieving a marriage was long and arduous. The artist Marina Abramović journeyed three thousand miles along the Great Wall of China to bid her husband goodbye. Caro had given Nick his three thousand miles, or so she'd believed. Yet tonight, when he lifted his champagne glass in pomp, there could be no denying the signature of desire that illuminated his face.

Maybe he had tired of her, like Matisse with his toys. Funny how one day, you were overanalyzing a wink in the copy room, and the next, you'd slept together so many times – thousands, she tallied – that the act had become, God forbid, tedious. She missed the days of their sneaking about, fondling each other in unfamiliar rooms. Neither toys nor lingerie could compensate for the impression that sex had become yet another item on their to-do list, no more exceptional than washing the dishes or walking the dog. But boring didn't equal unhappy. She and Nick were, for all intents and purposes, happy – weren't they?

The wine had gone to her head, its impasto obfuscating her thoughts. The darkness around her was thick, webby. Outside, the sea's surface made maracas of the rain. The clouds parted to reveal a sky staffed with stars and then abruptly swelled back shut. In the nightstand drawer was a red Gideon. She carried it into the bathroom, where the light was better, and flipped to a random page, trying to excavate the long-buried solace such words once provided.

Wherefore, my beloved, as ye have always obeyed, not as in my presence only, but now much more in my absence, work out your own salvation with fear and trembling.

A body-rattling sob overtook her. She cursed herself for imagining she could dodge the bill of her old sin; for dreaming that Nick would not come to resent her conventionality, when he had plainly been seeking in her youth a change from the mundane. She hugged herself, unable to prevent her mind from replaying the evening's awful toast. They had been Chagall's lovers, yes, but their descent had gone awry. They were tumbling toward earth at the wrong angle, threatening to burn up.

9

In his stoned state, it took Nick nearly an hour to deduce that Caro had taken Avery and departed the Boathouse, leaving him to divine how furious she might be. He hitched a ride back to the cottage from an old friend, a country lawyer who was considerate enough not to mention his unfortunate gaffe, nor the trouble that awaited him at home.

As he hurried through the corridor, he permitted himself the fantasy that maybe Caro was not angry. Maybe she'd fled the dinner on account of her nausea. Or maybe she *had* been furious but would be so overjoyed by his gallant return (he'd come the instant he realized!), she'd throw her arms around him and proclaim all forgiven. She would kiss him, and he would stroke back her hair, telling her what a vision she'd been tonight, and ... and ... *fuck*. He couldn't have been more of an ignoramus if he'd tried. Why the hell did he persist in wounding the ones he cherished most? Maybe he and his buddy George Proctor had more in common than he cared to admit.

In the suite's living room, Avery was asleep in her trundle bed, Matisse vigilantly beside her. She looked seraphic, her hair splayed on the pillow and her unicorn shirt swimming to her knees. Each morning, Nick would begin his day by dropping her off at camp, doing the choreographed carpool dance with the other parents. She'd tromp up the steps, turning back at the last second to lift a hand and wave at him. That gesture, that wave, the need to double-check that he was behind her, that he'd always be behind her – why did this stir in him the longing it did? He had grown soft, his armor showing its wear.

'Love you more, love you most,' he whispered, tugging the blanket up to her shoulders. He stooped to pet Matisse, who pressed his wet nose into his calf. At least someone still liked him. Nick silently communicated with the dog, relaying to him this evening's events as he might to a friend. He felt the dog alone understood him; the dog alone knew of his good heart.

'Daddy? Will you read me a book?'

Nick turned. Avery was holding her eyes wide open to the darkness as if to prove her wakefulness.

'Didn't Mommy read you one?' he asked.

Avery reached under the covers and pulled out a picture book about Dolly Parton. It was one in a series of books about famous women Caro had purchased to quote-unquote *inspire her*. If an alien were to beam his daughter's bookshelves into outer space, the entire extraterrestrial civilization would think planet Earth some feminist utopia.

He picked up the book and began to read, raising his voice so that Caro might hear him in the bathroom, model father he was.

'Why are their cheeks like that?' Avery asked.

'Like what?'

'Those little red dots.'

'Well, that's how the artist drew them.'

'Why?'

'Sweetie, let me finish reading.'

'Nicky?' She called him this sometimes, imitating her mother. Kids always wanted to grow up faster than they could.

'What is it, munchkin?'

'Is Dolly Parton alive in this world?'

In this world – dear God. Either his daughter had an innate understanding of quantum physics or a supernatural belief in the spiritual realm. Atheist he fancied himself, Nick didn't know which would be more astonishing.

'In this world? Yes, she's alive.'

'When's she gonna die?'

Look at her, his Avery, capably understanding the cycle of life and death – something he felt was beyond his own grasp even now. He felt guilty for underestimating her. Sure, she'd won her class spelling bee, but that was small potatoes compared to this. (Plus, Hazel Hollingsworth had peed her pants on the word *kitten*, which had likely distracted the other competitors.) Maybe she'd turn out to be a mini Einstein yet – one of those freakish children who attend college at fourteen and win a Nobel by twenty-three. A man could dream.

'I don't know, baby,' he answered.

'Is Dolly Parton gonna live forever?'

Oh, well. So much for that.

'I don't think so.'

'Where does she live?'

'In Tennessee.'

'What's Ten-seat?'

'It's in the South. It's the country music capital.'

'Nicky?'

'Avie?'

'I'm not feeling very good at sleeping tonight.'

'Try. Count sheep.'

'Sheep?'

'Just shut your eyes and count to ten.'

Her polka-dot rain boots were lying on the floor. Each boot had an easy-on pull handle, which made them look like miniature pocketbooks. Pocketbooks for dolls. He kissed her forehead and headed toward the bathroom, where a faint light spilled beneath the door.

Caro sat in her underwear on the lip of the tub, slathering shea butter onto each elbow. Her movements were slow, halting. The sink tap was running. Nick ran his fingers beneath it. The pillar of water broke and resealed. 'Jesus, that's boiling,' he said.

Caro continued working the lotion onto her legs, massaging each kneecap. When upset, she withdrew behind a mask of catatonia and ceased speaking, a habit he thought immature. His frustration only stoked her defensiveness. He imagined her tucking the softest parts of herself into a steel vault he could not access.

'So.' He assessed her. 'Let me have it.'

She removed a pair of tweezers from her cosmetics bag and set to work on her eyebrows. After each pluck she consulted her reflection, rotating her face one way then the other, as if a single absent hair might alter her entire countenance. Her movements carried a tense, embellished air.

'Nothing?' he said. 'No "Fuck you" or "Take a hike, buster"?'

She pivoted toward the bedroom, mechanical as a figure in a music box. At the nightstand, she popped a melatonin into her mouth. Nick debated asking her for one – not because he wanted it, but because if she withheld it, he'd have reason to nurse an anger of his own. Caro yanked back the covers with a swift motion.

'For chrissake,' he said, climbing in after her. 'At least let's talk about it.'

He burrowed into her shoulder in what he hoped she might regard as an adorable, puppy-like nuzzle. Beneath the laundered aroma of starch on the sheets lingered another smell: that of days when guests would return from the coast, their bodies pink and raw, their pockets flush with sea glass.

'Fine,' he said. 'You want to punish me all night, go right ahead.'

Caro's voice, laden with disappointment, floated to him: 'I'm not punishing you. I'm just hurt. Don't I have a right to be?'

Well, at least she'd answered. He ought to apologize, but he was afraid doing so would seem an admission of guilt. One would be better off, he believed, atoning through actions alone.

'Car, honey, honest to God, I didn't mean to say her

name. It just came out. I was bumbling up there. You know how I get.'

He envisioned each word as a blowtorch aimed at the icy block of his wife's anger. So grave were the contours of his contrition, he could do nothing but obscure them by making it seem like Caro was overreacting. If he condoned her feelings of victimization, there would be no recovery.

His only consolation: that Caro had not spotted him outside with Linnie, had not heard him reveal to his ex-wife the details of his financial distress. Telling Linnie had been a relief. She was practically a stranger to him now, and it was far easier to confide such truths in a stranger.

Oh, but why had Linnie felt the need to summon Alice's specter into the festivities? The weekend was now utterly wrecked. All Linnie had wanted, he knew, all she'd been seeking, was validation of their former life together. She wanted him to corroborate her account of the years that preceded their grief, when the worst possibilities were still incipient, not possibilities at all but mere wisps of them, abstract nothings that would rowel her at night. She had sought that validation, and Nick had denied her. Now, as if to punish him, Alice was here, in this room, hovering just beyond Caro's shoulder.

'What can we do?' he asked Caro, resorting to the plural in the hopes it might fuse them.

'Short of turning back time? Not a goddamn thing.'

'Baby,' he pleaded, snaking an arm beneath her waist.

He kissed the nape of her neck. She did not resist. Nor

did she pull away when he rubbed his palm over her breast. It would be easy for them to resort to this, a panacea they applied to the slightest agitating symptom.

When Caro next spoke, she did so tonelessly, as if recording a voice memo. 'You don't get it. It's bad enough being known as the woman who slept with her boss. But I still come with you to these family things because I know how important they are to you. And then you act like you don't even want me there. Like you're the school hotshot, and you're pretending to be with me for some stupid dare. You *humiliated* me, Nick.'

'I didn't—'

'You know something else? Your mother has never asked me a single question about my life. Not one.'

'My *mother*?'

'Before the stroke, even. She's got no desire to know me, and that hurts.'

'Honey, you can't let that get to you. She doesn't even recognize *me* half the time.'

'And now you're defending her—'

'I'm not.'

'—when once you were her harshest critic.'

'She's an old woman, Car. Is she a pill? Sure. But I sure as hell hope that at the end of my life, someone treats me with sympathy.'

'Sympathy? You want to talk about *sympathy*? Okey-doke, signor, let's talk about sympathy. Where should we start? Should we start with the fact that I'm the only one who pushed for your mother to even be here this weekend? Oh, no, it's too much, you said, she can't handle it, she'll be confused. But why not give her miserable life some *joy*? And now suddenly, *I'm* the enemy.'

'Fair enough.'

'You should've heard her yesterday. It was Linnie this and Linnie that. Tell me, Mr *Sympathy*, who's on the phone with the aides every day, hearing about her hemoglobin levels and every flippin' time she misses the toilet? I'll tell you, Nick – it's me. So, if you want to talk about *sympathy*, go ahead, I dare you.'

Nick nodded in the polite way a tourist nods when receiving directions in a language he does not comprehend. It was all right for him to speak harshly about his mother, but not anyone else.

'And another thing: Why didn't you tell me about running into Peter at Starbucks?' Caro asked.

'Because it wasn't a big deal, that's why. I ran into him, all right?'

'And kept it from me.'

'You're acting like I meant to keep it from you.'

'Yeah, you're acting like you did too.'

'I told you, I had a meeting.'

'In East Harlem.'

'Yes, in East Harlem.'

'I didn't realize you were colleagues with the underserved.'

'That's racist.'

'No, Nick, it's not.'

She licked a teardrop from her lip. The question hung in the air between them: *Are you cheating on me?* Nick realized, with a swift blow of shame, that he'd prefer her to believe he *was* unfaithful rather than unemployed. If she was this hurt now, how would she react upon learning about *that*?

'You came on to me, Nick. Way back when. You came on to me, and you sought my approval. It wasn't the other way around. You wanted to know that you could still hang, that young, attractive women were still into you. But what's gonna happen when I'm not the young, attractive thing anymore, huh? You gonna find some other young, attractive woman to stick it in? Or have you already done that?'

Their breath was heavy between them. A series of pops erupted out the window, followed by a long whiz-zing noise.

'Fireworks,' Nick said, to say something.

They resumed their bickering, though the interruption had chased the acrimony from their fight.

'The real problem is,' Caro said, 'you're not listening to me. Frankly, I can't tell if you lack self-awareness – if you honestly believe what you're serving – or if you think I'm just that dumb.'

'I *am* listening,' he sputtered. 'I made a boneheaded mistake tonight, I admit. But that doesn't change the facts – I chose you. I *choose* you.'

'Do you?'

'A hundred times over. A thousand.'

Silence condensed between them.

Yes, he had chosen Caro, but not entirely of his own accord. When the foundation of his first marriage showed initial signs of collapse, he'd arrived ready with a trowel and a bucket of stucco. Please, he begged, let him try to repair it. He accompanied Linnie to the grief support group held in the dingy basement of St Mark's Church. He purchased tickets to a retreat center in New Mexico where they performed a butterfly release ceremony to represent the letting go of wounds. Even as they did this, their hands joined on the box's lid, they remained isolated, each webbed in their own sticky grief. He pledged to do anything necessary: moving states, participating in an ayahuasca ceremony, even reciting the Hail Mary every day. He met with one therapist who assured him that conjugal stress was a natural response to the loss of a child; another who said he oughtn't blame himself for Alice's death – eighty percent of people who committed suicide denied nurturing self-destructive thoughts until their last breath.

'What were you thinking?' Linnie asked him once afterward.

'Clearly, I wasn't,' he said.

'Goddammit, Nick. You're the most selfish man alive. All this' – Linnie made a vague tossing motion with her hand – 'for some pussy.'

Pussy. The word was like a piece of paper she was biting, tearing in two with a violent thrash of her head. She spoke this way by then, with obscenities, as if to frighten him away, or prove that she too had a secret self, one who was duplicitous and capable of shocking him. He took this as an encouraging sign; it meant she still cared. So long as they persisted, he believed, things were bound to get better. It was the same advice he offered concerned clients: wait it out. The most fundamental rule of long-term investing was to weather the market's vicissitudes with clear-eyed detachment, understanding that what falls must eventually rise.

He held his thumb to Caro's cheek, rubbing in small circles as if she were a mirror in need of polishing. 'Let's go to sleep. We'll have more clarity in the morning.'

'All I've ever wanted is a fair chance. That's all I've ever asked for. Do you disagree?'

He winced, unable to look at her. It seemed to him the most punishing thing, that you could love someone so much and injure them so gravely. Or perhaps it was *because* you loved them that you were able to wound them, for the tender flesh beneath their shield was also the place the knife slid in.

'You deserve better,' he said, and watched these words ripple across her expression like a stone dropped in water. It was true. She deserved someone who wasn't embarrassed to bring her around his coworkers, inventing an excuse each December for why she didn't need to attend the Christmas party. Someone who'd accompany her to the gallery in Nyack and ask which piece was her favorite, how she'd gone about pricing the inventory, what efforts went into maintaining the exhibitions.

One summer's day years ago, Nick had surprised her there, at the gallery. Through the window, he watched her lead a pair of buyers through the pieces. She smiled brightly when he entered. 'Let me take you around,' she said.

That month's exhibition was devoted to color field

painting. Occupying one wall was a tremendous canvas sliced into a chromatic grid. Several interlocking orange panels hung on another. Nick found these pieces pleasing, if puzzling. As Caro gestured to the placard below the grid, he sidled closer and extended an arm to graze her breast. They each kept straight faces, staring ahead. Her breath quickened as he worked a hand into her back pocket and squeezed.

'*Nicholas.* I'm working.'

'Since when is this not workplace appropriate?'

'Come, I want to show you something.'

She guided him to the smallest canvas in the room. It was deep blue with textured splotches of color. The work was a meditation – on what, Nick didn't know. Its title, *Rhythm Angst*, offered few clues. He found himself absorbed all the same, drawn in by the movement, the life. To merely behold it triggered in him an avalanche of sensations. His gonads swelled, blood gushing forth. Good God, was he ... hard? The longer he contemplated the piece, the greater the effect.

'Do you like it?' Caro asked. 'It's not everyone's cup of tea.'

His tongue fattened in his mouth. He *liked* movie theater popcorn. He *liked* Duran Duran. Yet this feeling, this druggy rush verging on terror, transcended such commonplace affections. In the debauched red contours of the painting – more akin to slashes in flesh than brushstrokes – he witnessed a mind spiraling into madness, a mind eager to reach out and whisk him into its depths. He envied Caro for being able to bask in this

wild energy day after day, envied her for having pos-
sessed the genius to select this piece in the first place.
She was a maverick, a tastemaker. A thousand years from
now, the fact that she had selected this painting might
have real implications on the trajectory of art.

In theory, Nick understood he shouldn't feel insecure
around his brilliant wife. Still, his ego, as pervasive as the
ivy dripping over the sides of the cottage, hampered this
understanding. Even years into their marriage, these
blazes of Caro's inner life unsettled him – moments when
his aperture widened, and he was forced to acknowledge
that he'd been viewing her through a narrow lens; that her
perception was beyond his ken, as a crab under the sea
cannot fathom the view from the pelican's vantage above.

The cottage suite was hushed now but for the rain
percussing the windows and roof. Moonlight slid across
Caro's moisturized forehead as she rolled toward him. 'I
don't want you to speak to Linnie again,' she said. 'You
asked what you could do to make it better, so there.
Once this godforsaken trip is over, I want you to cut her
off. If she tries to call you, you hit ignore.'

'And if she asks why I'm suddenly the world's biggest
jackass?'

'I don't know, Nick. History has proven you're a good
liar. Make something up. Or tell her the truth.'

'Which is?'

'That your wife's wishes outweigh her comfort.
Besides, she's got Ezra now. I see no reason for her to
continue playing the damsel.'

Anger broke like a wave on the shores of Nick's mind,

and borne upon it was a profound sense of bewilderment. He felt Caro was requesting a sacrifice he could not give, but the vise grip of his circumstances offered no room for negotiation. He laid a hand on her stomach. 'If it'll put you at ease, then fine. So be it.'

Her ribs contracted. Relief.

'You're my everything,' he murmured.

'So you claim.'

He threw back the covers and snatched up the pillow as if to head for the couch. Testosterone pulsed through him in gratifying spurts. Had a plate or vase been within reach, he would've hurled it to the ground. 'God, you're such a *child*. I'm trying to make amends here, but it's like you'd rather be mad at me than resolve the problem.'

'Lower your voice, will you? Avie's sleeping.'

He squinted, trying to read Caro's expression in the dark. At some point over the past thirteen years, whether purposeful or not, they had started missing each other.

'What more do you want from me?' he asked. 'Please, tell me, because I honestly can't figure it out.'

'I don't want anything.'

She was lying, of course. This was the trait he found most peeving in members of the opposite sex – even when they appeared to accept his pleas for clemency, they still insisted on keeping him locked in emotional purgatory. Never mind that he'd bought Caro the Scarsdale house, invested in her money-hemorrhaging gallery, and paid for Avery to attend a Waldorf school so that she could have a 'holistic' education, though they lived in one of the finest school districts in the country. Nick had done his best to give Caro everything and to operate from a place of goodwill. But perhaps places of goodwill are as varied as countries on a globe, and his version no longer resembled hers.

She lifted a strand of hair from her shoulder, examining the split ends. As if the thought had just come to her, she said, 'You know who seems like a great guy? Ezra. He mentioned stopping by the gallery sometime. We chatted for a bit while you were off God-knows-where.'

'And?'

'He's a good listener. You can tell how much he cares. I think he's good for Linnie.'

'If you have something to say, come out with it. I can't stand this beating around the bush.'

Caro doubled her pillow and collapsed backward into it. 'I'm going to sleep.'

'Good night, then.'

They lay there in the dark, each absorbing the tension radiating from the other's body, two poised bows at the ready. Yes, the problem with women was their impetuousness. Yet wasn't it this very trait that had kept buffoons like himself captivated for millennia? After all, one never knew when Helen might flee Sparta for Troy, or when Eve would decide to pluck the apple from its gnarled branch, and you – loyal, logical Adam, foremost among men – sensed that, given the choice, you'd choose to remain an innocent child in your father's holy garden forever.

10

By midnight, the guests of Elizabeth Cottage had retreated from the Reading Room, where some had enjoyed a nightcap, and the fire pit, whose last embers expelled arabesques of smoke. The kayaks were shelved in their cantilever rack, the fishing rods filed away. Even Benji's most rambunctious friends agreed to fold up their poker game early to conserve energy for the following evening. To a passerby driving the slick ribbon of road that wound up to the cottage door, the estate would've appeared abandoned.

In the bridal suite, Morgan rummaged through her suitcase for the MR & MRS signs she had printed, which Peter was responsible for delivering to the appropriate vendors. 'I know they're in here somewhere ... Oh, wait, success – got them.'

She turned to find her father distracted by something beneath the couch. Without looking, she knew it must be the box of talismans Sequoia had shipped to her and Benji's apartment in Brooklyn. The box contained a piece of red thread, a strand of pearls, a faded photograph of the two of them, mother and daughter, with Morgan's arms wrapped around Sequoia's neck.

'It was nice of your mom to send this,' Peter said.

Morgan shrugged, annoyed by her father's prying.

She sat down on the bed and lifted her hairbrush from the nightstand. Its teeth glided through her tangles without a snag. A good sign, she thought. It was a girlhood habit of hers, to read into moments such as these, tallying them as evidence of how much the universe favored her. Opening the microwave on a zero or five: good. An uneven number of stairs: bad. No instance proved too feeble to invest with meaning, nor too inconsequential to hold sway.

Rains from outside blew through the cracked window. The air had a viscous quality to it, like pus leaked from a wound. A bad sign, indeed.

'Quite the night,' Peter said.

He was loitering. He had something to say before returning to his room, but Morgan refused to prompt him, denying him the release that her questions might offer. She removed her checklist from her planning folder and reviewed it. Ring holder – check, marriage license – check, vow books – check.

'Nick and that speech,' Peter said.

'It was rough.'

'The way he treats people is horrible. He's certainly not winning any husband-of-the-year awards.'

The chilly tone with which her father referred to Nick reminded Morgan of how he used to speak of her mother. At age ten, Morgan couldn't comprehend why her father withheld from her the chance to go live out in California with Sequoia. It sounded idyllic: foraging for herbs, crooning folk songs around the campfire, discovering methods to raise her consciousness – and,

217

most dreamily, falling asleep every night in her mother's arms. Yet each time she mentioned the ranch, Peter disparaged Sequoia's ragtag coterie of soul-searchers as suckers, Johnny-come-latelies to the counterculture revolution who were too coddled to handle the responsibilities of adulthood. With each biting remark, Morgan became increasingly convinced that his true agenda was to poison her against her mother so that he wouldn't have to vie for her affection. Was he hoping to perform a similar trick with the Weils? Convinced this must be the case, she felt a sudden rush of pity for her father and his petty motives.

'You seem mighty invested in this Nick and Linnie business,' she said.

'Of course I'm invested. This is the family my baby girl's marrying into – how could I not be?'

A croak entered his voice, causing her eyes to snap up. Their stares met in the mirror as if across a great lake. Was it just a trick of the glass that made him appear colorless, already slouching toward old age?

Throughout Morgan's childhood, Peter had functioned as both maternal and paternal forces, yin and yang. By the time she was six, he had grown expert at plaits and pigtails, Barbies, glitter art. When she got her period, he went to the Duane Reade on the corner and filled his basket with supplies. Once, upon discovering she'd been excluded from a sleepover, he permitted her to smear blush onto his cheeks in consolation.

'Anyway, I wanted to give you this.' He reached into his pocket and removed a jewel-encrusted barrette. 'For your something blue, and I guess also your something borrowed. It belonged to Granny Rose.'

Morgan was moved in spite of herself. 'I love it, thanks.'

'Try it on.'

She slid the barrette's lever beneath an inch-wide section of hair. The jewels glistened among the dark waves.

'You look like your mother.'

'Oh, Dad.'

'Sorry, it's just . . .' Peter danced his fingers over the sundry objects on the vanity. 'You could have told me about you and Benji sooner. There was no reason to keep it so hush-hush.'

'I wasn't trying to keep you out of it,' she said, managing to sound earnest.

For months before Benji proposed, Morgan had felt guilt gnawing away at her. Absent her father's approval, she struggled to merge the facets of her life into a gestalt. But she saw only the gaps, the betrayals that kept them apart.

This wasn't the first time she'd resorted to such deception. In high school, she and Alice used to flirt with older boys on Facebook – boys who lived nearby in the San Remo or the Dakota and attended Regis or Collegiate but were practically strangers, leading hermetic lives of lacrosse games and dinners at Eleven Madison. Morgan had fallen for one boy who messaged her every night. He told her he wanted to be a poet, though both his parents worked for Sullivan & Cromwell and expected him to follow a similar path. She made confessions of her own. Their budding intimacy remained tethered to the virtual realm – a stream of texts and photos. When she suggested they meet up in person, he ceased communication. Morgan was left heartsick and confused. She worried that the photographs she'd sent might circulate among the inboxes of other high school boys. She could've confided in Alice but chose not to, hoping to contain her shame within the anonymity of the web.

'We meant to tell you, honest,' she said to Peter. 'It's just, the more we held back, the easier it became to keep quiet.'

'And that's the whole truth?'

'Why would I make something up?'

'Maybe deep down, you were scared I wouldn't like it.'

'That's ridiculous. You might not think Benji is all that, but I do. He means everything to me, Dad – *everything*.'

'On the contrary, I think Benji is an exceptional young man. It's you I worry about.'

'You make it sound like I'm stuck at home, playing Susie Homemaker all day. I've got a job I love, one I'm damn good at.'

'Yes, and those kids are lucky to have you. Forget I said anything.'

How little her father understood. Even now, he assumed that her former life as a child violinist guaranteed her admission into the elite world of classical music – a risible notion. Since college, she'd auditioned for one or two independent orchestras and passed the initial rounds before faltering miserably at the callbacks.

Any attempts she undertook to alleviate the sting of these rejections proved useless. A small voice inside her said she was nothing but a striver, a phony; that the music directors had seen through her pretenses to the desperate animal underneath. The harder she tried, the hungrier that animal grew, feeding off some human piece of her soul until only a loathsome emptiness remained.

'Dad?'

'Uh-huh.'

'Why'd you never remarry after Mom?'

'Oh, I don't know. No one else, I guess.'

'But you didn't look, did you?'

Weariness slackened Peter's features. Morgan had never seen him depleted in this way, devoid of the usual fire that would propel him into the hospital at dawn. 'If you're wobbling on tomorrow . . .'

Heat smarted across her face. 'Why would you even say that?'

'Just an option, sweetheart.'

'You're trying to deflect from your own issues, is that it? You can't bear to see me and Benji happy and in love. You even wince when I say that word, *love*. But we *are* in love. Stop trying to control my life.'

'Control your life? Now you really sound like your mother.'

'Leave her out of this.'

'I'm just saying, maybe you could learn a thing or two from my mistakes.'

Peter closed his mouth, a shadow of regret passing over his face. As Morgan studied him – the liver spots on his forehead, the shocking whiteness of his hair – she felt a flash of anticipatory grief.

He softened. 'Your mother wasn't a mistake. We had many fantastic years together, and she gave me the most incredible daughter. I'm only asking—'

'I've thought about it, Dad. Benji and I have discussed it all – our future, where we plan to live, what we want. We're not kids anymore, okay?' Her voice caught on the word *kids*, a lump rising in her throat.

'And what about depression?' Peter said. 'Studies show that mutations in certain serotonergic genes are linked to that. If you and Benji have kids, God willing, and those kids have some chemical imbalance, are you ready to handle that? Is he?'

A seething venom surged through Morgan's veins, displacing her earlier pity. 'God, there's no point in even talking to you. You're so judgmental.'

'Oh, Morg. I'm just trying to help.'

'How? By spouting off on shit you clearly know nothing about? If you truly cared, you'd trust that I know what's best for me.' She folded her arms. She was being harsh, but she couldn't help it. The words were a poison that she needed to expel. 'I don't even think you're capable of love at this point. You think their hearts are frozen over, but yours . . .'

'Easy,' he said. 'Don't say something you can't take back.'

'It sucks that you're jealous of my happiness. I wish you could see it from my side. Maybe someday. Till then, let's not talk about it.'

Peter crossed to the chair where his jacket hung and

removed a folded piece of paper from the inner pocket. 'Look, I know I'm not the best at expressing myself, so maybe this will explain a few things.'

Warily, she took the letter. A moment passed in which Peter might've glanced down and realized his blunder. As Morgan's eyes scanned the first words – *My dearest Lin* – a rap sounded at the door.

The knock blessedly diverted Peter from his rocketing emotions. He opened the door to see Nick in his pajamas, his pants soaked to the ankles with rain.

'Jesus, are you all right?' Peter asked.

Sheepishly, Nick glanced down. He was breathing raggedly, the wet fabric of his shirt conveying each rise and fall.

Peter stepped into the hallway, closing the door behind him. In the dim light, the corridor appeared endless, each door identical to the last as if reflected in a hall of mirrors.

'Does someone need a doctor?' he asked. *Is it Linnie?*

Nick rubbed the back of his neck. A raindrop slid down the front of his coat and fell to the carpet. 'I was going out for a stroll and figured I'd pop in to check on the bride.'

'Ah, well, I'd say, "Have a seat inside," but . . .'

'No, no. I don't want to commandeer your time.'

That Peter had yet to change out of his rehearsal dinner attire while Nick wore a pair of damp pajamas emphasized some peculiar power dynamic between the two men. Ordinarily, being the one who was smartly dressed enabled Peter to tap into a latent sense of confidence. Opposite Nick, however, he experienced an upwelling of inadequacy, as if he'd dressed to counter-act some imbalance in their stations. He loosened his tie and waited. Nick continued to stare vacuously at a spot on the far wall.

'There must be something I can do for you,' Peter said.

'Actually, I came to ask you about a job.'

'Not for Benji? I was under the impression that things at the school were going well.'

'It never hurts to keep options open. I do the same for myself. What do you know about the hospital's in-house financing?'

A suspicious tilt of the head. 'Very little.'

'Oh, that's too bad. I wonder, for Benjamin's sake . . . is there anyone you could speak to about that, if it isn't too great an ask? It would be good for him to start making connections in other sectors. Long-term, social work isn't exactly, well . . .'

'Look, it's late,' Peter said, steering Nick a few steps down the hallway. 'Why don't you get some rest, and we can revisit this in the morning?'

Nick shambled forward. He rubbed his neck, tem-ples, and arms, as if ensuring these parts were still intact. Peter nearly changed his mind and invited him inside. They had never gotten along (Peter's view of the man severely hindered by all Linnie had revealed), but that didn't mean they needed to be rivals either.

'Hey,' Peter called.

Nick turned.

'You still owe me a check for the band.'

'Right.' Nick blinked a few times. 'I'll get that to you.'

By the time Peter had reentered the bridal suite, Morgan was by the vanity, a heating pad in her lap. The atmosphere of the room felt strained, as if all the air had sucked itself up around her – or was he only imagining it? Nick's visit had introduced an element of unrest into his ordinarily unflappable exterior. 'Your father-in-law has dug himself into a hole,' he said.

Morgan said nothing.

'Anyway, where were we?'

She motioned to the paper on the bed.

'What?'

He picked it up. It took only three words before the shock penetrated, his mind shifting into overdrive as he tried to work out how this letter, this accursed confession, had made its way into his daughter's hands.

He forced himself to meet Morgan's eyes. 'This isn't—' He faltered. What could he say? His feelings for Linnie had escaped their paddock; any effort to regather them into the privacy of his mind would be futile.

'So.' She folded her arms.

'Please, let me explain.'

'It's probably best if you didn't. It's all rather clear. You didn't want me to be with Benji because it would hamstring your chances with Linnie. Pretty selfish, even for you.'

'No, no. God, no. What kind of monster do you think I am?'

She didn't answer.

'Look, this doesn't negate what I said to you earlier. All that was true. You're making too big a deal out of this.'

She grabbed the letter from his hands before he could stop her. Mockingly, she read his words back to him: ' "I love how your nostrils flutter when you laugh, your lop-sided smile, the coconut smell of your hair. Would it be too forward to admit I've spent endless evenings imagining our life together—" '

'Enough,' Peter cried, snatching the letter back. Each word writhed beneath his gaze, the ink trying to unsew itself from the page.

'You love her,' Morgan stated flatly.

'I—'

Twelve years he'd stood by Linnie's side. Twelve years in which he might have taken action. Might have reached for her hand while they were walking in Tompkins Square Park and recited the soliloquy he'd composed in his mind on those bitter nights he'd remained at home, when Morgan would phone from Poughkeepsie to tell him about the compliment her English professor had left on her essay. He had wanted the best for his daughter and been willing to discount his happiness at her expense. All this was true enough, so why did he now feel walloped by guilt?

'I do not love her,' he said forcefully. 'I have loved only one woman my whole life, and she is you.'

Morgan's gaze shifted from the right side of his face to the left as if examining two variations of the same text, scouring for inconsistencies. He saw his reflection on her eyes, and behind it, the thoughts he couldn't reach. 'I love you too,' she said, a deceptive note in her voice. Over her shoulder, the dark waves of the harbor rose and fell, the mirrored moon sliding between them like a waterlogged boat. Peter hadn't known it was possible until then to fear what he'd glimpsed in his own child's face; to take her in his arms, yet still feel fantastically alone.

12

Sunrise found the waterfront a slurry of pebbles. Boats skimmed the glassy harbor. The Hoenig Islands, an archipelago of evergreen-studded masses, peeked out distantly through the woolly haze.

In the cottage's salon where breakfast was served, guests gabbed around linen-decked tables. A chalkboard at the front trumpeted the morning's fare: fresh-from-the-oven popovers, country sausage, and deviled eggs. Berry jams and fresh-whipped butter sat arrayed in hobnail jars, trembling with each swing of the kitchen door.

Morgan entered the salon and beelined toward Ezra. A penumbra of dark curls framed her face. She wore a button-down flannel so as not to disturb her makeup when she dressed for the wedding later – an event whose occurrence no longer seemed guaranteed. Between Nick's careless slip and her own father's baffling admission, she'd realized over the past twelve hours that Benji was sorely mistaken: no one had abandoned their grief; they'd merely found better places to hide it.

Ezra brightened as Morgan entered his field of view. 'Morning. I like your—' He traced a circuit around his face. 'Is Linnie up there?'

'She's getting her hair done. I was actually looking for you. Care for a walk?'

She waited while he set down his dish. Together they strolled outside, yielding onto the beaten trail that meandered along the shoreline. The trail went on for miles, disrupted only by the occasional gazebo or inoperative ferry dock.

Ezra removed his cigarette case from his pocket. 'To what do I owe the honor?'

Up ahead, two men strolled with their arms linked. Farther out, someone was running the path in a dark windbreaker. Was it—? Yes, Benji. Doing his morning laps, black headphones coiled around his ears.

'How was Linnie last night?' she asked. 'After the snafu with Nick – how'd she seem?'

'Oh, you know.'

Absently, Morgan lifted her hand to her hair; it was stiff as crinoline. 'It's funny,' she said. 'When I was a kid, I used to think Nick was the coolest guy. He was one of those dads who made you hate your own. Alice used to say she didn't get how he could be with someone as frigid as Linnie. Sorry – I hope that doesn't offend you.'

'It's fine.'

'Anyway, now I think she must've had it backward.'

'You were good friends with Alice, weren't you?'

'Until the end, yeah.' Morgan's thoughts were arrows shooting in too many directions, failing to meet their target. She kept talking, the words spewing out of her. 'She was the yardstick that showed me where my own talents fell short, so make of that what you will.'

'What do *you* make of it?'

'I don't know.'

'Try.'

'I remember, that final fall, she'd been assigned this wicked solo to play. The day before the concert, she comes up to me, saying how nervous she is, that she's worried she's gonna blow it, blah blah blah. She hadn't been open with me like that in a long time, and I guess I was a little pissed at her for cutting me out, so I said, "Are you for real?" She looked at me for a long time then – even now, it gives me chills to think about – and she said, "Guess not." And I said, "So you shouldn't be anxious about it anymore."'

'I understand.'

Morgan winced. She sensed that Ezra *did* understand – far more than she'd anticipated. She had curated this account precisely to ensnare him into confessing foibles of his own, and he'd seen straight through it. They were more simpatico than she wished to acknowledge. He too viewed relationships through a prism of transaction, each conversation functioning as a vending machine into which she'd insert her carefully minted tokens of charm or flattery and tap the requisite buttons until her desired response materialized.

'What's your agenda with Linnie?' she asked, keeping her voice light.

'Why do you assume I have one?' he replied, equally arch.

Her line of inquiry was leading to a dead end. Ezra was just as clever as she, and even more adept at this game of misdirection. At once, she altered her approach, turning haughty. 'So, it's just happenstance that you're here?'

Deftly, Ezra passed the cigarette between his fingers. His presence, the quietude of his demeanor, caused Morgan to wonder what it had been like between him and Alice. There had been so many stories. She recalled Akash Sethi leaning over in English class to whisper, 'Micah saw Alice and Mr N. leaving the subway together.'

It must have been late November. Morgan could picture the student council members replacing the autumn leaves on the bulletin board with shimmering paper snowflakes. She had gone straight from English to the cafeteria to confront Alice. Part of her wished Akash was mistaken, yet the pieces aligned too well: Mr N.'s wink in the hallway, Alice's growing withdrawal from their friendship. Probably Mr N. had flattered her, appealed to her intellect, persuaded her to keep their liaison a secret. But Morgan wasn't just anyone; she was Alice's best friend. As she slid into the bench at their usual table, she said bluntly, 'When were you going to tell me you're boning your philosophy teacher?'

'Hello to you too,' Alice said.

Around them, the cafeteria was abuzz. The air smelled of grease and dry-erase markers. The tiled walls quivered with the mood fluctuations of the school's three thousand pubescents.

'Are you sleeping with him?' Morgan asked. 'Because some people think you are.'

'Since when do you get your news from rumors?'

'Micah saw you together.'

Alice idly swirled her thermos lid, offering neither denial nor confirmation. While most students ate the cafeteria food or purchased a meal from the scrum of food trucks outside, Alice always brought lunch from home. Linnie would pack it for her, inserting small notes like 'Have a great day' or 'Good luck on your pre-calc test' – unheeded pleas for connection that Alice left unread.

'I can't tell you,' Alice said.

'Why not?'

'Just trust me.'

'Right, because trust is in such high supply between us these days.'

'Look, he doesn't like me like that, okay? He said so himself.'

'Why would he tell you that?'

'Because I asked him. I asked him point-blank.'

'And?'

'I don't know, Morg. It was, like, this bizarre, fucked-up thing. I really don't feel like talking about it.'

For a transitory moment, Morgan's purview expanded to include the entire cafeteria – the discarded trays chugging steadily up the conveyor belt, the grilled cheese suspended on the lunch lady's spatula, the computer game loading on a laptop one table over. It was as if they'd all been recruited to take part in an elaborate improvisation, and an actor offstage had just yelled, 'Freeze!' With a plummeting sense of dread, she waited to be tapped out of the scene so that someone else could occupy her place and resume the conversation. She heard a betrayed voice, her own, marvel, 'So, it's true. You really were at his place.'

'Jesus,' Alice said, 'when did you get so dense?'

Her tone was the same Morgan had heard Linnie take

with Benji when telling him to pick his clothes up off the floor, or Nick when calling to ask what time he'd be home. And when did you become such a bitch? she thought. But anger seemed too simple, too obviously what Alice was aiming to provoke. Little by little, understanding took shape in Morgan's mind, the edges emerging against the backdrop of her disbelief. 'Holy shit. You love him – is that what this is?'

Alice shrank into her seat, her arms pinned to her sides. She wore a pilling sweater that hid from view the cuts along her inner wrists – cuts whose existence only Morgan knew of. She was a portrait of loneliness, isolated behind whatever curtain of confidences she was keeping. In that instant, Morgan perceived the matrix that stretched over their lives. On one side of the matrix lay Alice and Mr Newman, with their clandestine meetings, their stolen kisses, their forbidden love. On the other side was mundane life as it had been up until then. How juvenile her and Alice's days of beading plastic bracelets and sipping vodka from water bottles seemed when cast in stark relief against the weight of true Adult Affairs.

Now, beneath the austere gaze of Elizabeth Cottage, Morgan felt a prick of self-reproach as she recalled that her initial response to Alice had not been to discourage the relationship with Mr N., that such a reaction hadn't even crossed her mind. Instead, she'd mentally pieced together the spotty details of their entanglement into a high-octane, will-they-won't-they narrative, casting herself as Alice's consigliere. By entrusting herself to such a role, she'd hoped Alice might view their friendship as an unburdening place; that the thrilling tribulations of her affair could reify their past closeness. And if Alice ended up wounded in the aftermath, Morgan would be there waiting to comfort her.

'Listen,' she said to Ezra, impatient, 'I don't know what you're playing at, but you have to tell Linnie about you and Alice.'

He shook his head. 'I know I'm not perfect. I know I've messed up.'

'Bullshit. You think you can perform self-awareness, and everyone'll clap you on the back and tell you not to be so hard on yourself. But that won't work on me.'

'Well, aren't you clever? Bravo.' He smacked his hands together in mocking applause. The sound echoed over the water. 'What if I told you *she* came on to *me*?'

This proposition was so outlandish, so far from the inference Morgan had drawn a dozen years before, she promptly shoved it aside. 'It's easy to say that when the other party can't refute it,' she answered tersely.

She looked out to Benji, who had completed his miles and turned back. His cheeks were flushed with effort, his lungs pumping the fresh morning air. He hadn't yet spotted her, though he soon would.

She angled toward Ezra, accusation seeping into her voice. 'I saw you wink at Alice one time in the hallway. I saw you. You can't deny it – or, wait, let me guess: You have some explanation for that too?'

'No, I don't. I have no recollection of that.'

'Liar.'

'Truly, I wish I could help you. But you've got me thinking, are you aware of the concept of infinite regress? It's the idea that all of life is a chain reaction, a string of falling dominoes. I initiate X, which causes you to do Y and prompts Benji to act on Z . . . do you see? And my X traces back to my childhood, V, which is linked to my parents' childhoods, U, and so on. Everything is interconnected, everything converges.'

Morgan folded her arms. 'Philosophize it all you want. Do your little song and dance till you're blue in the face. Linnie still deserves to know.'

'Deserves to know what, exactly?'

That Alice loved you, Morgan thought, the realization seizing her at once with shock and relief. It made sense now, the distress she'd felt upon seeing Ezra here. She'd believed him privy to Alice's innermost affections in a manner no one else had been or ever would be, herself included.

Just then, Benji glanced up. Morgan caught his gaze, reading the question in his eyes. He picked up his pace. As he neared, he sped up as if to blow past her, but she extended an arm to stop him.

'Can't chat,' he panted.

'Benj . . .'

Excusing herself from Ezra, she guided Benji aside, onto a cluster of mossy rocks. He removed his headphones and waited, regaining his breath. Morgan racked her mind for an explanation. Only yesterday she had promised him to leave the Ezra situation alone. Though the stones held steady and the summer air was static, she felt a sudden spike in G-force, as if her body were plunging through space.

'You look pretty,' Benji said.

Morgan had forgotten about her hair and makeup, which would need to be retouched before the ceremony. The supplicating look in Benji's eyes backed her up to a ledge inside herself. When she tried to speak, her throat pinched shut.

'Did you get my note?' he asked.

'What note?'

'About the family meeting I called for this morning. I left it under your door.'

A family meeting? Her head whirled. 'What for?'

'It's time we lay a few things out on the table.'

His distance from her seemed to widen, each word a kick that drove them further apart. Had they been alone, she would have settled him down on the rock, leaning him into her with their torsos touching. She would have relayed to him what Alice had divulged that day in the cafeteria. But Ezra was standing not ten feet away, exerting his peculiar force over her.

'Oh' was all she managed to say.

'Eleven o'clock in the turret,' Benji said. 'See you then.'

13

Benji waved goodbye to Morgan and zipped away as fast as he could. Only once he was out of sight did he stagger to a walk. Yesterday's raindrops plunked sporadically off the spruces lining the trail, dampening his shoulders. Sweat trickled in fat beads down his neck. On the ground, fragments of the gray-blue sky floated in mirrory puddles.

Benji had anticipated that this weekend would be difficult, but he had hoped that such difficulty would bear fruitful returns. Wittingly or not, he had re-created the fraught circumstance of reuniting everyone once more in order to prove that they weren't stuck in the past, that family harmony could be restored. Now he realized this task wouldn't be as straightforward as he'd believed.

Mired in these thoughts, he at first missed his stepmother, standing a few feet off the path. She was braced against an aspen. Groundwater had seeped through her canvas espadrilles, staining the sides. In the morning light, her skin appeared tallowy; she resembled a naiad plucked from a fountain. She distractedly twirled the fringe of her shawl between her fingers.

Benji was in no mood for conversation. Last night's terror had been his father's doing – why should he have to mop up Nick's messes? But some thrust of sadness in

Caro's face stalled him. He couldn't bring himself to hurry by and pretend he hadn't seen. He waved. 'Car, hey.'

Caro apprehended him with surprise. He waited for her to smile or inquire how he was feeling; waited for the desperate stoop of her shoulders to right itself. When neither occurred, he said, 'Everything all right?'

'Oh, sure. And you, sweating off the jitters?'

'Trying to. I've had this pit in my stomach all morning. You seem . . . If this is about my dad—'

'No, no, it's—'

'—he didn't mean what he said. He makes these sorts of faux pas now and again, and that's when he *isn't* hammered.'

'Don't worry about me, Benj. Please. You've got a lot on your plate.'

'Right. Well, I'm not trying to make excuses for him. I'm the last person to do that. But he means well.'

Caro's expression twitched, bucking against some internal doubt. She brought her thumbs to her chest and dug them into her sternum, kneading. Benji had anticipated breakdowns from both his mother and his father. He had even expected one from Morgan, who'd been anxious in the weeks leading up to today. But he'd not expected one from Caro, who was arguably the most even-keeled among them. He remembered once in college asking her why she'd choose to exhaust her prime years on his father. She'd laughed and said, 'Believe it or not, I love that old man of yours.'

'Are you nervous?' she asked, conspicuously steering the attention away from her own upset.

'Ish. Should I be?'

'You? Nah. You've got a remarkably good head on your shoulders. Now if it was me, on the other hand . . . At your age, I was all screwed up.'

At your age. At his age, she'd been not a few years shy of marrying his father. The idea made him shudder.

'It'll be great,' she said.

So reassuring were these words, an antivenin to the fear in his blood, Benji forgot as he lumbered away that it had been she, not he, who'd seemed in need of comforting.

14

That morning, beneath a sky so soft and iridescent as to seem liquefied, Caroline DeLuca woke to a queasiness in her gut that could not be imputed to her hangover. When she sat up, her breasts ached – it wasn't just in her head. Sickness pooled metallically in her mouth, and her insides were soused with heat. She managed to stagger to the bathroom, where the world reduced itself to a series of grainy essences: the water laboring through the pipes, the nauseating smell of wet porcelain emanating from the toilet bowl, the sibilant whispers of Nick and Avery on the other side of the door. Even before her fingers found the pregnancy test secreted in her cosmetics bag, she knew.

The emerging telltale line brought her no joy, only fear. When Nick called through the door to say he was taking Avery down to breakfast, acid swam in his voice. Caro understood, perhaps better than he, that his anger was but bells and whistles to divert attention from his crippling internal disappointment.

Now, standing outside Elizabeth Cottage, the truth she'd worked to ignore – that Nick did not want another child – sprang up with the force of a pool toy held beneath the water's surface. Perhaps he figured that by steeling himself against new love, he might likewise steel himself against potential grief. That made sense. That was the type of fool's calculus he would perform. Oh, Nick. With Avery, he had gladly stepped into the role of doting parent. He chauffeured her to school and soccer practice, prepared her dinner, and feigned amusement at each nonsensical story. When Caro had volunteered to chaperone the class trip to the Bronx Zoo, Avery had cried, 'Not you. I want Nicky to go.' Nick laughed and said, 'That's my girl.' It wasn't sufficient for him to be a *good* parent; he needed to be a better parent than she. He craved, always, the upper hand.

Last fall, Caro and Nick had attended a garden party thrown by Wilhelm Ziegler, a German artist from the gallery on whom Caro harbored a small but innocuous crush. Nick picked up on this at once, apathy and disdain mixing in his smile. Caro tried to counter his rudeness by assuming outsize cheer. When the talk veered political, Nick flushed the color of the Barolo in his glass. He believed that none of those artists knew how the world worked. Caro watched him squirm, perceiving his inner conflict at once. Expressing this view would only transform him into the very effigy of the conservative party the others despised. After all, was he not the lone *Homo economicus* at that table? Had he alone not chosen to partake in the game of private enterprise the rest of them mocked? And though he seldom flaunted his wealth (not like some of his parvenu coworkers, whose collection of fancy cars and expensive clothes belied their scrappy pasts), she knew that secretly, he evaluated his worth by how immediately he could gratify such cravings if he so chose.

'Boo, down with Wall Street. Down with the oppressors,' Wilhelm said, flashing Caro a sly smile.

Now he'd done it. She closed her eyes, mentally pleading with Nick to disengage. Nick, never one to back down from a challenge, cleared his throat and said, 'Wilhelm, do you have a girlfriend?'

'No.'

'A boyfriend?'

'No, why?'

'I just imagine they'd be jealous of the stick up your ass for hogging all the action.'

Wilhelm laughed, bumping Nick with his fist and saying, 'Good one, man, good one,' but Caro hadn't been able to hug their host goodbye; she was too mortified. On the ride home, Nick said, 'You were flirting with him, that Wilhelm fellow.' He smirked to himself. 'It's a relief, really. What a sorry state our world would be in if a married person couldn't indulge in a little harmless flirtation now and again.'

In his twisted way, she sensed that he was trying to make amends, reduce the sting of his immature behavior. They would go home now and sit brooding on opposite sides of the couch until eventually Nick reached out to draw her close. They would come together then, a blur of bodies. She would be underneath him at first, and then on top, the power seesawing between them, their vulnerability and hurt revealed only in awing snatches, like glimpsing a magnificent castle concealed behind a curtain wall. Afterward, they'd hold each other, feeding their accusations away to the rushing stream of marriage, the river Lethe. They would watch these wounds be carried off until only something else – something small and enduring and brilliantly clear – remained.

Suppose she told Nick she was pregnant, and he decided to leave. He had done it before, with Linnie. That time Caro assisted, supplying the knife when he requested it. Was this her karma? No, no. They were meant to be together. He loved her, and she him. She felt this love radiating behind his every small act: the tender way he'd hold her at night, tracing letters into her back; how he'd reorder her favorite coffee before she'd even clocked that she was running low; the moment when he'd scan the crowd for her at Avery's soccer games and, upon finding her, smile as if some impenetrable encryption had deciphered itself between them. Beneath their lust lay a steadfast friendship, formidable as mountains veiled in smog. So what if he was driven by the occasional unsavory urge now and again? Her father had been like that too. He'd play up certain harmless attributes while pursuing his true objective of scoring another drink. The trick to handling such men was to discern when you were being duped and to understand that the duper was no less a hostage to his subterfuge than you.

Two girls with tennis rackets sauntered down the path. Behind them unfurled the bay, brocaded with seaweed and sun. A breeze sheared off the water, scaring a flock of gulls from the jetty. The birds ascended silently, wings blading the sky. Caro's heart stirred in reply.

She placed a hand on her stomach, locating an inner

peace parallel to the one she'd felt as a girl, kneeling at the foot of her bed. 'God?' she called. 'Are you up there?'

Atop the wooden pier, a trio of birds halted their preening to glance at her.

Already she could sense this baby was stronger than the one she'd lost. Its heartbeat would grow so forceful that it would jolt the earth she strode upon. Nine months from now, it would emerge beneath another sky, another sun. This beautiful world – how it gave and took.

Yes, she thought, things would work out. They had to.

15

'So, you got the note too,' Peter said, as Linnie stepped into the turret.

'Do you have any idea what this is about?' she asked.

He shook his head. The mysterious summons to a *family meeting* had arrived that morning. As he absorbed the words, he felt a rash of hope spread across his neck. Surely this meant he had broken through to Morgan, and she'd decided to call off the wedding. In a paroxysm of excitement, he'd hurried downstairs twenty minutes before the appointed time, followed promptly by Linnie, who wore a fully painted face, her lashes long as spiders' legs.

Peter tucked his hands beneath his armpits to keep from fidgeting. He had, until now, successfully managed to evade Linnie. The turret felt infernally small around them, its lack of angles punishing as a padded asylum. Between the curved pieces of window glass, the bay shone in Rubenesque tranches.

'Well,' said Linnie.

She set her handbag down on a chair and made a single lap around the room, pausing at the broom closet to pull back the bifold door and inspect the contents inside. The closet was no more than three feet wide and crammed with paint cans, light bulbs, and cleaning supplies. As if these objects were of great fascination, she stepped inside to examine them further. Peter followed close behind, into the wave of stale air emanating from a candy box on the top shelf. Linnie spun, her hands landing on his chest.

'Well,' she said again.

Peter drew the door shut. A gold chain dangled from the light bulb above; neither moved to grasp it. The only lumination came from the slats in the door panels. A stunning heat issued upward through the chambers of Peter's heart. He was trying to keep his rational faculties from falling victim to this flame and, judging by the sensation in his groin, failing.

'I feel like I've hardly seen you this weekend,' Linnie said.

'This weekend?' he said. 'What about the last few months? If I'd known that your taking classes meant you'd desert me, I wouldn't have suggested it.'

'Desert you?'

'Kidding, kidding. I just miss your face, that's all.'

'Oh, Pete.'

A lilt in her voice evinced her hurt at his accusation. Her hands slipped from his chest. He gripped her wrists to hold them in place.

'I'm proud of you,' he said. 'With what you're doing with school and all that.'

She smiled, her lip gloss shining in the stripey light.

'If you could be anywhere in the world right now,' he said, 'where would you be?'

'Somewhere other than here, you mean? I feel like it's too predictable to say Paris.'

'Ever been?'

'Uh-uh. I bet it'd be blissful – all the new people, the sights, the food. A do-over.'

'Well, I for one would miss you if you left.'

She appeared not to register these words. 'I keep thinking about when I was the kids' age, walking along that triangle where Broadway and Columbus meet. I remember feeling then that everything around me was ending, and I could do nothing to stop it. It was a complete feeling – I mean, I felt it in every part of myself – but it wasn't scary. In some way, everything *other* than that feeling was scary.'

Peter leaned in. He did not like this version of Linnie. This version reminded him too much of Sequoia, who used her cynicism to navigate the world. Once, with his long hair and fruitarian diet, Peter had fit squarely into Sequoia's vision of a kindred spirit. Eighteen and unsure of himself, he'd surrendered to her proselytizing about free love and was duly rewarded when she praised him for being different. He hadn't been trying to trick her, merely to discover his own identity. Later, though, when he expressed to her his desire to leave for medical school, she accused him of deception, impersonating someone he was not.

'I used to play this little game in my head where I'd fold up time like a bedsheet' – Linnie pressed her palms to illustrate – 'the beginning touching the end. I remember thinking that neither of my parents would be alive in forty years. It didn't seem like such a long time then. But it is a long time, isn't it, forty years?'

248

'Say more,' Peter said, though he wished she'd say less.

As Linnie's lips shifted to accommodate her words, he let himself imagine how sweet it might be to kiss those lips, to undo her blouse. So absolute was his love, so stimulating her proximity in this cramped closet, he was convinced he'd burn up if he didn't snuff out the flame.

Still holding her hands, he bent forward and set his mouth on hers. She went rigid with shock, but she didn't pull away. An explosion erupted between Peter's ears – *pop, pop, pop*. His hands migrated up to her hair. 'Careful, I just got it done,' she whispered. The heat of her breath zapped his every nerve to attention. He touched the crotch of his pants, too apprehensively for it to be suggestive, and she pretended not to see. When he moved for her skirt, though, she held out a hand to stop him. No, she was right – they couldn't do it here. They ought to move upstairs into one of their bedrooms. But Peter was afraid to suggest this, afraid that even a single word could cause the fragile thing between them to snap. He took a step back. Linnie furtively wiped her mouth.

'Am I dreaming?' he asked.

'Don't.'

'No, really – isn't it obvious? I'm completely under your spell. Maybe you've guessed that by now, probably you have, I don't know. I love this' – he kissed the underside of her arm – 'and this' – her shoulder – 'and these' – her fingers.

Her body went limp, an unpleasant stench rising

between them. Later, looking back, Peter would remember not Linnie's response but the pause before she delivered it. In this breath, a vista unfolded. There they were, him and her, in Paris, strolling through a shopping arcade with a dizzying checkerboard floor. It was a vision disconnected from all that came before and after, an island floating in midair.

'Let's pretend this never happened,' Linnie said.

'Keep it a secret,' he said. 'Good idea.'

'No, not a secret – a nonentity.'

Peter didn't understand. Surgeon he was, he had mentally dissected every possible iteration of this conversation and had thus convinced himself that the tricky part would be summoning the courage to express his feelings. Once that step occurred, the rest would fall into place. There would be ramifications – he had gamed these out too – but the beautiful thing was that he and Linnie could face these together. Yes, it would be a most beautiful thing. And now, with this fantasy in hand, he refused to accept the reality gaining ground in his mind, the cruel knowledge that she had not responded in one of the thousand ways he'd anticipated but instead turned pensive. Absurd, impossible. He had *kissed* Linnie Olsen. He was no coward; he was a god, with iron flesh and bones of steel.

'I can't just take it back,' he persisted.

'And you expect me to do what with this?'

'I don't know.'

'Therein lies the problem.'

'Do you think you could . . . someday down the line?'

250

'You don't mean this.'

'But I do.'

'What about our kids, and everything else? I don't mean to stand on ceremony, but you're one of my closest friends. It's a bit incestuous, I guess.'

He cringed at that wounding *incestuous*, its pornographic valence. There was that stench again. It was coming from him, the residue of his nervousness and desire. 'Please, will you say it back, even if you don't mean it? I just' – he permitted himself a long, spiky breath – 'I'd really like to hear you say it.'

'Okay.'

'I'm sorry, that was uncalled for. You shouldn't say it if you don't . . . Let's rewind.'

Linnie reached up and twirled the light bulb chain. She sighed and said, 'There was a time I would've said it back to you. I would've said it to appease you and because it made me feel good to be loved.'

'Don't patronize me.'

'I wasn't trying—'

'You act so high and mighty, but you still lionize him.'

'Who?'

'You know who.'

'I most certainly do not, and I resent that.'

'You do, but you shouldn't. He showed up at my door last night in a bad way.'

'Oh, I know. It's this financial jam he's in.'

'You know about that?'

'Listen, I'm sorry for stringing you along, Pete. The truth is, you represent for me this awful period of grief

that I'm trying to . . . Well, I just can't . . . I worry that
the me you love is not the me I want to be.'

'I don't believe you.'

'Please do. I've never been more honest in my life.'

'I guess I should feel flattered by that.'

'Look, there's a future out there for me, and there's
one, a different one, for you.'

Peter took a step forward, two steps back. To scrub
away the humiliation of Linnie's reply, he resorted to
calumny – she was selfish, vain, mercenary. How many
nights had she resided on his couch, bemoaning her
former husband, leading him to believe he still had a
chance? He wanted to slap her – no, he wanted to fuck
her – no, he wanted, he wanted . . . oh, for God's sake,
what *did* he want?

'Shh,' Linnie said. 'Someone's coming.'

Peter's senses, which until now had restricted them-
selves to the closet's four walls, expanded. There were
footsteps, the sound of someone entering the turret.
Quickly, Linnie slid outside, shutting the bifold door
behind her, just in time for Peter to hear Benji's voice:
'Mom?'

Linnie's hand lingered on the knob. Peter watched
through the slats as she erased their conversation from
her expression.

'What're you doing?' Benji asked.

'Playing hide-and-seek.'

'Alone?'

'I needed a moment to myself, all right?' she said, adopt-
ing the vexed tone she used when holding back tears.

'Sheesh, sorry.'

Linnie glanced back at the closet where Peter knelt to the floor, beleaguered by a regret so intense it bordered on madness. He lay there paralyzed, like a man caught in the throes of insomnia. He felt as he did on the long nights when a surgery went awry, and he'd drag himself home replaying the events in his mind, searching for the precise instant the Angel of Death had swept in.

'Is this room large enough?' Linnie asked. 'Maybe we should find somewhere else.'

Before she could fashion an excuse to empty the room and give Peter a chance to sneak out, further steps sounded down the hall.

16

Linnie felt deranged. A tempest of rage, remorse, and dread spiraled through her. She had ended things with Peter all right, but she felt no triumph. Her stomach cramped; her feet ached. The whole weekend was a bust. She had lost her dearest friend, and yet he was still here, imprisoned in the closet only three feet away.

Morgan entered the turret chamber, looking pale. She and Benji regarded each other with tepid penitence, radiating that mysterious air exclusive to young lovers. They were a pair who preferred their shared solitude to any company. Linnie perceived this in a flash as Benji raked his hand up and down Morgan's spine – a tender gesture that she sensed he hadn't intended her to witness.

The door opened again to reveal Nick, pushing Judith's wheelchair.

'Linnele!' Judith exclaimed. 'How nice to see you.'

'We saw each other last night, Mom. At the rehearsal dinner.'

Linnie's eyes darted to Nick, a look that was not lost on the elderly Judith, who smacked her forehead and said, 'Oh, jeez. I must be having a senior moment.'

'That's all right,' Linnie said. 'I get them sometimes too.'

Judith waved her away. 'Compared to me, you're a

spring chicken. Tell me, how's my silverware? Are you making good use of it?'

Nick rapped twice on the table at the turret's center, repurposed from an old porthole window. 'Family meeting,' he muttered to himself, in the bemused tone one uses when repeating a slang term he's heard for the first time.

Linnie extended a hand toward his face. 'Hold still,' she said. 'You've got some—'

He recoiled. 'What're you doing?'

She wiped away a glob of shaving cream tucked below his ear. He'd never had good technique – he wasn't punctilious enough, too easily distracted. As her finger grazed his neck, she girded herself against the swift return of last night's emotions, when she had seen in Nick all the endearing qualities she had deliberately pushed from her mind. Then, suddenly, there they were, those ravishing glimpses of his humor and geniality, unmasked by the ebb of her anger. Dazzled by the strength of her longing and Peter's damning words ('You still lionize him'), she pulled away, relinquishing the flirtation before it could blossom.

'Where's Ezra?' she asked, to remind herself of his existence.

'I saw him at breakfast,' Morgan volunteered.

Benji glanced sidelong at her.

'That's fine. I can always take meeting minutes to fill him in,' Linnie said.

Nick scoffed.

'What's your issue?' she asked.

'No issue.'

'I don't see *your* people here either.' (Even now, she couldn't bring herself to utter Caro's name.)

'Yes, I'm sure *my* people would appreciate your talking about them in that tone.'

'Apparently, I can't say anything around you.'

'What's this?' Judith asked. 'Israel and Palestine? You two can't have a civilized discussion?'

Nick shrugged, skillfully transforming his expression into one of indifference.

'Daddy!'

Caro and Avery appeared in the doorway. Avery released her mother's hand and dashed toward Nick, who scooped his fingers beneath her armpits and hoisted her into the air. Obstinate wisps of cornsilk hair escaped the teeth of her headband; he smoothed these into place. Linnie looked away, unable to watch him enact such tenderness.

Benji clapped his hands. 'Let's begin.'

'Hold on,' Nick said. 'Where's Peter? I need to apologize to him for last night.'

'Last night?' Caro said, perking up. 'What happened last night?'

'Oh, nothing,' Nick said, activating a hat-in-hand smile as if to suggest he and Peter had engaged in a dose of locker-room banter that would be distasteful to repeat.

'Let me go check if there're any more chairs,' Morgan said. She advanced across the room.

'What're you doing?' Linnie asked, her voice hitched to a shrill cry. She practically tripped over Judith's wheelchair to reach the closet before Morgan could open the door and reveal Peter. She gestured to the bespoke bench beneath the window, built to the room's curvature. 'It'll be tight, but we can squeeze.'

Nick and Caro shuffled forward and sat upright, their backs pressed to the glass. Nick crossed one leg over the other in a figure four. Avery lay at her parents' feet, a coloring book open before her. Linnie sat on the far end of the bench, trying to put as much distance between herself and the others as possible. She perceived, with a cold glint of delight, that she could reveal to Caro all that Nick had divulged the previous evening. If she wanted, she could – what? Destroy their marriage? Unlikely. But stir a little chaos inside it, to be sure. The petty part of her, the scarred bit that would never forgive him, nursed a satisfaction at knowing she could wound him with such ease.

Benji began: 'The reason I've called you all here today is because I'd like to clear the air. We haven't been the best at communicating over the past few years, and I apologize for whatever part I've played in that. But, Mom, Dad, your behavior this weekend has been frankly appalling. I want to be clear: today is about me and Morg.'

'No one's suggesting otherwise, bunny,' Linnie said.

'Really?' Benji clasped his hands behind his back and strolled from one end of the room to the other, a watchman on patrol. 'You brought to my wedding some stranger I've never even met just to make Dad jealous. A stranger who, mind you, my fiancée isn't too fond of.'

Linnie felt a blush creep into her cheeks. 'That's not true.' Then, to Morgan: 'What's wrong with Ezra?'

Before Morgan could reply, Benji went on. 'Your

motives seem pretty obvious from where I'm standing. God forbid one weekend isn't about you.'

Linnie turned to the others. No one would meet her eyes. Nick squeezed Caro's knee – a slight movement, but Linnie caught it all the same. At the end of the row, Judith had folded her hands beneath her chin. A solitary rhombus of sunlight scaled the wall behind her.

'I didn't know you all thought of me that way,' Linnie said.

A vein pulsed in her forehead. Though Benji stood only inches from her, he might as well have been miles away. In the shadow of his chin swirled a galaxy of razor bumps. His jaw, once bound by childhood, had squared to manly proportion. The candidness of his expression threw her off-kilter. She felt as if she were meeting a stranger, albeit one she'd loved her entire life. No romantic flame had ever come close to that which burned for her children. She would do anything for them – a realization that had terrified her from the first moment she'd gazed into their small, wondering faces and thought: I will die for you. I will kill for you.

'I'm not going to sit here and let you berate me,' she said, rising. 'I'm tired of being the family punching bag.'

'Lin,' Nick said.

'What? Were you hoping to get your jollies in too? You haven't done enough? None of you have even a shred of respect for me.'

He started to protest but caught himself. When he looked over at Caro, seeking acknowledgment and maybe even approval for his restraint, it took her several seconds to catalyze the taunting glare he seemed to be expecting. Chastened, he sat down again and tried to appeal to his son: 'Look what you're doing to your mother.'

Benji waved a dismissive hand through the air. Linnie felt that wave pass through her like an axe through undergrowth, clearing a path for the advancement of her ache.

'If she wants to leave,' Benji said, 'let her. I'm sick of having to hold everything together all the time.'

Nick roared up. 'Oh nooo, we certainly wouldn't want to burden our resident White Knight with that. You think you're so good, so kind, so much better than the rest of us. So what? You think that entitles you to some reward? That the universe will see you basking in your golden naïveté and think: Oh, golly gee, this one has it bad, better put on our kid gloves for him? You think you're the first *nice* person this godforsaken world will wipe its ass on? If so, I've got some beachfront property in Arizona to sell you.'

'Nick . . .' Caro said.

'What? He wants to be an adult. I'm talking to him like an adult.'

'Fuck you,' Benji said.

'And let's not forget that you were the one who hid this relationship for *years*, and now you expect us all to respond with rainbows and sunshine.'

Benji wheeled. 'Did you ever stop to wonder *why* I'd want to keep it secret from you, Dad? You're a shitty, absent father. I'm not even sure you like me very much.'

'Oh, don't be ridiculous.'

'When was the last time you sat down with me and

said, "Hey, Benj, what's going on in *your* life? How are things with *you*?" Sure, I'm far from perfect, but at least I'm not the one who embarrassed this family last night. Better yet, I'm not the one who broke it apart to begin with.' He pointed a finger in Caro's direction. 'You want to tell her what I caught you and Mom doing outside last night, or should I?'

Nick sobered. 'We weren't doing anything.'

'Stop it, both of you,' Caro cried. 'Enough. I don't want to know.'

Linnie's heart skittered fast. She stole a glance at the closet, wondering what Peter was making of this spectacle.

Perhaps fearing Benji would swing his wrath her way next, Morgan reached out and clasped his hand. He resisted her a moment before surrendering to her touch. 'I'm going to count down from ten,' he said. 'If anyone has an objection to the wedding, now's the time to voice it. I don't want anything spoiling today. Ten, nine, eight...'

The first time Judith Weil experienced a lapse in memory, she was at her computer, trying to log into her email. She went to type in her password, which was her old street address, and found the number obscured by a cloud of smoke. 185? 174? Maybe the spelling was off. How *did* one spell *Brookby*? She made several attempts before the server alerted Nick to suspicious activity on her account. The episode rattled her. She'd forgotten things before – placing the ice cream in the fridge instead of the freezer, confusing the aides' names – but this was different.

Slowly, and not so slowly, the mephitic vapor spread. Some mornings she awoke believing she was back in her childhood room. She would tell Raina they had to go to the station and pick up her father. When Raina said that wasn't possible, her father had been gone sixty years, Judith grew addled. How could that be, when his voice resounded clear as a foghorn in her head?

Twice a day, she would ask after her late husband, Victor. She fretted that he wasn't eating enough, fretted that his bare feet would ache on the hardwood floors. Where were his orthotic slippers? Why were they not by the door? When Raina said that Victor was gone too, Judith wept as if she'd never mourned his loss before.

When they were young, she and Victor used to argue over which of them would go first. Victor said it was always the man. Judith said it wasn't so in her family. 'We're a who's who of every ailment in the book.'

'I hope it's me,' he said. 'I couldn't manage without you.'

'Phooey. Women'll be lining up down the block to take care of you.'

A child of one war and a decorated airman of another, Victor was less reserved by choice than by circumstance. He was hesitant to show emotion except when riled. When riled, he'd unleash a stream of anger that scalded every surface it touched. Judith, accustomed to men shrinking from her gaze, relished the challenge he presented. Throughout their lives, they served as each other's fiercest allies and most formidable foes.

'Seven, six, five,' a young man's voice cut in.

Judith looked up. She registered the turret, the unfamiliar faces. She struggled to align this image with the one in her mind, of her at seventeen, standing in a pink ruffled dress in the entryway of her house, her mother and father upstairs. They were laughing, her father practicing 'The Star-Spangled Banner' – the anthem of his adopted homeland. She walked through the light-drenched hall. In the music room that overlooked the Grand Concourse, a girl sat at the piano, blond tresses spilling down her back. She curled her fingers over the keys and, without glancing back, said, 'D major.' The chord swelled.

'Four, three, two . . .'

Judith tried to shake the memory free, but the girl from the piano remained hovering at the room's edge. 'Alice,' Judith said. 'Alice, is that you?'

With an incomprehensible smile, Alice skipped out the window, passing seamlessly through the glass, her ponytail streaming behind her. A cry extricated itself from the deepest layer of Judith's core. She braced against the sight of a body askew on the sidewalk, but when she keeled over to look, she saw only the bay, blue and sparkling as the folds of a ballgown.

'Ma,' a man said, shaking her shoulder. 'That's Linnie, you know Linnie. And Avery, your granddaughter. Say hi, honey.'

Nick's voice came to Judith distorted and delayed, as if via satellite phone. For a few seconds, she struggled to place it. 'Victor?' she said.

'Dad's not here, Ma. That's Benji, your grandson – he's getting married.'

'Married,' Judith repeated. 'You know what my father used to say? "When you're looking for a husband, don't look for looks, the looks can go—"'

'Forget it,' Nick said.

At last, the fog cleared. With a spark of lucidity, Judith saw her son, his face drawn in exasperation. She saw her grandchildren, their eyes filled with terror. They couldn't fathom the anguish of her condition, the merciless free fall into oblivion. She was poised on a precipice, the past on one side and the present on the other, with the first stars of twilight piercing the zenith overhead.

Benji clapped once, regaining the group's attention. His grandmother's outburst had dispersed the fight from his speech. Relieved, the rest of his family stood to go. He didn't try to stop them. All but Linnie scuttled from the turret in haste, perhaps afraid he might change his mind and decide to hold them hostage.

When it was just the two of them, mother and son, Benji glanced to Linnie and said, 'I know my words weren't kind, but you needed to hear them.'

'No, you're right. I've made my share of bad choices, and I regret that.'

'You do?'

'Don't sound so surprised. I do have some level of self-awareness, you know. Anyway, I wanted to give you something for today.'

She reached into her handbag and removed an envelope. Benji lifted the flap and shook it, dislodging a silver lapel pin from the bottom. He recognized the pin instantly, though he hadn't seen it since the day Alice vanished. It was the treble clef charm from her necklace, the one the police had found in the abandoned violin case on the bridge.

'Do you like it?' Linnie asked. 'I figured you could wear it when you walk down the aisle.'

'What happened to the chain?'

'I took it off.'

Benji struggled to imagine his mother extracting the necklace from the pile of keepsakes stored in her closet. She'd always been wolfishly protective of Alice's possessions. A memory: Christmas break, his senior year at Syracuse, when he'd lent Morgan a hat and gloves to wear, not realizing they'd belonged to Alice. When Linnie returned and discovered the matching knits on the table, she blanched. 'Who moved those?' she said.

'A friend and I went to see the tree at Rockefeller Center,' he replied, worried his mother might put the pieces together and unmask Morgan as that friend. They'd been dating only six months at the time.

Linnie's thoughts, however, were not on the girl who'd worn those gloves, but on the act of violation itself – as if handling Alice's belongings might rob them of whatever essence they still held. Nettled by what he viewed as her overreaction, Benji wished to reassure her that no harm had been intended. Before he could, she lifted a fist as if to strike him. 'Don't!' he cried. At the last second, she spun and slammed her hand down onto the table instead. The force of that blow echoed through the years; even now, Benji could feel it driving through his center.

Linnie's hands quivered as she affixed the pin to his lapel. 'Beautiful,' she murmured, tears swimming in her eyes.

'Mom,' he said, 'listen to this. I heard it on the radio yesterday. What's the key to making AI more human, do you think?'

'I don't know.'

'Take a guess.'

'Please, Benj. I'm not really in a guessing mood.'

'It's forgetting. We humans forget things all the time. Our brains know how to distinguish between what's useful and what's not, so we don't have to carry it all.'

Linnie shook her head. Benji could practically hear her thoughts: But some of us do have to carry it all. Some of us really do.

'I'm sorry,' he whispered. 'I wish my best could be as good as hers.'

'Oh, Benj, don't.'

With a movement unexpected to them both, Benji reached out and pulled his mother into an embrace, amazed at how defenseless she felt in his arms. It occurred to him how few times he'd initiated such a gesture. How many wasted opportunities, when such a touch might have conquered the space that twelve years had set in their way.

PART FOUR

PART FOUR

The Weil family took their seats in the front pew of the synagogue and waited for the memorial service to commence. The room was packed with hundreds of people – more than Benji had seen in the stands at any hockey tournament. There wasn't enough oxygen in here for them all. What if they asphyxiated en masse? (This was the current along which his boyish thoughts had bobbed for the past two weeks. Everywhere, inside of everyone, lurked the germ of death.)

The members of his peewee hockey team, a mixed group of eleven- and twelve-year-old boys, sat solemnly in the back, stuffed into their formalwear. They were a motley crew, aggregated from several Manhattan neighborhoods. The boys had bonded over rides to Wayne and Freeport, summer camps devoted to practicing intricate sequences. On days when they couldn't make it to the rink, they'd band together in Riverside Park for a game of roller hockey, using trash cans as goalposts.

Benji, jersey number 7, was explosive on the ice – all kinetic speed and sharp turns. Coaches praised his edge transition in drills, and his vaunted backhand could deceive even the stealthiest goaltender. He was a decent shot, a better teammate. He lived for the hour before puck drop, when he and his teammates would warm up together, basking in the camaraderie that arose from countless hours logged in the locker room and rink, each player embellishing the others' carvings on the ice.

In hockey, there was no pitcher, no quarterback. The center relied on the defensemen to block and the wingers to score. When the team won, it was due to the collective efforts of offense and defense alike. They trained together, won together, lost together. Benji liked this, liked being part of a team. When he watched Alice cross the stage to perform whatever étude she'd spent months perfecting, he recognized that she was playing both sides – both teammate and opponent, forever trying to outdo herself.

At the front of the synagogue, Rabbi Friedman took his place upon the bimah. Sunlight poured unevenly through the stained-glass windows above him, casting the room in stark chiaroscuro. Friedman's eyes skimmed over the tops of the congregants' heads to the trompe l'oeil mural of the Holy Land at the back of the room. He coughed. The sound echoed, carried by two small microphones at the lectern's edge.

Benji felt the familiar pull of his mother and father beside him. They looked respectively too small and too big for the confining pew. Nick placed his hand in Linnie's lap; she intertwined her fingers with his. She wore her engagement and wedding rings, and a silver bangle on her wrist. As Benji observed her, a peculiar sensation washed over him. Suddenly, Alice was next to him, teasing him: 'Such a mama's boy.' A spark of indignation ignited his insides. Am not, he thought, the words escaping him.

'What's that, Benj?' Nick asked.

'Nothing.'

Benji had never been close to anyone who'd died. He knew of people who'd passed, certainly – a teacher struck while on her bicycle, a friend's grandparent – but those losses were peripheral, quick as the darting tongue of a bullfrog. He'd wanted to believe, despite all evidence to the contrary, that death only affected characters in TV shows or books. Not him. Not his family.

Four nights before Alice disappeared, Benji had been in his bedroom, tossing a Nerf ball into the door-mounted hoop, when he noticed the house was unnaturally quiet. So habituated was he to hearing Alice practice into the odd hours of the night, the profound silence perturbed him.

He crept into the hallway. The scent of char lingered in the air; his mother had burned the Brussels sprouts while waiting for Nick to come home. Alice's door was cracked. She lay on the island of her bed, one elbow crooked over her eyes. Above her, the blinds shredded the moon into thin strips of white.

Benji stepped forward, relieved by the darkness. 'Can I come in?'

'No brothers allowed.'

'Allie.'

'Rules are rules.'

He crossed to her bed anyway and perched on the edge. Dozens of stuffed animals crammed the mattress, spilling from its sides. He ran his hand over the spotted back of a giraffe he'd won at Coney Island.

'What's up with you?' Alice asked.

'Just wanted to see if you were okay.'

'Why wouldn't I be?'

'I thought I heard you crying.'

'Buzz off. You're hogging my pillow.'

Benji reclined with his feet still on the ground so his and Alice's bodies formed a tangent. A few stars whose glow had faded were tacked on the ceiling. He listened to Alice's drawn-out exhales, a measured rhythm he tried to match. He waited for her to call him out, as she often did, for breathing too loudly. When he glanced over, though, she seemed to be elsewhere.

'Hey.' He nudged her. 'Remember at Grandma's in Maine, when we pitched the tent in the backyard and pretended we were camping?'

'It was last summer, Benj. Of course I remember.'

'That was cool, wasn't it? Wish we could've stayed in Maine forever.'

He waited for the assent of Alice's snort, which did not come.

'Is Dad home yet?' she asked.

'Don't think so. Why?'

'Just wondering.'

A fist clenched in Benji's stomach. Weeks before, Nick had shown up late to one of his hockey games. The match was the most important of the season; it would determine which team moved on to the playoffs. When Benji glanced out to the stands and discovered Nick missing, he panicked. A terrible accident must have happened: a car T-boning him at the entrance to the West Side Highway, a heart attack. He thought of the lockdown drills they practiced at school – what if a shooter had invaded his father's office? By the top of the second period, however, Nick was standing proudly in the spot he always occupied, beneath the farthest metal halide lamp, cheering as if he'd been present all along.

'Dad's sick, isn't he?' Benji said. 'Cancer? Is that why you're upset? I pinkie-promise I won't say a word.'

'Why all the questions? Can't sleep?'

'Big game tomorrow. We're playing the Badgers.'

Alice didn't reply.

'Mom and Dad aren't happy,' he said. 'I know that.'

'Benj.'

'They don't talk anymore.'

'What makes you say that?'

'Haven't you noticed?'

Alice chewed the inside of her cheek. She didn't seem to be doubting his statement but rather trying to figure out why it had evaded her own scrutiny. This spooked him. He relied on his sister's omniscience. If she couldn't forewarn him against the dangers ahead, who would keep him safe?

'Everyone's being weird,' he pressed, 'and nobody'll tell me why. I'm not a baby.'

Alice's features shifted, regrouping into an expression Benji didn't recognize. The transformation was so subtle, anyone less familiar with her might have overlooked it. Later, Benji would try to catalog what precisely had changed at that moment, like one of those 'Spot the

273

Difference' puzzles in his father's *Smithsonian* where you'd circle the misplaced balloon, the subtracted corner of sidewalk.

'I'll tell you a secret,' Alice said. 'But you gotta swear it stays between us.'

'Who would I tell?'

'Swear it.'

'Okay, okay, I swear.'

The siblings locked pinkies.

'I'm getting out of here.'

He frowned. 'To college?'

'Yeah,' she said absently. 'Here.' She passed him the giraffe, the one he'd given her.

'It's yours.'

'Take it.'

'Allie, you're freaking me out.'

'Boo,' she said.

Unsettled, Benji rose from the bed. He glanced back at Alice from the threshold. 'Sorry for bothering you,' he said.

'It's chill,' she replied. Then, so softly he'd later wonder whether he'd imagined it: 'Inway orfay emay omorrowtay.'

Win for me tomorrow.

Benji had kept this final memory to himself, a pebble in his shoe that dug into him each time he stepped. He wished he could extract it, hand it to his parents for safekeeping, but feared their response. Why hadn't he told them sooner? Alice had been the bridge between his world, the isle of youth, and that of adults. Now he was stranded.

On the bimah, Friedman bowed his head and muttered

a prayer. Benji flexed his fingers at each pause in the chant to ensure they were still attached. He felt disconnected from the words and the strings of melody upon which they floated. If Alice were here, she'd be trying to make him laugh – wresting her mouth into silly expressions, mocking the stuffy rituals. It was a game they liked to play in tense moments: Who could get the other to crack first? Alice always won. She could fix her features such that no amount of humor could displace them.

'We'll begin with the recitation of the Twenty-Third Psalm,' Friedman said, inviting mourners to follow along.

He sang a series of honed, glottal cadences with more showmanship than necessary. To block out the sound, Benji clasped his hands over his ears, as he used to during thunderstorms. Beside him, his parents politely bowed their heads, though he sensed neither was truly listening. They had fireproofed their hearts against today.

Once Friedman completed the prayer, he slipped off his glasses and shuffled his papers. On the wall beside him glinted a gold tablet of names, a memorial plaque. 'This morning,' he said in a tone laced with pathos, 'we join to honor and mourn the life of Alice Mackenzie Weil, whose time on earth came to a tragic end too swiftly. Alice was a cherished friend, an outstanding sister, and a beloved daughter. On days like today, each of us is Job, wondering why the Almighty has brought upon us this suffering.'

Friedman sought out Benji's eyes in the crowd. The instant their gazes met, Benji darted his sights away. The walls of his being were still porous, and so he felt, treacherously, that every person he met was a tentacular extension of himself, no different from the characters in his video games. In this way, he accepted total blame for his sister's disappearance and believed he alone must have failed her.

His foot had gone numb. He lifted his leg and slapped his shoe against the floor to work the blood back in. He did it again, harder. Nick clamped a hand over his thigh, fixing him with a stern look. *Quit it.*

Friedman continued: 'My grandmother had this expression: *Mit a lefl ken men dem yam nit oys'shepn* – you can't empty the ocean with a spoon. Maybe that's how Alice felt, that she had too much ocean, not enough spoon. Who can say? What I do know is that in times like these, we must come together as a community to support those who are hurting. To keep their joy safely tucked away in our own cupboards until there's room again on their shelves.'

Benji squirmed in his seat, seeking solace in the crowd. Some congregants' faces were imbued with ascetic resolve, while others were teary. None was looking at him save for Morgan Hensley. Their gazes joined. She lowered her chin slightly, a nod of communion. Earlier, when she'd retreated to the coatroom, he had wanted to go to her, but the sight of her sobbing had rattled his nerves. She had always been his favorite of Alice's friends; more than his favorite. He hadn't given his feelings for her a name until now. Now, he understood. He had loved her, quietly, for as long as he could remember.

2

Ezra Newman's Survey of Philosophy seminar took place during the last period on Wednesday afternoons, in the hour reserved for electives. During the rest of the week, his second-floor classroom served as the setting for five sections of World History, when eager tenth graders would fill the space with their thoughtful (if misguided) pontifications on the Silk Road, the Enlightenment, and both world wars. Presiding mutely over these discussions was the porcelain bust of Descartes Ezra kept on his desk. On the last day, he'd use the bust as a prop for his yearly recitation of the 'Alas, poor Yorick' speech.

Unlike his colleagues in the English and drama departments, Ezra refused to invest his meager budget in classroom frills like soft-glow macramé lamps or plushy beanbag chairs. The lights remained a harsh, fluorescent white. The walls were bare. Long black tables with laminate tops, as might be found in a science lab, replaced traditional desks. Consequently, class discussions tended toward the austere – a tendency that Ezra strove to mitigate with his sardonic humor.

On the first day of what would become the defining year of his teaching career, Ezra directed the dozen philosophy students who filed nervously into the classroom to rearrange these tables into a square. His hope (as he expressed to the students) was that such a setup would facilitate discussion. It was imperative that his pupils not view him as their teacher in this space. Yes, he'd be leading discussions, but they should feel free to parry him as often and as forcefully as they did their peers.

If this directive intimidated the students in classroom 213, they didn't let on. A paucity of feeling marked their unlined faces. It was one of the attributes he found most perplexing in people this age: they were simultaneously driven mad by some emotions and aseptically estranged from others.

'Right, then.' He sat atop one of the tables. 'Questions before I go on?'

A scrawny redhead raised his hand. 'Are our discussions going to be graded?'

Every year some version of this question was raised. Manhattan Tech was a breeding ground for the best and brightest, a public magnet school with a grueling three-hour entrance exam and an acceptance rate so astonishingly low, it rivaled that of the nation's top universities. The classes were small and individualized. Obsequiousness was prized, and students were trained to participate in discussions not for learning's sake but to receive the good marks that would bolster their National Merit Scholarship applications. They would stop at nothing to achieve this. One had been caught copying answers onto her water bottle label, another disseminating a calculator program that contained formulas meant to have been memorized.

'So long as you show up,' Ezra answered, 'you'll do well. I won't lie to you: the concepts in our readings can be dense, frustratingly so. You might want to throw your books at me, or bang your heads against the desk. That's fine, though my inner Kant does discourage violence on principle. I'll try to guide you and illuminate the finer details where I can, but I won't coddle you. I won't breathe down your necks to make sure you're up to speed. In fact, I'd like to amend my earlier statement and say that you don't even need to show up, though I certainly hope you will – it would be boring to stand here talking to myself. My rules are simple: put away your phones, avoid side conversations, tempting though they may be, and try as best you can to be present with me, your peers, and your own burgeoning minds.'

He sounded discomfitingly earnest, but the students, who were still young enough to be persuaded by such impassioned discourse, met his words without defiance. They watched him as if he were Socrates, striding across the stones of ancient Greece. Philosophy wasn't dull – far from it. Philosophy was the study of human nature. It was where the vertices of reason and desire, the natural and the supernatural, converged.

Other instructors at Manhattan Tech had, in private meetings and with subtle and not-so-subtle turns of phrase, accused Ezra of striving too hard to elicit emotional reactions from his charges. Indeed, he liked young people best when they were agitated. In these moments he softened, passing them the tissue box he kept on his desk for precisely this purpose. The sight of a teary-eyed jane invigorated him, prompting him to sit up a little straighter in his chair. To teenagers, the ultimate little narcissists, the entire world consisted only of their lives – their friendships, families, hopes, and dreams. When any aspect of that world fell into turmoil, it felt as if the whole universe was crumbling. Ezra reveled in this – the totality of it. He often wished he could feel as intensely about any one aspect of his life, let alone all of it.

There were worse roads to take, he supposed, than that of a high school teacher. He liked to think of himself as a protector, a valiant instructor who fought on behalf of his students against the Evil Administration and Parental Overlords. His students readily bestowed upon him the title of Favorite Teacher. They showered him with gift cards and fruit-and-nut baskets during Christmas, and flowers during Teacher Appreciation Week. He stoked their affections any way he could, perching himself on the edge of his authority to test its limits. He was, in essence, no more at fault than a child who proceeds to bop his little sister on the head after his parents have told him to cut it out. He simply desired to measure the seriousness of those in charge, to see how many times he could transgress before they rained the truncheon of punishment down on his shoulders.

Ezra wasn't attracted to the juveniles who filed into his classroom each year (God no, he wasn't one of *those* sick fucks), but he was, admittedly, attracted to how he felt in their presence. By winning their admiration, that most precious currency, he could become the Cool Kid he'd never been. Still, the spell lasted only so long.

Eventually midnight struck, and the horse-drawn carriage transformed back into a pumpkin.

Each year, Ezra had to resort to greater measures to garner the affection necessary to sustain his perceived coolness. This meant coloring his speech with an increasing number of vulgarities and divulging more personal details from his life to compel students into sharing their own. And share they did – stories of drug use, sex, parental affairs. Teenagers were more advanced than adults wanted to believe. He never failed to be amused by the parents who described their little Jenny or Nathan as an innocent cherub on back-to-school night. Which kids are those? he wanted to say. Surely not the ones in *this* classroom.

Naturally, treating his pupils this way caused many to harbor crushes on him – which was fine, he knew where the boundaries lay. He also knew that in skirting such boundaries, one could make a high schooler feel singularly special, and that these gooey feelings of specialness could in turn fuel better work, more probing insights. Was it manipulative to kindle such sentiments in an adolescent for the sake of improved learning? Perhaps. But seduction seemed a less detrimental tool than sternness, and plenty of instructors relied on the latter for their winning results.

'Right, did that answer your question about grades?' he asked the scrawny redhead.

The word *grades* spurred on the group like a starter's pistol. Would there be tests, essays? By what scale did he plan to judge those? It wasn't fair, one disputant argued, for all students to receive the same marks. What about those who dedicated more time to the readings? Should not their efforts be reflected in some quantifiable way?

Ezra nodded at each inquiry. 'This is good. Very good. This is exactly what we're after. I want you to interrogate everything — not just the big questions but the small ones too. Take nothing for granted. Don't assume you're right, and don't assume I am either.' He rapped on the table beneath him. 'For instance, consider this table. Is it really here, or are your senses playing tricks on you? How would you go about proving the existence of an object external to your own mind? Can you prove it with absolute certainty? To what extent does our interpretation of reality differ from what's objectively there? If our senses deceive us, can we provide any conclusive proof that the world itself exists?'

He turned to his right, where a blond girl sat, arms folded across her chest. A promontory of freckled collarbone jutted out over the neckline of her T-shirt. Her features remained immobile, as if someone painting her portrait had instructed her not to move. A clear, penetrating intellect flickered beneath the surface of her skin and upon her face like a play of light.

'What's your opinion?' he asked.

'Sorry?'

'Grades — should we have them?'

'I don't know.'

'Give it a shot.'

He forced himself to steady his eyes on hers.

'It's not that I want grades,' she said, weighing each word. 'But I don't think you're allowed not to give them.'

'Ah. This introduces the question of rules: who sets them, and what's the benefit of our following them. An astute point by Miss—'

'Weil.'

'So what you're saying, Miss Weil, if I may try to summarize, is that by accepting my position here, I've entered into a social contract whereby I agree to somehow algorithmically account for your efforts.' He crossed to the chalkboard, pleased with himself. *Algorithmically account* – how poetic. 'Does everyone have a piece of paper handy?'

A brief hesitation, then a salvo of zippers as the students opened their bags. A girl with a florid updo volunteered extra sheets for anybody in need. She waved a few loose leaves through the air, setting the feathered pendulums of her earrings asway.

On the board, Ezra wrote: 1. COOPERATE, 2. DEFECT.

'Everyone settled? Here's how this will work. On your paper, you'll each write a number corresponding to one of the words on the board. If everyone votes for option one, to cooperate, you'll all get a B for this course.'

An obligatory groan.

He held up a hand. 'If you cooperate, you'll get a B. If everyone cooperates except for one person, the defector will get an A, and the rest of you will get a C. If more than one of you defects, everyone, collectively, will get a D.'

'This isn't for real, right?' the redheaded boy asked.

'It's completely for real. Shall I review the options again?'

There was a pause, followed by a few dubious nods. Ezra repeated the instructions, relishing the students' undivided attention. He had them now.

'This is bullshit,' the boy muttered. His classmates snickered at his boldness, their amusement strengthening him. He kicked out his legs.

'What's your name?' Ezra asked the boy.

'Harry.'

'Harry what?'

'O'Neill.'

'All right, Mr O'Neill. Tell me why you think it's bullshit.'

'Because it's rigged. Either way, we lose.'

'Hold up now. That's not entirely true, is it? All of you could get a B – that's above average. It's even possible one of you could get an A. See, I'm giving you possibilities, Mr O'Neill, leaving the choice in your hands. That, my friend, is independence. I'd imagine that for some of you, it's a new feeling.' He smiled. 'Hence why it's so scary.'

Outside, the sky darkened. A tassel of rain whipped the roof. Ezra set the chalk in its holster. 'Put your name and year on the left-hand corner of your paper. Below that, write your choice: one for cooperate, two for defect. No talking, please – this is an individual assignment.'

The students hunched over their papers with an air of seriousness. Some used their forearms as makeshift partitions to keep their neighbors from peeking. A few finished instantly, while others took their time. Harry cast suspicious glances around the room. The girl with the dangling earrings smiled at Ezra with a sycophant's broad eagerness.

'All right, everyone. Pens down. Flip your papers over and pass them to me.'

The students made a show of averting their eyes as they shuttled the papers along the conveyor belt of their hands. Ezra carried the stack to his desk in the corner. 'I'll take attendance while I sort these. When I say your name, raise your hand to let me know you're present. If there's a nickname you prefer, now's the time to speak up.'

He turned over the first page. 'Cooperate.' He shared only the student's name with the class, keeping their choice private. 'Robbie Apter?'

A lanky boy in a beanie raised his hand. 'Here.'

The second: 'Cooperate.'

He paused at the surname, pronouncing it with a hard 'j': 'Devan Macejka?'

'It's *Ma-sake-cah*. Present.'

The following few, including wisecracker Harry O'Neill, voted the same: cooperate. High schoolers – predictable. No one wanted to swim against the current. The only thing worse than academic mediocrity was social ostracization.

The eleventh selection was penned in loopy, uniform letters, the sort of enviable handwriting that indicated a considerable care of presentation. Ezra glanced at the girl with the earrings: 'Denise Shapiro?'

Another toothy smile. 'Yep, that's me.'

The rain picked up. The drops fell without reprieve, a single gray curtain. There were screeches as the students angled their chairs outward. Any weather, any glitch in the norm, could arouse a room full of high schoolers.

A locker slammed in the hallway. One more vote to go.

Ezra turned the last page over. The writing was so tiny, it took him a second to decipher: 'Defect.'

He lifted his head. Only one student was watching him now: Weil, Alice. Her eyes were slit with intent, possessing the delphic quality of liquid mercury. A tremor passed through him. After a delay, he checked off her name and regathered the pages into a stack.

'I've recorded your responses,' he said.

'I swear,' Devan mumbled, 'if any of you screwed this up . . .'

A hush fell over the group. Before he revealed the results of this experiment, he said, they ought to discuss the activity at hand. As he spoke, he crafted a narrative to later share with colleagues about the enrapture that inflamed his pupils' faces at this moment.

'What you all just partook in is a modified version of the prisoner's dilemma. The dilemma presents a paradox, a Chinese finger trap, if you will. On the surface, the guiding principle of rationality would urge you to act out of self-interest – to pursue the personal good. But if you'd done that, you'd each be worse off than if you'd acted for the collective. So the question is, what risk justifies what reward? Let's see what you decided.'

He strolled to the front of the room, a hollow pit in his stomach. Alice Weil – the sole defector. She had challenged his experiment, testing him to see whether he'd stay true to his word. Now the power game, the dilemma, existed solely between her and him. Should he do as he'd promised, granting her the A and the others a C (an action that would no doubt earn them both blowback), or should he exercise his authority to show her who truly held supremacy in this room, flashing his cards at her beneath the table where only she could see them? Impulsively, he grabbed the chalk and traced a large circle around the word *Cooperate*.

The students erupted in cheer. Harry jabbed two fingers into his mouth and let out a sustained whistle. Denise high-fived her neighbor. Among the merrymaking, Ezra's eyes flew to Alice. She sat sedately, a sphinxlike smirk playing at her lips. Well played.

Alice's smile lingered in Ezra's mind now, as he lifted the prayer book from its cradle. He opened it, grazing his fingers over the densely inked pages. The references to God stirred in him first a feeling of revulsion, then of wonder.

Beside him in the pew, a woman wept, her entire body convulsing beneath her fur coat. Ezra had half a mind to offer her his handkerchief, but when he reached into his pocket, he discovered it missing. The woman tucked her chin into her collar and continued to sob, dabbing her nose with the corner of her sleeve. The taut lines of the other attendees' backs told Ezra they too were unsettled by the violence of these sobs. He wondered how the woman was acquainted with Alice. It must have been quite well, to produce such an intense reaction.

3

Caro herself could offer no explanation for her brimming emotion inside the synagogue. She didn't consider herself prone to hysterics. But seeing Nick today confirmed what she'd already surmised: they were finished. A sheet of dejection slid over her. She should have heeded the omens, been more prepared. Nick had warned her from the start that his family was his proudest achievement, and nothing was worth sacrificing that. Rationally, she understood this; emotionally, she did not. Despite her better instincts, she had fallen in love with Nick and stoked a small flame of hope that someday he might feel the same.

She blew her nose into her hand, wiping off the residue on her skirt. Such effort she'd put into her appearance this morning, and for what? Nick had barely looked at her. On the contrary, he'd gone out of his way to *avoid* looking at her. Another swell of dejection passed over her, followed quickly by anger. She despised the woman she'd become: one who viewed a man's gaze as a dangling carrot, fantasizing about the sorts of encounters with him that a person like her – to wit, a Catholic – should never dare dream.

The problem was, Caro had framed her life around Nick. Her entire day was bookended by his text messages wishing her a good morning and good night. When they didn't speak, she felt he was administering a test to see who could outlast the other. Such interstices tore her up. She couldn't eat, couldn't sleep, couldn't handle thinking that she'd inadvertently lost his affection. She was addicted to him and, like all addicts, had winnowed her worldview so that he was the only stimulant capable of bringing her joy.

Two months ago, when her mother called to ask about her plans for Christmas, Caro replied that she intended to skip the holidays this year.

'*What?*' her mother cried. 'How come?'

'I have work to do.'

'On Christmas? What about our ricotta cookies?'

'I'm sure Bridget can help.'

'What about Santa, and gifts, and *Charlie Brown*? It's Christmas, Caroline. Fa-la-la-la Christmas!'

'Gee, thanks. I nearly had it confused for the rabbit holiday.'

'What's gotten into you?'

Shaking, Caro slammed down the phone. An entire week without Nick – she couldn't bear it. Even a handful of hours outside his presence granted her enough clarity to see the warped reality she'd bet on. The only remedy was to draw nearer, narrowing her field of vision until the stark meridian of her predicament was no longer visible. She felt a deep kinship to the ancient saints, understanding at last what it meant to love another so consumingly that your passion obliterated all sense of self. As she brushed her teeth before bed, she swore she could see stigmata blooming in her palms.

She wouldn't confess these thoughts to her psychoanalyst, a Serbian woman upon whose mid-century sofa she lay every Friday, recounting all the Bad Actions she'd undertaken since their last session in an approximation of intimacy. (The details she shared were intimate; the act of sharing them was not. Caro frequently divulged this – that though she was sharing transgressions her analyst might *perceive* as sensitive, she felt no more exposed than if she were relaying her lunch plans.) These sessions abraded the surface of Caro's defenses until several long-buried truths emerged.

The first truth was that Caro had wanted children since she was thirteen, when her cousin Norah was born. She'd kept from sharing this with partners, fearing they'd judge her either (a) selfish, for wanting to bring children into a world of economic insecurity and global instability, or (b) antifeminist, for restricting her appetites – which had been exposed to all sorts of gustatory delights, from sports to music to literature – to the very sphere from which women had long fought for emancipation. A self-sabotaging part of her desired Nick precisely because he obviated this procreative inclination, effectively spaying her with his age.

The second truth was that below her revealing V-necks and self-deprecating humor lay a vast trove of body image issues stemming from adolescence. She'd had the largest chest of any sixth-grade girl in Syosset – a fact that embarrassed her each gym period, when she'd wait for the others to depart the locker room before peeling off her own sweaty top. Now, at the age of twenty-six, she suspected an attraction to men who complimented her figure, and even more so to those who refrained.

Third, Caro was shadowed by her family's sinister history of addiction, her father having been an alcoholic who expertly hid his drinking beneath an affable Italian facade for years. It wasn't the addiction itself that most troubled her but the manipulations that upheld it. Once, when Caro was eight, her father persuaded her in secret to pawn her favorite gold bracelet, the cash from which he used to buy booze without her mother's knowledge. His actions were despicable, yet she understood them, and that understanding terrified her.

The fourth and final truth: Caro feared disillusionment. She feared it more than she feared grief, loneliness, or despair. She lived in dread of the day a force beyond her control would sweep in and reveal her entire reality to be a farce. In her overreactive childhood, she'd once sucker-punched a classmate who mocked her belief in Santa. In college, she'd slashed the tires of a boyfriend's car upon learning of his infidelity. She had loved that boyfriend unconditionally, hearing wedding bells every time they were together. He claimed he had not misled her, pointing out that he'd disclosed his philandering nature during their very first hookup. Thus, any vision she maintained of him throughout their dating as some upstanding partner was, he said, completely of her own deluded design. Could it be unjust to resent someone for being true to themselves rather than your vision of them, when your vision was clearly superior?

So, this past Christmas.

At 9:00 a.m., Caro set off from her place in Murray Hill for the Upper West Side. Northward she walked, up streets gradated with sun, the cold barely touching her. She bypassed Times Square, crossing west in the Sixties instead. She had copied Nick's address from one of the bills he'd asked her to file. When she reached Eighty-Seventh and West End, she peered into the cozy brownstone she identified as his. There, through the parlor window, she saw Alice and Benji, watching TV.

Caro mounted the stoop steps, her eyes fixed on the children, waiting for them to turn and spot her. The kids were in their pajamas. Alice tilted her head to the side, a barely perceptible movement. Her mouth opened. She was calling for someone, summoning them. Linnie appeared, floating into the room. She crossed to the window. Caro, spooked, descended the stairs two at a time and hurried away toward Riverside Park. Had Linnie seen her? Had Alice? She didn't know, but she did. Deep down, she knew.

A few stragglers were sweating off the morning's calories, pumping their arms in excited circular motions. Their eyes darted over her like lasers. *You harlot*, she imagined them hissing. She dropped onto a bench facing the Soldiers' and Sailors' Monument, an imitation of a Greek temple. The art did not move her. It hardly compared to the majesty of her love.

Her breath made clouds in the air. She had on a flimsy skirt, unfit for the winter's demands. Frost terrorized the backs of her thighs. The world twisted grotesquely before

292

her, the sidewalks writhing like salted slugs. She tugged the scarf from her neck, letting it slip over her wrists. The Escher staircase of her conscience offered no way up, no way out. What did it mean for a choice to be right or wrong, good or bad? To love was wholly good, the most beautiful thing there was, but to love a married man? Well. History would be her judge on that.

At some point, Caro must have shut her eyes and drifted off. In her dream, snowflakes fell upward and injected themselves back into the clouds.

A few days later, she was at her desk when the phone rang. 'Kerr & Company, how may I direct your call?'

'Caroline, hi.'

She recognized Linnie's voice instantly, the unnatural way her pitch lingered in the lower register. Nervous laughter rose in Caro's throat. This happened occasionally, to her chagrin – an emotion she couldn't explain would assail her, and her shock at its presence would emerge in the most inappropriate way.

'Sorry to bother you – Nick isn't answering his cell. I've tried him a few times. Is he around?'

The question triggered a series of vulgar words inside Caro's head. Now was her chance to reveal all, sack the citadel. She was Joan of Arc at Orléans, the favor of the gods in her hands.

Too quickly, the fantasy slipped and the office re-appeared, with its fishbowl rooms and drab gray furniture.

'He's tied up in a meeting,' she said.

'Oh. Right.'

The compressed quality of Linnie's voice betrayed a

masked strain. Caro couldn't resist probing. 'Everything all right?'

'Honestly, no. It's Alice. You're closer to her in age, maybe you could make sense of it.'

Caro's heart surged, meeting this confession with voyeuristic delight. She pictured Alice and Benji in the parlor room, curled up on the couch. In truth, she'd hoped that Linnie might reveal a hidden cache of marital struggles, but this unexpected peek into her and Nick's domestic life offered its own intrigue.

'What's going on?' she asked.

'It's just . . . we're not getting along, Alice and I. She's been – I don't know how to say it. She wants to go to this New Year's Eve party tonight.'

'And?'

'I know, you're probably thinking, Oh no, here comes another one of those helicopter parents. I'm not one of them, I swear.'

'I wasn't thinking that.'

'In all honesty, it isn't the party I'm afraid of. It's Alice herself. Nick hasn't said anything?'

'No.'

'That's funny. Here I am, pouring my heart out to a literal stranger because I don't know where else to turn, and he manages to carry on whistling through his days.'

Caro felt the slick curve of the receiver against her cheek as if it were a cavernous maw, threatening to suck her down. She blinked a few times, tethering herself back to the office.

'It's like some devil has sunk his fangs into her,'

Linnie went on. 'I can't say anything right. I tell her how beautiful she is, she looks at me like I have four heads. I tell her I'm here for her, and she twists her face in disgust.'

'Maybe she should talk to someone.'

'Oh, believe me, I've tried. We're on two therapists' waiting lists. I love her, obviously, but I'm finding it harder and harder to like her. Does that sound hyperbolic?'

'She's a teenager, so—'

Suddenly, sniffles, raw and penetrating, sliced through the line. Caro shrank back. An ill feeling seized her, bile ascending the walls of her throat. She considered offering a word of solace but was aware that even the meekest expression of comfort would sound hollow. She needed to end this call immediately.

'You should go for a walk,' she said, assuming a strange formalness. 'I'll let Nick know you called.'

Linnie coughed. 'Great, yeah, thanks. Happy New Year.'

The line clicked. Caro sat back, her nape prickling. What she'd previously taken for partnership – the keeping of a secret between her and Nick – was, she saw now, closer to abetment. A home-wrecker, that's what she was. The realization sent a burst of shame through her. The only option, the only sensible course, would be to quit, relocate, start over in a faraway city. This was what she would do.

'Oh boy, I know that tone,' Michelle said. 'Creepy Grimaldi from research?'

Everything was wrong, the needle of the speedometer trembling at its peak. Ahead loomed Linnie, and

Alice, and Benji; Caro was due to ram into them with full force.

'I need a sip of water.'

She went and knocked on Nick's door. He was by the telescope, his face inches from the eyepiece. 'Your wife called,' she said. 'She's been trying to get ahold of you.'

Nick righted himself, a shaft of sunlight snagging his gaze. Surprise flickered in his expression for only an instant – surprise, regret, and perhaps fear. The emotions dissolved too quickly for Caro to pinpoint them. Nick extended his arm to the park across the way. 'My old man used to take me there whenever we came into the city. I remember once, there was this kids' show put on by the guy who'd walked across the Towers on a tightrope – you ever hear about that? Dad couldn't figure out why anyone would be so stupid.'

'I don't feel comfortable with this,' Caro said. 'All this lying and sneaking around. I want you to end things with her.'

'It isn't so simple. This is my life we're talking about.'

'And what about mine?'

'You didn't say anything . . .'

'How dumb do you think I am?'

When he didn't respond, she sighed and said, 'Of course not.'

'Good, that's good.' He beckoned her closer. 'Come see.'

Caro had no strength left to argue. She leaned over the eyepiece. The city – vertiginously grand and indifferent to her plight – came into focus. People were revolving in doors, cooks framed in the glass cages of their delicatessens. Taxis sped along the avenue, a bright blur of colors. Sequins and steel, and everything at once too large and too small. From a distance, the Great Lawn appeared arranged to perfection. The harmony felt oppressive.

Nick massaged her shoulders. 'Stay late tonight?'

'I—'

'I'll make it worth your while.'

'Sure,' she managed, her voice small and deplorably weak.

Now, only a month and a half later, Caro found herself in the synagogue at Alice's memorial service, watching as Nick looped an arm around Linnie's waist, presenting a unified front. The rabbi was still speaking, though she'd long ceased comprehending his words.

How could Caro have known that several rows ahead of her, Nick was recalling that same afternoon, the thought having migrated from her mind to his? The same memory, slightly altered.

He'd been on a conference call when his phone buzzed. He'd missed several calls from Linnie, and a text too: *I'm worried about Alice.*

He'd retreated to the telescope by instinct. Of telescopes, he most loved the story about Percival Lowell, an astronomer who spent years studying the surface of Mars. In 1906, Lowell published a series of drawings depicting the intricate canals he'd observed on the red planet, which he hypothesized were a sophisticated irrigation system established by the Martians. Many scientists would later offer explanations for Lowell's bizarre conclusions. To Nick, however, the explanation was simple: Lowell's mind had naturally marshaled the random streaks it saw into a pattern. The most human instinct: to make meaning out of chaos.

Linnie had cause to worry; Alice was not well. Enveloped in a gloomy torpor, she'd sit through meals with her cheek on her hand, studying her place mat as if it held some oblique code. One night Nick found her wandering the hall at 2:00 a.m., a photo album tucked beneath one arm. Her expression, once vibrant, was somber and withdrawn. Her eyes, though still pale as ocean shoals, possessed a darkness that frightened him. The album, she said, was for a school project. She lifted her chin, daring him to object. He didn't object, not then. But when he walked into the bedroom, he warned Linnie that no child could handle the stress they'd put on Alice. Linnie refused to hear it. So vicariously did she thrive off their daughter's triumphs, the idea of quitting amounted to a kind of death.

Eventually, Linnie would have to come around. Alice had no intention of attending Juilliard, the Curtis Institute, or any of the other music conservatories for which her mother daily left brochures on the counter. She couldn't stand the idea of being penned up in a studio for several more years – she'd confided this in Nick during one of their trips up the Palisades. He listened with sympathy, aware that the sense of ambition that propelled his wife forward, the ambition that once attracted him to her, was the very trait that risked rending their family in two. He wanted to be on Alice's side, he did. But to be on her side meant opposing Linnie, and Lord knew their marriage was already skirting as close to the cliff's edge as physics would allow.

He remembered Alice at age eight, her spring recital. All week, she'd pleaded with him and Linnie not to make her perform. When the recital finally came, she refused to remove her violin from its case. Nick and Linnie found her backstage, crying in a corner beneath a complex system of pulleys and ropes. Around her, the other students were occupied with their own last-minute preparations. 'Please, Daddy,' Alice whimpered. 'Don't make me.'

'This is just a touch of performance anxiety,' Linnie said. 'I used to get it too.'

Nick knelt to his daughter's level, smoothed back her hair. The terror in Alice's eyes was depthless. He recalled the story about his father and the airplane, plummeting through the sky. Sometimes a thing could fall and fall, and the person inside had no way of knowing if Fate would intervene, deus ex machina style, to save them.

He rubbed his daughter's back, radiant with heat. She'd worked herself into such a state. 'Tell us, sweet pea. You want to go home? We can do that.'

'What she *wants*,' Linnie said, 'is not to disappoint her fellow players. So, let's pull ourselves together and go out there with a big smile. Afterward, we'll celebrate at Serendipity. Sound like a plan?'

As they made their way back through the auditorium, Nick refused to meet his wife's gaze. He couldn't look at her for fear of how his anger would manifest. He hated her then more than he'd ever hated anyone. 'Children have to learn,' she said, squeezing his wrist as they took their seats. And then, as if it were an afterthought too pressing not to voice: 'I do it because I love her.'

Weeks from now, after the stream of sympathizers had trickled to a drip, after the memorial service had been heaped in with the month's other horrific events, it would occur to Nick that he ought to check the photo album, the one Alice had been carrying on the night he ran into her. Beneath the yellow orb of his desk lamp, he opened the cover. Sweat gathered on his lip as he scanned the pages, his eyes pinballing between pictures. There they were at the San Francisco aquarium, the Children's Museum, the New Victory Theater – he, Linnie, and Benji, with a jagged space between them, like a swath of earth deleted by snow. Alice had painstakingly cut herself out of each image. Nick held his finger over the empty circles, feeling his daughter's invisible hand beneath his. I spy a missing girl. I spy what she forever damaged.

'Oh, Alice,' he whispered. 'What have you done?'

4

Linnie sidled out of the pew, deploying every reserve of strength to maintain her composure. She made her way to the front of the synagogue, aware of her posture, the eyes on her back. Through her head echoed the faint voice of Mr Andreyev, her old ballet instructor, who used to align a broomstick to her spine, prepared to whack her if she dared slouch. She contracted her gut, suppressing the flutters inside, and smoothed down her hair. An age-old riddle: What came first, the ballerina or the perfectionist?

She took her place upon the platform, her toes bumping up against the hard inner shells of her shoes. Each tooth in her mouth vibrated to its root; she envisioned them falling out one by one. Even that prospect didn't sound so bad. What was pain now, after she'd known the greatest sorrow of all?

The congregants waited. She stared out at random as if their faces were not faces but a conglomeration of swerving atoms. The enormity of the task at hand punctured whatever flimsy courage she'd assembled moments before. She was not, and had never been, someone who felt comfortable in idleness. At parties, she'd bustle about, as if even a moment's rest could leave her open to others' scrutiny. This is a performance, she reminded herself. You are a performer.

'Thank you for that, Rabbi,' she said. 'And thanks to all of you for being here today.' She lifted her eyes. The guileless expressions of the crowd goaded her. She had a twitchy urge to fling out her arms, unhook her bra – do something, anything, to unleash the insanity coursing through her veins.

She slipped into a mechanical mode. 'I'm humbled by the many people who've traveled great distances to honor my daughter. The outpouring of love we've received from each of you has buoyed our spirits in this challenging time. I wrote out a little something, so we'll see how much of it I can get through. Let's start at the beginning. From the day she was born, Alice filled our lives with song. Our little blessing.'

Indeed, Alice had defied the odds. Dance had exerted its merciless toll on Linnie's body, as had her severe caloric restriction. Her monthly cycle, if it occurred at all, was alarmingly irregular. When the thin blue line finally materialized, she felt as though God himself had descended to kiss her forehead.

The actual pregnancy proved another matter. Linnie was used to having complete mastery over her proprioception – knew how many pliés she could do before her legs shook, how to perceive a nanometer-scale shift in her center of gravity. This new creature swept in like a houseguest who decided to rearrange the furniture behind her back. Whenever any well-meaning acquaintance asked how she was feeling, she would say fine, but deep down she felt alienated from the process. Alice had taken the connection she felt with her body – the strongest bond she had – and corrupted it.

She read on:

'When Alice was a baby, she made me sing to her all the time – which, for those of you who've been tortured by my off-key rendition of "Happy Birthday," is rather comical. Let's just say she didn't get her musical ear from me. But Al – or Owl, as I liked to call her – didn't care. She would look up at me with those big eyes, drinking it all in. When she was three, she saw a violinist on TV and said, "I want to do that." We were reluctant – she was so tiny, and children's wills can be fickle. But, well, I'm sure you all know what happened next.'

Those initial few years, Linnie had accompanied Alice to each of her lessons at the teacher's apartment in Lenox Hill. The teacher, Darlene Frasinello, had refused to let Alice even touch bow to string for the first couple of weeks. Instead, she emphasized proper posture, instructing Alice to tuck the violin beneath her arm in rest position, then raise it to her shoulder. 'Don't slouch,' she'd bark. 'Keep your shoulders relaxed. There, hold it.'

Many children might have been bored by the tedium and rigor of these lessons. Not Alice. She wielded her instrument as if it were the aegis of Athena. When Frasinello ordered her to loosen her wrist, watch her intonation, and mind her dynamics, Alice did not cry. She improved at remarkable speed. Frasinello cautioned that talent was not enough – a musician needed grit. A musician needed to play until the music pervaded her veins and marrow.

For days, months, years, Alice practiced with ferocity, as if to soothe a wailing inside her, or else release it. Each evening when Linnie went to bed, she heard the violin through the wall – Alice running Wohlfahrt studies to the tick of a metronome – and was reminded of the exacting standards to which her fellow dancers had held themselves in the studio, borne along on the dream that they might one day *make it*.

There lived in Alice a strain of what infected those dancers, some medley of prowess and yen that had always eluded Linnie, who glimpsed in her virtuosic child a second chance at glory. Disguising her festering ambitions beneath the cloak of dedicated mother, she shuttled Alice to auditions, rehearsals, and music festivals around the country. So many nights spent on the road, staying in nondescript hotels, eating All-Bran from a Continental breakfast spread among strangers. Everything – Linnie had sacrificed everything for her daughter. Sacrificed with the belief that what she'd given up today would return to her twofold tomorrow.

Years ago, while Alice was attending a chamber music master class downtown, Linnie stumbled upon a children's dance studio next door. Beyond the window, several girls in leotards and tights stood at a portable barre, sliding their tapered legs from front to side to back, compasses tracing a perfect circle. Mesmerized, she stared, each revolution drawing her further in.

'Heel forward,' the teacher, a lean Israeli woman with

a shaved head, called from across the room. She pressed a button on a speaker, and a perky mazurka trumpeted its opening bars. 'Breathe in, breathe out.'

The girls lifted their arms from first position to second.

'And one, open two, back on three, arm at four. And five, knee bends, stretch on seven, and close.'

The steady count lulled Linnie into a memory of sixth grade, when she'd walk to the store every day before dance class for a box of donut holes. She'd eat them in the bathroom, forcing herself to watch her reflection, berating that inferior self for every bite. She wanted to be graceful, a girl in a Degas painting, with luminous skin that glowed from within. Ballet is my ticket out, she thought. If I become good enough, I'll get away from here, like the Sanderson sisters.

The Sanderson sisters were famous in Little Falls. Four of them, all blue-eyed and porcelain-faced. Every autumn, when the trees were ablaze and the light subdued, the girls would return from Duluth, where they were members of the Minnesota Ballet company. Linnie watched through the curtains as they posed on the porch for their annual Christmas card. Her house was several yards from theirs, but in her memory the two homes were jammed so close that with a simple extension of her arm, she could grasp the hand of the youngest sister, Elsa. Elsa was in her class at Mr Andreyev's Ballet Academy that spring. She was the studio's golden child, the star of the spring show, *Coppélia*.

After rehearsal one day, as Linnie waited outside for

her mother to arrive, another dancer announced she'd left her shoes inside. Eager as ever to impress Mr Andreyev, Linnie volunteered to retrieve them. She walked back into the stillness of the lobby. Music spilled through the corridor. Upon reaching the studio door, she stopped. Through the glass panel she saw Elsa, one knee in *passé*, the toes pointed, her face frozen and blank. Mr Andreyev stood behind her, his hands exploring her slender waist. A bolt of righteous anger surged through Linnie. Elsa was neither special nor gifted after all; she was just a toy that Mr Andreyev had wanted to play with, a doll he'd wanted to hold.

On the bimah, Linnie swallowed. The letters on the page broke into squiggles. The bulwark of her Midwestern decorum crumbled as the moment's grim reality reasserted itself. The congregation waited for her to resume speaking, but she couldn't. A child dying – *her* child – this was the ultimate contravention of the natural order.

'I'm sorry,' she whispered. A scream mounted at the base of her lungs, tearing through her with violent force. The walls shook as the sound unraveled into mangled sobs.

The guests were not prepared for this. Even death – that annihilative X – was expected to operate within the scaffolding of routine. Teenagers turned to their parents, parents to one another. A sense of calamity, palpable as a vapor, permeated the room. Friedman looked hopelessly around as if in search of a shepherd's hook to yank Linnie offstage. No one knew how to restore the ruptured equilibrium.

Benji stood to assist his mother down from the platform. Though his limbs reached out, he did not advance.

'Don't you see what you've done?' Linnie whispered, tears slipping off her chin. She was posing the question to everyone, yes, but chiefly herself: *How had you not noticed? How had you failed in the only job you had?*

Above the altar, the light pouring through the stained-glass windows dimmed, casting the room into shadow.

5

Outside the synagogue, Ezra lit a cigarette, relieved to have escaped the oppressive service. Around him, wind purled, the sky growing lighter with intimations of snow. Trees planted at even intervals along the sidewalk waved their branches. Ezra jammed his free hand into his pockets, stirring up the gathered lint.

The door behind him opened. Out hurried the sobbing woman in the fur coat, her flight arrested by his presence. Her impulse to escape seemed to collide with some habitual politesse inside her, because when a cab zipped by, she stuck out her hand only tentatively, as if swiping it through a candle flame.

'You'll have to do better than that,' he said.

She folded her arms. 'I'm debating whether I really want to go.'

'Can't say I'm a fan of funerals myself. Smoke?'

'No, thank you.'

'Suit yourself.'

'Well, maybe one.'

He made a trick out of igniting the lighter before he'd fully withdrawn it from his pocket.

'I'm Caro, by the way.'

'Ezra.'

They smoked in a companionable silence interrupted

every few seconds by Caro's hiccups, a remnant of her earlier sobs.

'So, what's your connection to the family?' Ezra asked.

'I work with Nick.'

'Ah. Cubicle buddies.'

'Something like that.'

'It's nice of you to come.'

'I'm not so sure he agrees.'

'Why's that?'

'He despises me.'

'I doubt that. You seem like a lovely woman.'

'Hah. In that case, you might need to get your radar checked.'

Through the curling smoke of his cigarette, Ezra held Caro's eyes.

'It's not worth getting into the details,' she said. 'Let's just say I made a stupid mistake.'

'Happens to the best of us.'

A cold wind enshrined them in its vigorous arms. The phrases they exchanged traveled only so far before fading away.

'Did you ever purposely do something you knew was awful?' Caro asked.

'All the time.'

'Now I know you're lying. You're not the type.'

'The type?'

'My type. The kind who sleeps with her boss, then doubles down on her idiocy by falling for him. Oh, God—'

She clamped a hand over her mouth, her gaze fixed on the empty space before her as if waiting for her secret to become incarnate. Ezra remained stoic, trying to exude the same professorial calm he extended toward upset students. His mind whirred to piece together the timeline. Had Alice known . . . ?

Caro stubbed out her cigarette on the brick wall and said, 'You're lucky. It's a lonely feeling, regret.'

Lonely. He heard the word in Alice's voice: 'Do you ever get lonely, Mr N.?'

Ezra didn't, or at least struggled to attach the word *lonely* to the sensation in his gut, which hewed closer to spiritual emptiness than any craving for human company. Solitude had always seemed to him the natural way of things. He'd spent his childhood on Cape Cod, buffered by the roar of spindrift in winter and the spray of ocean waves in summer. His parents' marriage had been one of convenience. One time, he caught his father at the mall cinema, engaged in a tryst with his math tutor, Mr Paul. 'You don't tell a soul about this,' his father warned. Ezra promised he wouldn't, a promise he kept. Yet still he sensed his father despised him for having been there, for having seen him.

At thirteen, Ezra was granted admission to a preparatory school in rural Massachusetts. The boys at the school wore blazers and ties to class regardless of the season, shunning winter coats as a sign of weakness. Their faces looked startlingly aged, as if their skin had been worn by the centuries of Harvard men who'd come before them. They referred to ninth grade as the *prep year* and to dorm leaders as *proctors*.

A hidden order of monies underpinned the school's

social web. Ezra, on scholarship, lacked even sufficient funds to go with the others to the general store in town. To combat this embarrassment, he cultivated an air of thriftiness, pretending his threadbare dorm was a reflection of some inner asceticism. If others saw him holding his head high in situations that might otherwise bring them shame, they'd presume he had a hidden source of confidence, a talisman in his breast pocket that rendered him untouchable.

Soon, Ezra eked his way into the fringes of popularity. The other boys revered his command of counterfactuals in debate tournaments. Teachers praised his intellect. Such success was, he believed, the source of his ultimate stagnation. The problem with touting children for their early genius was that these same students were likely to mature into validation-starved adults whose entire sense of self-worth hinged on a belief that they were superior to their peers. Inevitably, though, even the most belated late bloomer caught up, and the once-special child, the *gifted one*, was forced to endure the loss of his youth.

As he meditatively savored the last drag of his cigarette, Ezra wondered whether he and Alice were not so dissimilar; if her loneliness wasn't just the realization that her many achievements had prepared her for a future rife with disappointment. *What were you promised?* he asked the younger self within him. The answer, he knew, was nothing. No promises, only perceived ones; illusions he'd mistaken for prophecy. Hope had been his vice, and he'd indulged in it liberally, without anticipating the comedown.

'I oughta head back in,' Caro said. She stroked the hem of her coat, the bristles paling one way, shading the other. 'You won't tell anyone what I told you . . .'

He lifted two fingers. 'Scout's honor.'

There was the creak of the synagogue door, and then she was gone. Ezra turned his back, aware as any seasoned smoker of the wind's direction. He pictured Alice in his apartment that afternoon she'd come over, standing in her socks, a rubber band around her wrist with threads of hair caught in it. She moved with queenly grace, sliding her hand up and down along the violin's neck. Her body was so expansive, it seemed to contain everything and nothing at all.

6

The service ended, and it was time for the Weils to pro-
ceed back down the aisle. Benji took his mother's hand
and steered her past the network of relatives, coworkers,
friends, and parents. He gritted his teeth, willing her not
to make another scene. Behind his teammates stood
Morgan. Her gaze bolstered him once more.

'You should've seen Mom,' he imagined telling her
and Alice later. 'It was like she was drunk.'

The girls would be seated on Alice's bed, braiding
each other's hair. 'Like you know what drunk is, sped,'
Alice would say, affecting the contempt older siblings
were obligated to exhibit toward their younger counter-
parts. Morgan would stand up for him. Morgan would
tell Alice to be nice, to cut it out.

At the back doors, Linnie paused. 'I'm going to the
restroom,' she said.

Nick assessed her. 'Do you need me to come with you?'

'No, no. You stay here.'

She started down the corridor. Benji called out after
her, but she didn't turn. Nick wiped his brow and
removed his suit jacket. Sweat patches showed through
the underarms of his shirt. The floral notes of a woman's
perfume – a treacly scent Benji neither recognized nor
liked – hung in the air.

The guests paraded out the synagogue's doors with faces grim and bodies hunched. They patted his father on the back, shook his hand, remarked upon what a moving service it had been. Nick reminded them of the reception planned back at the brownstone. Of course they'd be there, they said. Did he need them to bring anything?

'Have you just met my wife?' he answered, winking at Benji. 'She's got Russ and Daughters on speed dial. I caught her ironing the tablecloths last night.'

Benji looked away, repulsed by his father's lame joke and by the guests' delight as they imagined his mother laboring for their pleasure.

Once, as a boy, Benji had asked Nick what he'd do if he or Alice died. 'I'd kill myself,' Nick answered blithely, as if charmed by the question. If he'd told the truth then, how could he be laughing now? For a blinding instant, Benji wished it was his father's funeral they were attending instead.

'Hey, B-man,' one of his teammates called.

He crossed to his peers, relieved to reenter the company of boys his age. The entire gang was there, inconspicuously trying to shove one another into the other mourners.

'Sorry about your sister,' AJ said.

'So it goes,' Benji answered, aping an expression he'd heard his father use earlier that day.

'Did you hear we creamed Bryker on Friday?'

'Didn't Schmidt get a concussion or something?'

'Headfirst into the boards,' AJ confirmed. 'It was gnarly.'

Bit by bit, Benji saw AJ's face break open and sadness rush up through the cracks. AJ had always had a thing for Alice. Last spring, at the Weils' brownstone, one of the boys had dared him to open Alice's door. Benji protested, grabbing AJ's shirt collar with such force it tore. AJ shoved Benji into the shelf of trophies, the plastic gold hockey stick pricking his underarm. AJ broke free and ran down the hall. He turned the knob. Inside, Alice stood by her armoire in her underclothes, her hair in a towel. The room around her glowed violet with evening light. She shrieked as she caught sight of the boys in the corridor. AJ froze. Benji saw his sister, and for a moment he saw what the others saw – her body, her skin, her beauty. Alice lifted the hairbrush and tossed it, with all her might, at AJ, who ducked just in time, laughing.

The longer Benji pictured the image, the more his sister faded, like a photographic negative exposed to light. He tried to visualize her neck, shoulders, and hands, but soon those were dissolving too, as if Alice were being devoured from within. Campbell Truman had once claimed that the nails of the deceased continue to grow underground. Benji imagined Alice's nails extending for miles beneath the Hudson. One day, a boy like himself might be swimming in the Atlantic and brush up against what he assumed was a whale carcass – Alice's nails. He shivered. It was the most concrete image of his sister he could conjure.

'You coming to practice this week?' Getz asked.

Getz was the largest of the crew. His height inspired deference in those who opposed him on the ice. He also had a notoriously foul sense of humor, which garnered him many a wary eye from parents. The first time he entered chez Weil, he bolted to the fridge and exclaimed (to Benji's dismay): 'I wanna see how rich people eat!'

'I think so,' Benji said, his features veering toward a frown.

'Really? My mom said—'

'What? What did she say?'

'Don't worry about it, dude.'

Benji's hope shriveled as he considered his friends' faces. Until now, he'd thought that life would return to its normal proportions, that the past few weeks were a spooky nightmare from which they'd all soon wake. He hadn't imagined that he might have to sit out the rest of the season, or that if he did play, he'd do so without enthusiasm; that he'd feel no connection to the puck or his own body, flailing on the ice as if he'd never skated before. He hadn't considered that his father wouldn't be there to cheer him on.

Ice hockey was the glue that bonded father and son. On Sundays, when Alice was at rehearsal, Nick would take Benji to practice at the Chelsea Piers Sky Rink. Benji would rise before the rest of the house to set his gear by the door. Nick took this as evidence of his love for the sport, but Benji would've been content had they merely ridden the subway together for hours.

'Coach wasn't sure you'd be back, is all,' Getz said.

'I will be.'

'Cool. Hey, if it snows tomorrow, you should come sledding with us.'

Benji gaped at his friends, at their stupid dress suits, their childish concerns. *Sledding?* Anger wrenched his bowels. They didn't care about him or his family. His mind zoomed ahead to the glorious day when he'd be free of every last one of them.

'Where at?' he asked, instantly realizing his mistake. Suicide Hill – the steepest slope on the Upper West Side, where all the kids went on snow days.

'Hey, buddy.' A British accent, a tap on the shoulder. Benji turned from Getz to see Peter Hensley. 'I just wanted to see how you're doing.'

There was no condescension in Peter's gaze, no artificial concern. In his eyes, Benji detected the solemnity his own father lacked. He sensed Peter might understand how alienated he felt, if only he could articulate it.

7

Linnie located the ladies' room at the end of the corridor connecting the lobby to the rabbi's office. The scent of potpourri within was suffocating. She leaned over the sink, her knuckles paling on the porcelain. 'You stupid, stupid cow,' she whispered.

Several days had elapsed since she'd last seen her reflection. Judith had draped black cloth over every mirror in the brownstone, a tradition to avoid making permanent the mourner's defiled image. Defiled, indeed. Linnie looked haggard: her skin bloodless, her lips chapped. She could see every pore, dusted with a trace of powder. Her eyes were puffy. The hot poker of grief struck her with every breath. The longer she stared, the more demented her face grew – her brows, cheeks, and nose all receding into her skull.

The door opened. In walked Caro. She moved with her shoulders pitched forward, as if preserving heat against a cold front. She hesitated before setting her clutch down on the vanity. 'How are you holding up?' she asked, reaching for a tissue. 'Can I do anything for you? Get you anything?'

'Can you do anything,' Linnie repeated, her numbness black and bitter and oozing.

'It's a hard day. I truly can't imagine.'

'No, I suppose you can't.'

'Nick – you know how he is, well, of course you do – he'd always come into work bragging, Alice did this last night, or Alice won such and such award. Anyone could see by the way he talked—'

'Ha.' Linnie's own stridency surprised her. She gripped the handle of the wicker amenity basket, a nerve jumping in her wrist. 'Ha, ha, ha.'

'Sorry, is something . . . Did I say something . . . Are you okay?'

'Oh, dandy, peachy. It's just a bit hilarious, don't you think. If it were up to him, Alice would be nothing, another nose-picker of a kid. But of course he'd find some way to take credit for her success – why does that not surprise me.'

Linnie could feel herself stoking her fury, using it to smother the flame of her grief. She unspooled her contempt word by word, as if extracting a swallowed hair from her throat. 'God, you're a snake. You're a snake, and I'm a fool.'

The women locked eyes in the mirror. Caro opened her hand, the tissue fluttering to the ground. 'I didn't realize . . .' For a scintillant moment, the possibility of denying the accusation must have presented itself. Then her expression shuttered and she said, 'Anyway, it's over now.'

From the farthest stall came the sound of a toilet flushing. Caro and Linnie turned. A pair of black flats peeked out beneath the stall door. Linnie's mind skipped to the worst: that the flats belonged to one of the nosy neighborhood mothers who hoarded secrets like mah-jongg tiles, playing them when they'd prove most inflammatory. How long before word of Nick's affair spread like head lice into every household on the Upper West Side? She had to leave him now. A wife could ostensibly recover a quiet dignity in staying with her hus-band if no one knew, but if everyone knew, she'd be deemed spineless for choosing to stay.

On some level, Linnie sensed that her shock was compulsory. Fair or not, her chosen métier of dance had prepared her for Nick's infidelity. In ballet, boys were scarce and valuable, while girls were not. Linnie had learned early to stay mum about her grabby partners, her licentious teachers. If you complained, they'd pass your track off to someone else. Women, she'd learned far too young, were replaceable.

What stung most, then, was that Nick hadn't come to her first. If he'd been frank about his desires, Linnie might have agreed to let him have his fun. They could've made a game of selecting a third party together. In exchange for Linnie's good sportsmanship, she'd receive Nick's eternal groveling at her feet. *The best wife. Too good for him; much too good.* The other woman – the mistress – would remain a smear of pixels in cyberspace, a utilitarian orifice. Linnie might think of her as a coatrack. Ah, yes, once a week my husband hangs his coat on that rack instead of mine.

'Did you hear me?' Caro said. 'It's over. We're through, and I'm sorry. I really am.'

'The lousy part is, I trusted you. I let down my guard to you. And you, you . . .'

'I wasn't – I mean, you weren't really opening up to me personally, per se.'

'Is that supposed to be an excuse?'

'No, it's not.'

'Do you love him?'

'I . . .' Caro glanced around as if the answer were scribbled somewhere on the wall. 'Would you prefer I say that I do or don't?'

'So you do, that's fine. But I do worry you're in over your head. Do you have even an iota of sense what it's like to be married to a man like Nick, going round and round the carousel of laundry and meals, praying that someone will reach out and save you?' Each word replenished Linnie with fresh acrimony. 'He's a dud of a father too. With Benji's travel games, sure, *those* he cares about. But ask him who checks the homework folders, plans the birthday parties, mops up after a stomach bug.'

Caro winced.

'I'm only trying to prepare you. It isn't all fucking and fun.'

Linnie lifted the metal tissue holder from the vanity and slammed it against the floor, no longer caring about the mysterious figure tucked away in the stall. A metal flower snapped off the holder's side. She picked it up, pinching so hard the petals left indentations in her finger pads.

'I get the picture,' Caro said weakly.

'Don't flatter yourself. You couldn't possibly.'

Through the opaque cloud of hurt gathering around

her, Linnie forced herself to meet Caro's gaze. Brown eyes; sensitive, despite the levee she'd raised to protect herself against Linnie's vitriol. The women exchanged a look that, with a hummingbird's fragile effort, hovered near compassion. Their shared love had made them enemies, though under other circumstances, it might have made them friends.

Changing tack, Linnie reached out and gripped the cross around Caro's neck. 'You're a Christian?'

'Yes.'

'How much of a Christian?'

'I don't . . .'

'You get down on your knees every night and say the Our Father?'

'On good days.'

'Let me hear it.'

'Let you . . .'

'I want to know that you're telling the truth. I have no reason to assume you are.'

'Our Father, who art in heaven, hallowed be Thy name. Thy kingdom come. Thy will be—' Caro broke off, tears in her eyes.

'Good. That's what I wanted to hear. That means you'll spend the rest of your life atoning.'

The room around Linnie spun. In some lowly nook of her consciousness, she'd held fast to the possibility of a different outcome; the chance that Caro would refute the allegations. For years, she had chosen to dispatch what she perceived as Nick's less savory attributes to the outskirts of their union, preserving his image as a flawed but tender husband, a devoted father. She had forgiven him everything, but he had not extended her the same courtesy. Instead, he'd gone out and tried to right her wrongs in the bosom of another woman, a woman with a surfeit of prospects before her – much like the one Linnie herself had once been. Twenty-one years they'd been married – Nick and Linnie; Linnie and Nick; the Weils; Mister and Missus – twenty-one years; a full-fledged adult. Fury clawed at her gut, twisting her organs like a sharp hunger. Fearing sickness, she lurched toward the stalls, and there, again: the black ballet flats, crossed at the ankle. Instantly, Linnie recognized those ankles: Morgan.

When Caro spoke behind her, it was in the small, cowed voice of the demoralized: 'Is he the one who told you about us?'

Linnie spun and barked out a laugh, appearing to grow several inches as she drew energy up her spine. 'If you think Nick had some come-to-Jesus revelation, you really are deluded.'

'Then . . .'

'Alice.'

The name hung between them, a spell.

For Caro, it conjured a memory of the evening six weeks prior. New Year's Eve: the same day Linnie had called the office asking for Nick. The day Linnie had divulged to her the details about Alice. The day that changed everything.

Caro had entered Nick's office that afternoon at six, after the others had gone. She climbed into his lap, dotting his neck with kisses. Just as their mouths met, a knock sounded at the door. Nick blanched, shoving her away more gruffly than he'd perhaps intended. 'Didn't you check to make sure everyone left?'

'It's probably the cleaning lady. She arrives early sometimes.'

'Tell her I'll be a minute,' he said.

Caro slipped her feet into her heels. She was an *administrative assistant*, helping her boss with urgent matters. No foul there.

'Wait – you've got lipstick on your cheek.' Nick reached out and swabbed her face with the cuff of his sleeve. A red smear shone on the fabric.

Caro made her way to the door. She opened it. On the other side stood a girl, rangy and blond. Caro recognized her from the previous week at the brownstone and from the frames on Nick's desk. In the flesh, however, Alice possessed a quality that no photograph could do justice, a certain fluidity that would inevitably cease the moment someone tried to capture it. Caro recalled that morning's conversation with Linnie: *It's like some devil has sunk his fangs into her.*

'Is my dad busy?' Alice asked, her evident beauty frustrated by a coldness in her eyes. 'I need my violin.'

'He's just finishing up a call. Excuse me.'

Caro walked to her desk, a walk that might well have spanned a mile. Her legs shook as she curved her fingers over the keyboard, enacting a pose of busyness. She registered her ghostlike reflection in the computer screen: the lipstick ringing her mouth, the misaligned buttons on her blouse. Alice's gaze remained locked on her. Caro volunteered the girl a smile, which went unreturned.

The air remained noxious with paranoia even after Alice had departed, clutching the spare violin she stowed in her father's office. The encounter seemed to pierce Nick to the heart, and Caro watched as the guilt he'd managed to keep at bay for months flooded his eyes. He asked whether she thought Alice had detected anything amiss. Caro soothed him. No, she said – though she knew just how perceptive teenage girls could be.

Now, in the ladies' room, her suspicions were confirmed. She wanted to press Linnie for details, but the other woman's eyes were closed; she was caught in a memory of her own.

8

That final Tuesday, a frigid February morning, Alice entered the kitchen at seven. Blue rings hovered in the translucent skin beneath her eyes. Dressed for school, she skulked through the room with an adult weariness that unsettled Linnie, who sat nursing a cup of coffee at the table.

'There's oatmeal in the pot,' Linnie said.

Alice fished an apple from the fruit bowl. She'd been eating less and less recently, a habit Linnie recognized from her own adolescence, when she'd exercised relentless control over her diet, recording her daily weight on a log she kept tucked beneath her bed. She had measured her worth by that number, by its diminishment. She suspected Alice's newfound diet had less to do with losing weight than with leveraging her body to make her misery manifest. Teenagers acted out in these predictable ways.

'How was rehearsal last night?' Linnie asked.

'Dumb.'

'Please don't roll your eyes at me. I was just asking a question.'

'Oh my God, I wasn't rolling them *at* you.'

'Don't forget your violin again,' she said, a purposeful provocation.

'Whatever.'

'It's not whatever, Alice. You don't want them to kick you out.'

'I should only be so lucky.'

'Watch the attitude, young lady.'

'You make it sound like I just decided this on a whim. I told you: I'm done playing.'

Alice crossed to the fridge and stood haloed a moment in its sterile light. She moved with jarring sangfroid – the same impassive demeanor Linnie herself adopted when aggrieved. It was the same impassive demeanor she adopted now, in fact, as she picked up her coffee mug and sipped. The yoke of parental authority that once assured her control over her elder child swung futilely in the air. In a desperate attempt to resecure it, she said, 'Why don't you take a week off and think it over.'

'Fuck that.'

'Excuse me?'

'You're missing the point.'

'Which is what, exactly?'

'I just don't want to.'

'Since when? You remember when you were little, you used to ask me to play that Perlman tape for you every night.'

'I fucking hate it, Mom.'

'Can we stop with the language?'

'Fuck, fuck, fuck, fuck.'

'Do you feel proud of yourself? Do you feel like an adult?'

'I. Hate. It.'

What was *it* – the violin, or the dream of greatness for which the violin stood as a cipher? Faltering, Linnie gripped her mug and gazed down at her runny reflection. Alice had what so many yearned for, what she herself had once yearned for: a natural gift.

Thousands of dancers possessed faultless technique, yet still fell short of greatness. To Linnie, this was the most damning fact on earth. Better to have no talent at all. For someone deficient of skill entirely could acknowledge the sizable gap that spanned between themselves and greatness, whereas someone who was very good, as she herself had been, couldn't fathom how they might expend both the necessary time and energy and still come up short. Friends of hers, the ones too headstrong to waive their dreams, had stayed on in the corps de ballet of various companies across the country. Though a part of her envied them, she schooled her conscience into mistaking this envy for pity. Those dancers would carry out their lives striving for the impossible, unable to account for the emptiness that slowly gnawed away at their hopeful hearts. Yet here was her daughter, who had every marking of propitious talent, and didn't even care.

'You said if I played through the season, I could stop,' Alice said.

'I said we'd consider it.'

'Okay, so?'

'I'll have to discuss it with your father.'

'Right, because you don't have a mind of your own. You're just Dad's pawn.' With a violent gesture, Alice wiped at her nose. 'No, you're worse – at least a pawn knows what they're fighting for.'

'Boo-hoo, the world's out to get you, we're the worst parents in the world – does that about cover it?'

'You never see things from my side.'

'Boy oh boy, are you kids spoiled. We could give you the moon from the sky, and you'd still find a reason to complain. If you had any idea how I grew up—'

'As if we *chose* this.'

The wildness of Alice's cry jolted Linnie, just as it had on the day she was born – six pounds, four ounces; a crown of downy hair, so blond it was white; the perfect baby, the embodiment of life itself. I will die for you. I will kill for you. Where was that child, so far from the one who stood here now, with febrile cheeks and agate eyes? The expression in those eyes was so tortured, it nearly moved Linnie to surrender. Then she drew in a breath that washed this compulsion from her mind.

'So, what? Help me understand. You want me to tell you it's okay, quit, throw away everything we've spent the last twelve years working for? Is that really what you want?' She softened. 'It's only a little longer, Owl. Someday you might even be grateful for this.'

'Everything *we've* worked for?' Alice lunged forward, reaching for Linnie's hand. With a jerky motion, she lifted it from the table and pried apart Linnie's fingers. 'Where are *your* calluses, hmm? Where's the tendinitis in *your* wrist?'

Linnie, startled, extricated herself from Alice's grip.

329

She stared into her daughter's face, waiting for embarrassment, shame, humor – anything that might acknowledge the undue fervor of her reaction.

'Back when I was dancing—' Linnie began, instantly wishing she hadn't. She detested her need to sound relevant, to make prominent the past self that her choices had eroded. She tried again. 'I know this is hard for you, sweetie. I know it is. Try to keep the long-term in perspective. All the doors it will open—'

'What doors? Where are they? Because all I see is a never-ending tunnel. I go off to college, get a job, and then? Enlighten me, Mom: What comes next in this perfect little world of yours? I get to be as happy as you and Dad? If that's all there is, it doesn't mean shit.'

'Your father and I *are* happy, Alice. And yes, that's what we want for you too. For you and your brother both.'

Alice gazed out, her eyes flat. In that instant, the voltage between mother and daughter clicked off, the circuit irreversibly snipped.

'Why are you being this way?' Linnie heard herself ask. 'Did something happen? Did someone touch you?'

'God, Mama. Don't be so dramatic.'

The coffee in the mug beneath Linnie rippled – no, it was only her hands around the mug that were shaking. 'What am I missing?' she asked.

There was a strangled pause. At last Alice said, 'Dad's cheating on you. With his secretary. Very original.'

These words cast out shock waves that acted promptly on the kitchen: warping the countertops, stretching the windows in their frames. A shooting pain radiated through

Linnie's sternum. She remembered a production of *The Bacchae* she'd once danced in, where King Pentheus was torn limb from limb in a Dionysian ceremony. She had become that king.

'Good grief,' she muttered.

'Are you sad, Mama? Does that make you sad? Do you want to wring his neck?'

Alice smiled, but the smile was false, inhuman; it reflected no soul.

A burst of anger crackled inside Linnie – an anger that, later, she would not be able to resummon, not even for Nick; an anger that was already fraying into defeat at its edges. She lifted her hand and slapped Alice, hard. Alice recoiled, instinctively reaching for her cheek. There was no astonishment in her eyes, only a flash of condescension, a haughtiness that refused to yield. Hatred – gone as swiftly as it had come.

Over and over, in her memories, Linnie will repeat this action: extending a hand to strike Alice. With strength. With deliberation. So you think you're better than me, she thinks, her palm smarting as she draws it back. That you'll grow up to be the sort of woman no man would dare cheat on. Believe me, child, I wish that for you.

Only under the auspices of dream can Linnie undo the slap and kiss her daughter instead. Does it change anything? What if she tells Alice to stay home that day, that she's worried about her – how about then? How many particles of the past must she alter to mend the future, and what gives in its place? It's the classic grandfather paradox. A man travels back in time and meets his grandfather as a young man. In doing so, he tinkers with some mechanism in the space-time continuum, rendering it so that he himself was never born. Rules, contingencies, climbing her way back up the ladder to see what changes if she reaches for rung A, or B, or C.

But there in the kitchen, the slap occurred only once. Alice cradled her cheek in her hand. She looked at Linnie with restrained tears glittering in her eyes, withdrawing into herself like a wounded animal. She said, 'I'm sorry I make you so miserable, Mama. I'm so sorry.'

Linnie couldn't think straight. These words failed to reach her. Her mind was far away. And so she said the strangest thing; she wasn't even sure why: 'Oh, Owl, don't act so smug. Obviously your father and Caro are sleeping together. As if I didn't know that.'

Gradually, Alice's expression changed, hardened. She tossed the apple into the air; it seemed it would never come down. At last it landed in her palm, her fingers denting the waxy coating. 'If that's the case, then you'd see why I find it ironic – you thinking I'd want to grow up to be anything like you.'

She tugged her coat from the back of the kitchen chair and strode from the room. Linnie waited in a spreading pool of sunlight, counting her daughter's footfalls. The lock on the door clicked. Silence.

PART FIVE

PART FIVE

TOGETHER WITH THEIR FAMILIES

MORGAN HENSLEY

&

BENJAMIN WEIL

invite you to join them
as they embark on
the journey of a lifetime
and become husband and wife.

SATURDAY, THE TWENTY-THIRD OF JULY

FOUR O'CLOCK IN THE AFTERNOON

ELIZABETH COTTAGE, SUGAR HILL, MAINE

RECEPTION TO FOLLOW

I

Benji took his position by the French doors and watched as the guests gathered in folding chairs on the lawn, beneath the midday light. Some perused the wedding program, while others discussed upcoming summer plans. A handful had extended their trips beyond this weekend, with stopovers in Kennebunkport or Acadia. Many had departures planned to more exotic destinations (Croatia, Iceland, Saint-Tropez) – a final dog-day hurrah before the revving up of school and work.

Judith sat in the front row, scrutinizing the hydrangeas spilling out from garden urns. 'Look at them wilting,' she said. 'And that chuppah – it's like the Leaning Tower of Pisa. Who'd you say was getting married?'

Suspended on a plane of ceremony, the guests pretended not to hear this. They pretended too not to notice the empty chair beside Judith, with a blush rose laid across its seat. A memory chair, Linnie called it.

Beside the altar, the children's chorus Morgan had conducted for years filed into view. Benji had arranged for them to sing during the processional as a surprise. Morgan's colleague lifted his arms, and the children began a harmonized rendition of 'Over the Rainbow.'

Linnie looped an arm around Benji's neck, bending

him to her level to kiss his forehead. The treble clef sparkled on his lapel.

'Ready?' Nick asked.

The doors swung open. Beyond the guests, a slice of bay held Benji's concentration. Each step vaulted him further into memory until he was not in Maine at all, but Washington Heights. Eighteen again, on the George Washington Bridge. He looked first at the nested spires of Manhattan, and then at the considerably flatter shore across the way. Finally, he turned to the river itself, staring straight down the middle passage toward Ellis Island, where his ancestors had arrived, taking those first tentative steps onto the edge of hope.

He had assumed that the world without Alice would sound as disconcertingly quiet as their brownstone had on the night she'd vanished, when both parents went out to look for her. Instead it was the opposite, everything turned up too loud. As if she'd just ceased playing, and every person and object – every cloud, leaf, and grain of sand – held her song.

The conductor lifted his arms, and the chorus began the opening arpeggios of 'Hallelujah.' Amid a chorus of *awws*, Avery promenaded down the aisle. She wore a puffy white dress with a tulle skirt and pink satin sash. Tiny sequins shimmered along the bodice. She reached into her basket and grabbed handfuls of petals, scattering them. Sunlight fell between the branches like specks of pollen to garland her hair. Benji gave her a thumbs-up.

The music changed. A single soprano voice hovered

lucidly above the others. The guests rose to behold Morgan, arm in arm with Peter, her hair cascading in silky waves down her back. As she moved, the word *sensational* trailed her, held aloft from one set of lips to another.

She stepped carefully, as if the aisle were filled with lacerating particles. The wind lifted her veil slightly off her skin. Benji recalled the promises they'd made to each other over the years, words whispered in secret across lonely miles when they were apart. Shiny, unspeakable hopes bloomed like signal fires inside him.

Upon reaching the altar, Morgan circled Benji three times, and he did the same. They then wove a single circle around each other, as if braiding a maypole. She was so close, he could smell the hairspray ballasting her coiffure, yet her eyes were faraway – turbid pools on whose surface reflections of the wedding scene floated. He squeezed her hand.

'You may be seated,' the officiant, his father's cousin Elliot, said. 'Friends, family – today we gather to celebrate one of life's greatest miracles: the union of two souls. Morgan, Benji: you have the rare distinction of having known each other since childhood and so have witnessed each other grow throughout the years. Now you're here, on this glorious summer day . . .'

Benji leaned in and whispered, 'I've dreamed of this for so long.'

'Shh,' Morgan said, her gaze bright and mirthful. 'How long?'

'Before we go on,' Elliot said, 'I'd like to acknowledge someone who joins us today in spirit. Like many who have gone before her to the World to Come, she is held forever in our hearts.'

There was the sipping of wine, the reading of vows, the exchange of rings.

'I am my beloved's, and my beloved is mine,' Benji said.

He felt mortared to the earth, a temple column: ancient, immovable. Beside him, the bay waltzed to the pier's edge. Above, gulls; their wingspan prehistoric. In no time, the wedding would be over; the honeymoon too. Years from now, he might only recall the nervousness he felt as he looked out; how the breeze, grown suddenly bold, contained in its summer freshness the faint promise of winter's return; how, when he leaned in to kiss Morgan, she laughed, and his lips grazed the enamel of her teeth.

2

Afterward, Morgan and Benji sat on an old white bench in the courtyard, where they'd adjourned for a few minutes of seclusion. Behind them stretched a wall of espaliered pear trees; beside them, a trellis covered in coiling green vines. Honeysuckle filled the air. Morgan imagined that some woman had planted this garden long ago, a wife like herself who wished to create a garden that would rival the harsh Maine winters; who dreamed of saturating the world with beauty.

She and Benji nibbled on the flaky egg rolls the caterers had brought out and threaded fingers by the fountain. Mayflies coasted over the algae-ridden surface, pricking their dressed-up reflections. Morgan had hoped that the words *I do* would trigger some transformative current that would right their affairs to order, yet everything remained as unresolved as before. Benji must have felt the tension too, because he cleared his throat and said, 'Well, so that's done.'

The garden around them hummed. The sun hung low in the sky. A squirrel stalled, petrified, in his journey up the tree.

'Listen, love,' she said, 'can I just say one last thing about Ezra? And then I promise I won't bring him up again.'

Benji released her hand, not shoving it away exactly, but not holding it either.

'He and Alice, they had a thing. That's why I couldn't stand him being here. That's why I went behind your back to seek him out. I caught them once together in his classroom.'

She saw Benji relent to curiosity in spite of himself. 'When?'

'Before Christmas. I wasn't snooping or anything, just worried. So I followed her.'

'And?'

'Well, that's just it. They were in his classroom. He got angry, and then – I don't know. I was scared of what he'd do, of how I'd deal with it, so I turned and ran.'

Benji rose from the bench, his expression inscrutable. Morgan felt a cold fear slide over her, an awareness of how much she'd entrusted to him. 'It was so long ago,' she said. 'I wouldn't have mentioned it, but then he strolled in here with your mom, and I worried . . .'

'You worried he'd screw this up too.'

'Kinda, yeah.'

Benji stopped and faced her squarely. The look in his eyes was the same as he wore on the ice, a penetrating beam of concentration. It struck her that this was the same expression Alice used to wear while playing violin, a look of utter focus, as if the very earth spun on the axis of the siblings' devotion.

'Any other secrets?' he asked.

She shook her head.

'I have one, actually,' he said.

She waited, trying not to let the terror show in her eyes.

'Alice told me she was leaving.'

'Told you?'

'She didn't spell it out, obviously. But I knew. There was something in her – I can't explain it. And then she went. She went, but she didn't go.' He reached out and grasped at the air.

Morgan put her arms around him. They held each other, hearing neither the gulls agitating the airspace overhead nor the guests' celebratory cries from within. In sharing the torments each had kept close for so long, they managed to tip the balance, which held on one side all the losses they'd suffered, and on the other the infinite joys they'd shared: the wintry day they'd skated together at Wollman Rink in Central Park; the lazy late afternoons on the pier, when they'd watch the sun descend into the East River; their first kiss. All the tiny moments – the coffees, subway rides, and glances across crowded rooms – that fostered in each the resilience to build a home in life's vast wilderness.

When they could put it off no longer, they clasped hands and traversed the lawn. They walked into the ballroom, temporarily blinded by the lights bouncing off the waxed floors. The crowd cheered for them. Goodness was falling faster and faster, gathering like rainwater in a pot.

And out in the garden, where the flowers continued to perfume the air and the bees grew drowsy off ambrosia, a handful of fireflies clicked on their lights. Spiders took to their weaving. Tomorrow stood far away yet. In the grass and on the pavestones, Morgan's and Benji's footprints remained for hours, inexplicable in their persistence, until the chimney sweep of night descended to brush them away.

3

By the band's fourth rendition of 'Hava Nagila,' Judith had issued Nick a dozen complaints about the ruin the music had wreaked on her hearing aids. Sweat stains proliferated across the men's shirts. The women gratefully supplanted their heels with flip-flops from the basket by the door. In true Weil fashion (in true *Linnie* fashion, Nick thought), no detail went overlooked. Even the slight hiccups – the microphone cutting out during Peter's toast, Benji slipping off the Chiavari chair as several men hoisted him overhead – could not rob the evening of its gaiety.

Shimmying out from the underbrush of skirts, Avery dashed to her parents, colliding with the cocktail waiter setting down entrée plates. 'I lost my tooth,' she cried, depositing the offending triangle into her mother's hand.

'We'll store it in the napkin for safekeeping,' Caro said. 'Don't forget.'

'Can I sit on your lap?'

'After dinner, princess.'

Undeterred, Avery sprinted back to the dance floor.

Nick opened his wallet and flashed Caro its contents: four twenty-dollar bills. 'I guess the Tooth Fairy needs to ask the concierge for change.'

Caro speared a mushroom with her fork. The metal

screeched against the plate. Nick's eyes traipsed over her place setting: the country-style skirt steak, the water goblet where her lipstick had smudged, the untouched glass of wine. 'You aren't drinking?'

Her complexion crimsoned. He raised his eyebrows quizzically.

Oh, fuck.

Had any words been exchanged, he might have asked whether she was sure, and she'd have confirmed it. She'd have said, 'What if this pregnancy turns out like the last?' He'd have comforted her, confessing in turn his own fears: that he was a rotten father, destined to become as caustic as Judith. 'Baby,' he'd plead, 'don't you see how afraid I am? Every day, I enter the world and feel an enormous weight on my chest.' She'd have pledged to stick by his side, no matter the troubles ahead. For a fleeting moment, the illusion of bliss would sweep them up and hold them in an embrace high above the dance floor. But this reality remained elusive, a vision that slipped Nick's grasp as soon as it appeared.

'I have something to tell you too,' he said. 'My job . . . well, let me preface it this way: it's bad. We might lose the gallery.'

He tried to smile, already doing his best to mitigate the aftershocks, but Caro sensed the emotion that ran counter to this smile. Her brows knitted in concern.

'I don't understand,' she said. 'My gallery? What's that gotta do with anything?'

'Technically, it's ours.'

'Cut the crap, Nick.'

346

He swallowed, relieved and terrified to realize that he'd at last wedged himself in too deep to turn back. He noticed a couple across the way, friends of theirs. They were pointing at him – no, they were pointing beyond him, at Morgan. Of course. The room buzzed, an electric saw slicing through his brain.

'It's difficult to say, that's all,' he said. 'I don't want you to see me in a bad light.'

Caro's expression grew more drawn by the second. Her eyes stayed tolerant but firm. She'd neither yell at him nor release him from the burden of disclosure. So, while the rest of the room celebrated, Nick relayed to his wife a summary of the past six months. He said the words quickly, without feeling. Even a momentary pause might cause the fragile enterprise to collapse. Caro's gaze drifted as she listened, replotting her memories in real time. He started with Kerr summoning him to his office and how he'd sensed, walking past the cubicles he'd passed thousands of times, the mounting pressure of what was coming. Oh, yes, he knew.

Well, so it was true he'd had a poor performance year, or a couple of poor performance years, if one were keeping track ('Dismal,' Kerr had said). True that his clients, whom he'd believed to be loyal, had come to him wringing their hands, apologizing and presenting him boxes of See's chocolates while pulling their assets. There was the packing up of his office, removing the certificates from the wall, gathering the photo frames, stroking the gabardine sofa where he and Caro had . . .

He looked up at her. She winced and gestured that he should keep going.

Naturally, the termination had thrust him into a state of shock. He kept expecting Kerr to phone and say there'd been an error, a different Nick Weil was meant to have been fired. The firm granted him several months' severance, which prolonged his incredulity. Once the money dried up, the shock oxidized to fear, then self-pity. He had no job and no job prospects.

All this he recounted calmly, speaking out of the corner of his mouth while continuing to wave at the guests and receive their handshakes. He hoped that his smile, whose edges he could feel straining downward, conveyed a sense of general gaiety. Look at him and his lovely young wife engaging in a cordial chat.

'So, that's the long and short of it,' he concluded. 'It's bad. No sugarcoating that.'

'Bad? Jesus, Nick – that's the understatement of the year. Try disastrous. All these months you were lying to me, hoping the problem would just go away?'

'I wouldn't put it like that, exactly.'

'What kind of solution is that? What the hell is wrong with you? This whole time, I kept thinking you were so different from my father, but you're not. You're the same. That's what my analyst said. She said I'm drawn to you because I want to fix you. I want to re-create the patterns I'd had as a kid, when I felt so helpless, and force them to play out differently. But it's the same. The same goddamn horror show on a loop.'

He was aware of her volume and how near the other guests were. He resisted the urge to point this out. Instead, he stretched his smile farther, fighting against that terrible strain. She looked at him as if he were deranged. He sobered some, enough to say, 'I'm sorry. If I could do it over, I would.'

Caro set a protective hand on her stomach. What was she thinking? Nick hadn't even a guess. Perhaps she was mentally paging through her book of threats, trying to figure out how to use her newfound position to her advantage. No; she was not spiteful like that. He softened his vision and thought, not for the first time, how sublime she was, how capable and wise. Over the past decade she had blossomed, while he alone had stayed the same – a patch of scorched earth beside a towering redwood. Let me try again, he begged some unknown force above. Grant me one more chance.

'This is going to take a while to process,' Caro said.

'You know that Kerr had it in for me—'

'It's not about the job, you idiot. Oh, the job, the job – I don't *care* about the fucking job. It's the fact that you came home and lied to me every day for months. Doesn't our marriage mean anything to you?'

'It means everything to me,' he said, surprised by the force of truth behind these words. 'Why do you think I couldn't tell you?'

She stared at him with detachment, ignoring the couple – friends of theirs from Scarsdale – who lingered a few feet away. The couple was pretending to be engrossed in their own conversation, yet every few seconds their eyes would dart over to Caro and Nick's table, evidently assessing whether it was an opportune moment to sweep in and offer their congratulations.

'Here's what's gonna happen,' Caro said. 'Monday morning, you'll drop Avery off at camp, and you'll start applying for every position within a forty-mile radius you're even remotely qualified for. As for the rest, I don't know.'

'Don't know what?'

'Honey, please.' She released a small cry. He could tell she was holding back, trying to preserve the emotion for when she was alone and could thoroughly analyze it.

'But are we—'

'God, Nick, enough. I still love you, if that's what you're asking. Even when you drive me up the wall.'

The declaration surprised him. He felt his smile wane, something genuine breaking through. His eyes moved across the room to where Benji stood, entertaining a crowd. His son. Nick watched him with a mingled sense of admiration and envy. How sure Benji was on his feet, how quick to see the good in others.

Nick recalled a day from long ago, when Benji was eight and Alice twelve. He had devised a little experiment to teach his children about the stock market. He created what he called the Weil Stock and gave them each twenty dollars to invest in it. Every day he'd tell them, 'The Weil Stock rose one percent today,' and illustrate how their money had grown. The Weil Stock only ever went up. Alice wanted to keep her money in it, demonstrating the makings of a shrewd investor, but

Benji wished to withdraw his immediately. Nick said, 'You don't want to do that, bud.' Benji became willful. He said, 'Yes I do, it's my money.' Alice looked over with a devious smile and said, 'I'll buy his shares, Dad. Isn't that how it works – Benji can sell if there's a buyer?' Nick tried to reason with his children, to show Benji his shortsightedness, but Benji refused to listen. Nick seized him by the collar. 'You're being a twerp!' he shouted, seeing an impulsiveness in Benji that he loathed, a trigger-happy urge he thought it necessary to quash before it was too late. As he shook his son, he felt the anger leave his body; only, it wasn't going into Benji; it dissolved at the moment of contact, as if neutralized by some counterforce within the boy.

He heard Benji's harsh words from earlier that day: *I'm not even sure you like me very much*. It couldn't be further from the truth; he loved his son more than anything. The only parts that disappointed him were those he couldn't face in himself.

'I just feel like a big loser sometimes,' he mumbled to Caro. 'That's why I was afraid to tell you.'

'Sweetheart,' she said, setting a hand on his knee, 'you're far from a loser.'

Her words rang out with a treacherous sense of falsity. Both knew there were further fights to be had, interrogations about the supposed meetings that had required Nick to return home after dark, the bevy of lies he'd spent months perpetuating. For now, though, each was content to entrust such arguments to the future.

'And you,' he said, gesturing to her stomach.

'Yes,' she said, tears rushing to her eyes. They were happy tears, she insisted. Happy, grateful tears.

Nick stood up and guided her to the dance floor. In anticipation of dinner, the center had cleared. A few couples remained rocking back and forth, ensconced in their private worlds, only seeing a tiny corner of their partner's heart. How little truth each of us can bear. As God tells Moses: *No man shall see my face and live.*

4

'Thanks again for coming,' Linnie said to Ezra.

They were on the dance floor. One of his hands gripped hers; the other rested on the small of her back. She twirled lightly, as if on a marionette's strings, possessing stewardship over every muscle in her body.

'By the way,' she said, 'where'd you disappear to this afternoon? I couldn't find you anywhere.'

Cold perspiration pricked Ezra's hairline. His guts churned with the whirling motion of the other couples. 'I just had some things to mull over.'

'Well, that's certainly ominous. Anything you want to run by me – the truth, maybe?'

Truth. The word reverberated like a church bell through his mind. On the other side of the ballroom, Alice appeared: 'Do you want to play a game, Mr N.?'

They were in his classroom a week before Christmas. Alice had on her slate-gray raincoat and heavy eyeliner. Recently, Ezra had spotted her hanging out with a group he identified as 'the Misfits' – the students with piercings and tattoos and neon hair who filled the desks at morning detention. (Even a school as prestigious as Manhattan Tech, with a Wikipedia page dedicated to its esteemed alums, harbored its fair share of dissidents.) Exactly when Alice had fallen in with them, he didn't know. He was startled one afternoon while teaching about Napoleon to glimpse her through the window, fleeing the premises. He intended to ask her about it but lost his nerve when she appeared at his door. It had been a long seven weeks since he'd invited her up to his apartment. He feared that if he called out her behavior, she'd throw that day back at him. He still wanted, needed, to be seen as her ally.

'Going somewhere?' he asked, half joking. There were still several hours left of the school day.

Alice didn't smile. She slid out a chair and set it across from his desk. 'Do you want to play?' she asked again. 'The game is called Truth.'

'What are the rules?'

'One of us asks a question, and the other has to answer it honestly.'

'And then?'

'We go back and forth.'

Had any other student proposed this, Ezra would've immediately exercised a sense of unwelcome and said he was too busy. A person in power could never tell the truth. But there was Alice, dazzling and calm, standing with one hand outstretched, as if beckoning him up a grand staircase.

'You first,' he said.

She picked at her cuticles, imitating abstraction. Her face possessed a peculiar vitality Ezra recognized from class discussions, when she'd sit and silently surveil her peers. Behind her proposed game he sensed another game, a shell game, and he watched, increasingly unsettled, as she maneuvered the ball of her intent from one cup to another.

354

'Do you like me?' she asked.

Her straightforwardness disarmed him. 'Of course I do.'

'You know what I mean.'

'I'm not sure I do.'

'Forget it.'

She slouched deeper into the desk, tugging at the sleeves of her sweater. Her gauntness made her appear sickly. How hadn't Ezra noticed it before?

'You go,' she said, reaching to unfasten her hair clip.

She clamped the plastic clasp between her teeth, sweeping her hair back with the practiced movements of both hands. A dusting of fine gold hair shone on her arms. Desire nibbled at Ezra's flesh. He imagined pulling her toward him. Other things he imagined too – things he couldn't articulate, even to himself, but whose phantom power nevertheless excited him. The more he imagined ways to resist the thrill, the greater his inclination grew to succumb to it.

'Mr N.?'

He snapped to. There was no trace of seduction in Alice's face. She looked oddly depleted. At the bedrock of her pretty looks, beneath the unblemished skin and pearly teeth, he found not hubris but fear. What others took for snobbery – what he himself had taken for snobbery – was nothing but crippling self-doubt. *And if thou gaze long into an abyss, the abyss will also gaze into thee.*

He reshuffled the papers on his blotter to distract from his shaking hands. 'The first day, when we played our little social dilemma game, you were the only one to defect. Why?'

Alice smiled; she'd been waiting for this. She reached into her violin case and removed a beige book. 'Do you remember the piece I played for you?'

'Bach,' he said. 'Sublime Bach. Sublime Alice.'

She slid the book across the table. Centered on the cover, in a baroque script, were the words *Sei Solo*. 'Notice anything funny about the grammar here?' she asked.

'*Sei* should take a plural noun?' he ventured, conjuring his rudimentary knowledge of Romance languages.

'Right. The title should read *Sei Soli* — six solos. Bach would've known that.'

'So?'

'Soooo, *sei* has another meaning too, from the word *essere*: to be. *Sei* — you are, *solo* — alone. It's a code: You are alone.'

Her voice had grown to a manic pitch, her eyes darting furiously across his face, refusing to land. Her entire being was aglow, some raw element combusting inside her.

Ezra frowned. He crossed and uncrossed his legs, his discomfort manifesting as a dampness in the air. 'Let's get something clear,' he said. 'I'm your teacher. My job is to educate you, to expand your horizons just a hair. If I've done that successfully, you might feel a little bit transformed. You'll start to question things you previously took for granted. You'll go to bed with thoughts you've never had before knocking around your head, and this is a kind of magic, learning is. Now, if those feelings of transformation have led you to other ones – romantic, or what have you – then fine, so be it, *iacta alea est.* But I need you to realize, Alice, and I need you to realize this hard, so please try to put all your mind to it, that whatever story you've concocted in your head about me, us, is pure make-believe.'

The wall clock ticked loudly above his head, counting each unendurable second. Alice's arms went limp, the bubbling cauldron of her psyche wheeled behind a curtain. She looked at Ezra with such vacancy that he shivered.

'You wanted to seduce us,' she said at last, 'and you wanted us to seduce you.'

'I never said that.'

'You didn't have to.'

Ezra gazed out to Amsterdam Avenue. One of his colleagues was struggling to shove a sheaf of papers into his briefcase, wrestling against the wind.

'Alice, I'm going to need you to leave now.'

Leave, leave, leave, the devil inside him chanted. His eyes flickered to the door, where he detected a flash of movement. No, no one was there; he'd only imagined it. The links of time and order were breaking before him, unseen networks coming undone. Blood rushed to his loins. The perversity was so rich, he could laugh. Alice twisted her fingers nervously around one another. How he'd like to take those fingers into his mouth, suck the sweetness out of each one . . .

'I thought we were friends,' she said.

'Alice, I'm twice your age.'

357

'That didn't stop you from inviting me to your apartment. I'm sure the administration would love to hear about that.'

'Yeah, what would you tell them – that I caught you in a bad state and wanted to make sure you didn't go slit your wrists? Don't get ahead of yourself. You think you're so smart, that you have all this leverage over me, but you know what everyone else will say? They'll say you're reading too much into things, that you have an overactive imagination.'

Alice stood, the hurt plain on her face. It accentuated her youth, this tactlessness. Ezra reached across the desk for her hand, but she didn't give it.

'Fine,' he said, exasperated. 'You don't even know what you want, what you're asking for. You come in here playing coy, do you like me this and that. What if I *did* like you, hmm? I'm a morally questionable person. I can't love in the way you can.'

He waited for her to disagree. This was a trick he'd learned from his father, to divulge his shortcomings before someone else could point them out to him.

Alice, cowed, advanced to the door. She paused at the threshold, running her hand along the painted frame. When her voice reached him, it was a relief. 'Mr N.? You wanted to know why I defected, and I told you. My turn: Why did you change my answer?'

Ezra had nearly forgotten he had. The easy excuse – that he wanted to protect her; that to elect herself the Brutus of the group could've gotten her crucified – seemed too transparent. Presumably, Alice had already

358

recognized the real reason and merely wanted him to admit it: he'd wanted to assert his dominance over her. He glanced at the music book on his desk. *You are alone.*

'I'll still give you an A if that's what you're worried about,' he said.

The line of Alice's mouth quivered. Self-loathing trickled down Ezra's throat, every breath rappelling him deeper into his own pit of depravity.

Outside someone was burning leaves, the acrid scent drifting through the cracked window. Life would go on whether she hated him or not. The seasons would change, and new students would fill these desks.

'You should leave,' he repeated. He was conscious of his malice, of how he'd mobilized against her the anger that ought to be directed inward. His eyes traveled down to the papers he had been grading before she'd entered. It made him feel better to remember that she'd interrupted his work. If anyone asked, he would say she had sought him out on his lunch hour, and he had turned her away in good faith. This idea ossified his resolve. 'I have business to attend to.'

Alice listed until she was at last slumped against the doorjamb. She readjusted her coat where it had slipped from her shoulder, refusing to glance back as she left.

He had not expected her to return to class after that. Students' schedules were often shuffled in the first few weeks of the new semester. He wouldn't have minded if she had dropped the seminar – he wished it, in fact. But in January, she arrived at the bell's summons and took her seat with disquieting calm. She did not approach him afterward or seek him out at lunch. For over a month, until the day he received notice that she had disappeared, Alice Weil remained as remote to Ezra Newman as any other student. It was what he had requested, that she not stray outside her role. Later, this struck him as the most tormenting blow of all.

If only . . .

No, he forbade his thoughts from traveling that route. He knew the rest too well – how she had drifted apart from even the Misfits, wandering the city alone during class hours; how she'd allowed her grades to slip; how, in those final few days, he detected a lightness about her and hoped, against all odds, that the old Alice had returned. The other teachers who encountered her on the city streets didn't question her, assuming she had permission to be out. Afterward, they would wonder what in her strut made them believe she lay beyond their purview.

Only Alice's English teacher had flagged her behavior to the guidance counselor. Ezra often imagined the walk Alice had taken through the halls to reach the main office. The counselor, a tenderhearted Scottish lady named Susie, was relieved when Alice said she had been missing class for rehearsals and that her mother had notified the school of this. Susie said she'd need to call Linnie to confirm. Go ahead, Alice said. Susie must have frowned a little, her ears pinkening as she forced herself to mention Alice's sliding grades. Ezra guessed Alice would have hesitated only a beat before her fear found its way to insouciance. 'I did the work, Miss Susie,' she said. 'Maybe my teachers haven't recorded it yet.'

Susie would have smiled, not believing Alice but wanting to. 'Let me write you a late pass.'

'No need. I have a free now.'

She gave Alice a pencil emblazoned with the Manhattan Tech logo and told her to drop by whenever. She didn't pull up Alice's schedule on the computer. If she had, she would have seen that Alice should have been entering math right then.

If only . . .

A jagged guitar solo punctured Ezra's reverie. Linnie, in her beaded dress, came into focus. As the ballroom spotlights swept over her face, he caught a glimpse of concern in her eyes. With that, every battlement he'd erected to protect himself vaporized. The last thing she needed was for him to wreck tonight too. With a miserable shudder, he drew away. 'I'm sorry. I have to go.'

He dashed out into the evening. The sky was streaky, gray. Clouds hung in tatters. Workers had finished dismantling the altar on the lawn and started in on the rows of folding chairs. Harbor lights floated atop the water's surface, breaking apart with each ripple.

Ezra gulped the fresh air. The taps of Linnie's heels sounded behind him. He turned. She seemed newly radiant, a star burning up as it charged through the skies.

'What's going on?' she demanded.

'It was . . .'

Could he tell her? Should he? He had taken pains to reassure himself of his irreproachability when it came to Alice. If he'd committed any fault, it lay in the opposite of what Morgan had accused – he had not been close enough to her. He had pushed her away when she needed him most, sealing himself off to avoid indulging the very perversion that he feared crawled beneath his skin. At every moment, he had operated with circumspection so that if anyone were to present his case to a jury, they'd uncover not a single shred of evidence.

Linnie Olsen was no jury, however. She was a mother who deserved to know the truth. But which truth? There was his – the one that lay embedded like a splinter in his heart – and Alice's. There was Morgan's truth, and everyone else's. Even if these accounts were to be melded, no objective version would emerge. He had done nothing wrong and everything wrong.

'It was about the tick repellent,' he said lamely. 'I forgot to tell you it never arrived.'

Linnie laughed, a mechanic honking sound that the seabirds swiftly picked up and mimicked. 'That's all? Well, goodness. You had me worried for a second there.'

Every inch between them crackled. It was a short road from resignation to nihilism, and once you'd arrived, you began resenting anyone still naïve enough to remain hopeful. They'll learn, you'd think, from your fortress of solitude, with its impenetrable walls and slow drip of darkness.

Ezra forced himself to turn away from Alice's mother, shutting the door on the past once and for all. It's for her own good, he thought sadly but definitively, as he made the choice to walk away.

5

Peter stood at the bar, nursing a drink. He swiped at his phone until he found Sequoia's name. He dialed and waited. No answer. Damn her. He couldn't bear to stay in this ballroom any longer. It was an inferno of sweaty bodies, guests urging him to join the festivities. Something in his demeanor must have warded them off, because each accepted his declination without protest. Only Benji dared to approach. Sweet Benji. Staring out through his eyes was both the man of today and the twelve-year-old boy who had looked so lost at his sister's funeral.

'What're you drinking?' Benji asked.

Peter held up his glass. 'No clue. It's good.'

Benji ordered one for himself. The bartender, a middle-aged woman with capable hands and a healthy complexion, shoved the metal scoop into the ice. 'To the happy couple,' Peter said.

'To family,' Benji replied.

Peter blotted his neck with his cocktail napkin. All afternoon, the thought of facing Benji had niggled him. In the turret's closet, he'd had no choice but to confront his folly in coming on to Linnie. Never in his life had he acted so brashly. On reflection, he could see that his proposition to her had been born out of fear – fear of losing her to Ezra; fear of Morgan growing up; fear that some insecure part of him wished to hold both women under his thumb so that they'd continue to depend on him as Sequoia never had. He'd defined his worth based on his usefulness to others. When suddenly that worth threatened to plummet, he had done what he needed to fortify his position against defeat.

He had not lost, though. Look at his daughter, wiser than he, capable of opening her heart to romance. Look at his son-in-law, who bore no grudge against the world and likely possessed sufficient optimism to save them all. Look at the family he'd gained, flawed as they might be, but nonetheless his.

'You doing okay over here?' Benji asked.

'Couldn't be better.'

'For what it's worth, she loves you a lot.'

Peter was startled until he realized Benji was talking about Morgan, not Linnie. He was about to reply when a group of Benji's Syracuse friends trooped over, intent on hauling the groom off for a picture. Peter said, 'Go on, I'll hold down the fort.' The boys jostled Benji to the photographer, cheering, 'Make way, make way.' They hoisted him clumsily between them, holding him horizontally like a prize check.

'I didn't realize I was in the presence of wedding royalty,' the bartender said.

'Peter, father of the bride.'

'And British,' she said. 'Royalty, indeed.'

'Yes, well, no. Bred abroad, but not British.'

'I'm Margaret.'

'Princess Margaret.'

'And you, Peter Townsend.'

'How do you do,' he said.

Margaret paused her task of drying glasses to shake Peter's hand. The humorous gleam in her eyes struck Peter as both familiar and strange, like a sight he'd glimpsed long ago. Her fingers were calloused.

'What instrument?' he asked, turning over her palm.

'What? Oh. Guitar.'

Her hair, the color of cranberries, was pulled into a ponytail. She wore the usual bartending outfit, and she wore it well. She made a silly air guitar motion with her hands. Peter laughed.

'Well,' he said, 'it was lovely to meet you.'

'Likewise.'

He gave her a wave and hurried away, pretending as if someone across the room had summoned him. He needed to go to the bathroom, splash some water on his face. But her spunk, her charm, that alluring smell . . .

No sooner had he crossed to the dance floor than he turned and doubled back.

'Forget something?' she asked.

'Margaret, I was wondering, if it's not too forward – and mind you, if you knew me, you'd know this isn't something I typically do – but would you like to go out sometime? Or, tomorrow? I leave in the afternoon.'

She slid his cocktail napkin back to him. Her phone number was on it. She must have scribbled it down in the time it had taken him to realize his error. He felt a surprised jolt of delight at her forwardness and at his own lack of restraint. Could it be that Linnie was right? Could there be a future for him too?

'Already one step ahead of you, Captain.'

6

Once the guests had departed with their organza bags of saltwater taffy, the flower arrangements divvied up, the top tier of the cake put in a box for Morgan and Benji to enjoy on their first anniversary; once the sign-in book had been closed, the dishes stacked, the leftover programs discarded – once all this had taken place, Linnie sat in her dress on the stone steps, nursing her aching feet. She had performed the evening's duties efficiently enough: smiling when approached, posing for every photograph, attending to Benji's every need. There had been relief after all in Sequoia's absence; Linnie's role as a mother not subjugated to anyone else's.

'Knock, knock.'

She turned to see Morgan by the French doors. The bride's hair had fallen from its updo, the curls freed from the hairspray's clench. She had replaced her gown with one of Benji's T-shirts.

'What're you doing here?' Linnie asked. 'You should be upstairs.'

'I could say the same to you.'

'Care to sit?'

Morgan crouched and pressed her hands between her legs. For a moment the two women were quiet. The music from earlier, long absent, rang in Linnie's ears.

'I think there's ducks there,' Morgan said, pointing into the distance. 'See them?'

On the open water, two ducks roosted. Nearer by, planes of light from the rooms overhead fell across the fountain, catching the coins at its bottom.

'So,' Morgan began.

'I'm guessing whatever you're about to say has to do with Ezra,' Linnie said.

'It does.'

At the alarm bells of these words, Linnie felt tiny hands of fear batten down the hatches of her heart. She lived as a woman prepared at any moment for an air strike. A woman with blackout curtains over the windows, a taser in the drawer. She recalled Ezra's outburst from earlier. She had known then that he was lying, the same dim way she'd known Nick had been lying about Caro all those years ago, but chosen not to pick the scab. It was better to live in a blissful world full of lies than in one ravaged by truth.

'I'm not sure of the details,' Morgan went on. 'I know that they spoke, often. Alice told him things.'

'What things? Things about me?'

'You should ask him.'

'He already left. Earlier tonight.'

Morgan shrugged, unsurprised. 'He runs when he feels the heat. Your garden-variety narcissist.'

The girl's indignancy touched Linnie, her childish conviction that people could be plotted along the axes of good and evil. She wished she too could reenter that state of ignorance. But life, in her experience, was more ambiguous. The old witch in the optical illusion could transform into a fetching maiden with a sleight of hand. Once the world had revealed the full scope of its contradictions, it balked at any efforts one made to arrange them into a neat package.

'Right, so that's it, then?' Linnie asked. 'He and my daughter were close.'

'Well, yeah, but . . .'

'Did he fuck her?'

She was trying to be provocative, using easy shock to throw Morgan off-balance. It worked. The bride scrambled to her feet. A look traveled between them, a signal firing across synapses. Morgan frowned. 'I thought you'd be madder.'

'Oh, I'm plenty mad.'

'But . . .'

'Will knowing what happened to her turn back time? No. Will it bring me peace? Also no. Knowledge can't rewrite the past. You could tell me every detail, every secret, and still.'

'But maybe—'

Linnie sealed off her expression, pretending the conversation left her unfazed, though every cell in her body throbbed with loathing. If Ezra were near, she would've throttled him. She'd sooner be damned, though, than let Morgan in on her hurt. She had been burned by the girl once before, twelve years ago, for evincing such vulnerability. She could still taste the bitter peel of that day on her tongue, could still hear the terrible accusations Morgan had lobbed at her in the chapel, could still feel the helplessness she'd experienced in the bathroom, knowing Morgan had overheard every word of her and Caro's fight. No, she refused to grant the girl even the slightest window into her pain.

'What I suggest,' Linnie said carefully, 'is that you forget about all this. Go up to your husband and let this evening soak in.'

Gently, she swatted Morgan's behind and watched the girl trot back to the door. At the last second, Morgan turned. Backlit by the golden light of the ballroom, a question mark in her eyes, she looked so like her father. Oh, Peter. Linnie hadn't yet processed what that morning's rejection meant for their friendship. Yet she suspected that Peter would ultimately forgive her, in his standup way. Her stomach twisted. It was wretched to have another accept what you could not accept in yourself.

'I'm sorry for the nasty things I said to you all those years ago,' Morgan said. 'I was a dumb teenager, not that it's any excuse.'

'Oh, that?' Linnie waved her hand dismissively, as if she hadn't been brooding on that same day.

'I thought I knew more than I did. I was cruel to you, and you didn't deserve it.'

'No, I didn't.'

'Can you forgive me?'

'I think so, yes.'

It took effort, but Linnie compelled herself to step forward and embrace the girl. She cradled her in the manner that she had yearned, almost thirty-five years

370

earlier, for Judith to hold her on the eve of her own wedding. Forgiveness forced its way up through the cracks in her heart. Maybe she and Morgan could reshape their circumstances, break the cycle. The ice between them was thawing, the silent creatures beneath it gasping to life. Linnie felt Morgan's body open, creating a space to accommodate her own pain. How close in stature she was to Alice – a woman of twenty-eight – yet how dissimilar; how unfathomably distant from what Linnie, in that moment and all others, desperately wished.

7

In the ballroom, the last musicians loaded their instruments into their cases. They did not notice Linnie weaving between the deserted tables. Nor did they see Nick, who entered from the rear and strode toward his ex-wife with purpose.

'You scared me,' she said as he tapped her.

'It's late,' he said.

'I just came to see that everything got packed up.'

He fixed her with a dubious stare. No doubt he too had witnessed her dramatic exit with Ezra and her solo return half an hour later.

She removed a place card from one of the tables and ran her fingers over its edges. 'Have I done something to upset you?' she asked.

'Not in the least. Why?'

She shrugged, allowing Nick to guide her by the elbow to the corner of the room, away from the superior ears of the musicians. From his pocket he withdrew a paper scroll.

'What's this?' she asked.

'I told you yesterday: I brought you something.'

Warily, she took the paper and pulled at the satin tie belting its middle. The paper unraveled, revealing a drawing of a brownstone – *their* brownstone, with its grand

Romanesque arch over the doorway and helixes of orna-
mental ironwork adorning the window guards. Her eyes
stalked from room to room, each no larger than a postage
stamp. Every detail had been wrought to precision. When
she reached the second level, she paused. The windows
were shaded, but if she squinted, she could detect some-
one there – the version of herself that had never left.

'Nick . . .'

'Yes?'

They were standing with shoulders touching by the
French doors. While they were inside, the varnish of
midnight had peeled away to reveal the tender belly of
dawn. No passage of time would settle what had hap-
pened between them. Certain events could bend the
hours, break a body in two, unwind all the miles you
thought you'd put behind you. Certain events could
shine like a floodlight on your interior, making you aware
that everything was snowing sideways.

'Do you remember when I told you I was moving in
with Caro?' Nick asked.

'How could I forget.'

'I actually want to apologize for that day.'

'Nothing to be sorry for.'

'I shouldn't have sprung it on you. It wasn't right. I
guess I was hoping you would . . .'

'Stop you?'

They stared at each other. 'If I'd tried, you would've
gone through with it anyway, only to have wound up
hating me in the process.'

'I could never hate you, Lin.'

'But you did.'

'Caro actually said no, the first time I asked. She thought I was in love with you and had too much self-respect to wed a man who couldn't love her back.'

Were you? her smile asked. It was too obvious a question. She couldn't pose it, and even if she could, what good would the answer do?

They advanced toward the harbor, cutting through clouds of bugs, the grass yielding to their steps. An invigorating breeze fanned over them. If they were to track that scent along the coast, they'd eventually find themselves homeward. The planet was so small, just landmasses and watery weft.

'Did it ever cross your mind, though, to stop me?' he asked. 'Friend to friend, did you want to?'

Linnie trailed a hand over the stone blockade. 'Friend to friend, I wanted you not to make a mistake, sure. But you're happy now, so I guess you made the right decision.'

'I do feel more at peace, I have to say.'

'How so?'

He couldn't articulate it; it was too shameful. She understood. For so long, he'd wanted nothing more than to be a different person, someone incapable of hurting the ones he loved. Toward the end of their marriage, he hadn't even been able to look at her. Looking at her made him think of Alice, forced him to see his worst self. Maybe he believed that if he left, married Caro, fathered another child, he could step into a new life.

She reached for his hand. His palm was worn, his

374

fingers dry and cracked beneath hers. She had the sudden urge to tend to them, as Magdalene with her jar.

'That day she died—' he began.

'Nick—'

'—is tied for the day I replay most.'

'Tied?'

'March 5, 1986.'

'What's that?'

'The day we met. Penn Station.'

'That was another lifetime.'

'Was it?'

'Life is full of them,' she said. 'Moments the old you dies, and you become someone new.'

'How jaded.'

'You told me that.'

'Well, even if you don't want to hear it, I truly am sorry.'

'Water under the bridge.'

'I've always avoided that expression.'

She laughed. He did too.

There was an opening in their conversation. Would she tell him what had happened with Ezra? If she didn't say it now, she never would, and the film reel of what occurred between them would resplice itself in her dreams, like that surveillance footage of their daughter walking through Washington Heights. She shivered. Nick removed his jacket and draped it over her shoulders. He tried to combat his sorrow by smiling, but she sensed his strain.

'Let's go in,' she said.

The musicians had departed the ballroom. Only a single woman with dark hair remained. The violinist. Slowly she lifted the instrument to her shoulder and played – softly at first, then with brio, her body swaying in time.

Though Linnie faced the woman, she did not see her. She saw instead, cast in the ballroom's parquet floor, the grand sweep of her days, every moment that had led her here. Nick could do this, disarm whatever illusions she'd succeeded in erecting. She both cherished and despised him for this, the two feelings augmenting each other in her breast.

On the dance floor they stood close, his stubble brushing her temple. Around them, revenants of their past and future selves constellated; the people they had been, the ones they were destined to become. He kissed her cheek. She grabbed his wrists and squeezed so tightly that the circulation fled his fingers. 'Why do I feel like this is goodbye?' she asked.

'Don't be so sentimental.'

But after a few minutes, impelled by the same ineffable force that had brought them together, they parted, not to see each other again for several years, at the birth of their first grandchild.

In Linnie's room the bed was made. Ezra's suitcase was missing from its spot in the closet. He had left her his toothpaste; she'd forgotten her own. A note of apology lay on the nightstand. She tore it up, allowing the pieces to snow to the ground. Maybe the evening's events had served as a referendum on her fate. In exchange for releasing a bit of the past, she'd be granted more of the future.

Restless, she stood to pace the hallway. The magnolia-patterned wallpaper was flaking. Down the corridor a door opened. Peter emerged in his bathrobe. They nodded at each other, joined in their plight as two strangers passing on a boardwalk at night, beneath a sky blurry with stars.

How far into oneself could a person recede? The answer lay somewhere in the infinite. You could halve a number over and over and still stave off nothingness. You could recede until you were only surface and still find further to go.

As they passed, Peter gently extended a hand to Linnie's arm. Friendship flowed between them, as once it had flowed between their daughters. They stood for a long time together in stillness.

Epilogue

High above or down below, depending on how you look at it, there is a window that gazes onto earth. By this window sits a girl who watches over her family as they go about their lives.

She sees her mother in a café, a gilt book in her lap. She looks like she belongs here, in this city. Far from sprinkler-fed lawns. Far from a certain suburban insularity she's always found oppressive. Her mother lifts her gaze to the couple beside her. The man looks like Nick. She stares a moment too long. The man turns. It is only a feint of the imagination.

She closes the book and gathers her hands atop the cover. French. Everyone who meets her wonders if she's done something different since she last saw them – a new haircut? A change in diet? To each she responds with a veiled smile. Her sadness is confusable for so many things, as is her joy. She has a new husband now, a carpenter, older than she. Theirs is a steady love.

At the table next to her mother, the man and woman – the ones who look uncannily like younger versions of the girl's parents – join hands. Their touch releases tiny sparks like winter static into the air. The man picks up a raspberry from his plate and spins it so each drupelet catches the light. The woman's laughter is the sound of a bell.

The girl leaves her mother there, to the privacy of her thoughts.

She sees her father and Caro, cheering on their younger daughter at her soccer match. Later: the elder daughter's voice recital. Routines of a family in motion. Her father making waffles, tracking the growth of both children with a Sharpie on the back of the pantry door. The way he looks at those girls – that is how he once looked at her.

Across the city, Morgan riffles through the sheet music on her stand. There is a text on her phone from her father. He and Margaret have gone to Maine and sent a photograph of Elizabeth Cottage, which stands proud as ever. Morgan lifts her violin to her shoulder. The sound emerges choppily. She winces but carries on, immersed in the work. A colleague knocks. It sounds good, he says. His voice opens a doorway through which Morgan sees another path unfurl.

Ignore it, the girl in the window thinks. That path isn't for you.

But this is someone else's life; try as she might, she cannot interfere.

She flashes to her brother in his office at the school. His desk is laden with photographs of his four-year-old son in hockey gear, the ice glossy as the coated pages of a magazine. He types a name into the computer's search bar and waits. Always he has been waiting, the cursor blinking on the final letter. He presses the backspace key. He cannot, must not.

Then there's Ezra. The girl visits him often at his house on the Cape. She comes as a wind or the shade of a willow tree. Today he is reading a book by Berkeley. She perches beside him. He senses her, though when he turns, he perceives only the visible world, the world as it is – wingbeats in motion. He is incapable of perceiving more, much as he wishes he could. Mozart said: *The music is not in the notes, but in the silence between.*

Through the window that gazes onto earth, time assembles around the girl's absence. If she cared to know how all this would play out, she could approach the shelf of hourglasses, where the grains of sand stream like rain. Every hourglass is inscribed with the name of a person she loves. She has glanced at them only once; it is perdition to know.

In numberless other universes, things play out differently. In some, she is alive. She approaches the bridge but turns back at the last second. In one, she goes to Yale; in another, she studies at a conservatory; in yet another, she forgoes college altogether. She meets a man and falls in love; she meets a woman and falls in love; she does not fall in love at all but flourishes into a revered professor. There are many worlds in which her parents resolve their difficulties and stay together. But it is this present from which she cannot turn away; here where her absence is most fully felt.

In the café, an intoxicating smell wafts from the kitchen. Sunlight gladdens the patrons at the tables. The man and woman stand. As the girl glances back, the day empties itself into spring. If she keeps watching, maybe she will be pardoned.

Acknowledgments

This book would be nothing without the tireless labors and brilliance of Bret Anthony Johnston, Allison Lorentzen, Jamie Carr, Camille LeBlanc, Madeleine Woodfield, Emily van Blanken, Jenny Meyer, Heidi Gall, Julie Barer, Carolyn Coleburn, Yuleza Negron, Raven Ross, Mary Stone, Elizabeth Yaffe, Claire Vaccaro, Randee Marullo, and Andrea Monagle. I am beyond grateful to you all. Thank you, too, to my incredible family and friends, my silliest bunnies, and my dear husband: *l'amor che move il sole e l'altre stelle.*